Democratizing Urban Development

In the series *Urban Life, Landscape, and Policy,* edited by David Stradling, Larry Bennett, and Davarian Baldwin. Founding editor, Zane L. Miller.

ALSO IN THIS SERIES:

A list of additional titles in this series appears at the back of this book

Maureen M. Donaghy

DEMOCRATIZING URBAN DEVELOPMENT

Community Organizations for Housing
across the United States and Brazil

TEMPLE UNIVERSITY PRESS
Philadelphia • Rome • Tokyo

TEMPLE UNIVERSITY PRESS
Philadelphia, Pennsylvania 19122
www.temple.edu/tempress

Library of Congress Cataloging-in-Publication Data

Names: Donaghy, Maureen M., author.
Title: Democratizing urban development : community organizations for housing
  across the United States and Brazil / Maureen M. Donaghy.
Description: Philadelphia : Temple University Press, 2018. | Series: Urban
  life, landscape, and policy | Includes bibliographical references and
  index.
Identifiers: LCCN 2017051562 (print) | LCCN 2018011720 (ebook) |
  ISBN 9781439914076 (E-book) | ISBN 9781439914052 (cloth : alk. paper) |
  ISBN 9781439914069 (pbk. : alk. paper)
Subjects: LCSH: Low income housing—Government policy—United States. |
  Low income housing—Government policy—Brazil. | Democracy—United States. |
  Democracy—Brazil.
Classification: LCC HD7287.96.U6 (ebook) | LCC HD7287.96.U6 D664 2018
  (print) | DDC 363.5/969420973—dc23
LC record available at https://lccn.loc.gov/2017051562

♾ The paper used in this publication meets the requirements of the American
National Standard for Information Sciences—Permanence of Paper for Printed
Library Materials, ANSI Z39.48-1992

Printed in the United States of America

9 8 7 6 5 4 3 2 1

For my parents, James and Linda Donaghy

Contents

Acknowledgments

This book is the culmination of five years of work, during which numerous individuals gave generously of their time and energy. First and foremost, I acknowledge the time and patience of all the people I interviewed for this project. In São Paulo, I express my sincere appreciation to Benedito Roberto Barbosa and Osmar Borges—in addition to many other individuals who have fought every day for the right to housing—for taking the time to explain the challenges they face, the long-term frustrations their work presents, and the determination they maintain in pushing forward policies and programs for the benefit of the residents of the city. In Rio de Janeiro, Theresa Williamson of Catalytic Communities and the members of the community of Vila Autódromo, in particular, conveyed to me their passion for and dedication to ensuring global recognition of the many strengths of the low-income communities of Rio that are threatened with displacement. In Washington, D.C., Elizabeth Falcon of the Coalition for Nonprofit Housing and Economic Development generously welcomed me to the Housing for All Campaign and explained the evolution of the campaign's extraordinarily successful strategies. And, in Atlanta, Mtamanika Youngblood and several other members of the city's housing community graciously showed me the complexity of gentrification and affordable housing in this rapidly changing city.

This project would not have been possible without the financial support of Rutgers University, where I am very fortunate to have begun my career as an assistant professor. Through grants from the Centers for Global Advancement and International Affairs and the Faculty of Arts and Sciences in Camden, I was able to complete the fieldwork for this book. My colleagues in the Department of Political Science and the Department of Public Policy and Administration also provided me with invaluable support throughout the project.

In addition, the book benefited greatly from the advice and comments of numerous reviewers. In particular, I thank Larry Bennett, one of the editors of the *Urban Life, Landscape, and Policy* series at Temple University Press, who worked tirelessly to make this book a much better product (any errors that remain are, of course, my own). Aaron Javsicas and the rest of the team at Temple University Press were a pleasure to work with, and I sincerely appreciate all their efforts toward the production of this book. I also thank the reviewers who read the book manuscript, as well as those who reviewed various versions of related conference papers and journal articles. I am forever grateful to the scholars who have encouraged me along the way, especially—among countless others—David S. Brown, Susan Clarke, Brian Wampler, and Clarence Stone.

My family and friends continue to be a tremendous source of love and support, allowing me to pursue the kind of work I value and enjoy. To my husband, Robert Naranjo, who always believes I can do anything I put my mind to and without whom this book would not have come to fruition, I express my sincere appreciation. I thank my daughter, Caroline, who was born in the early stages of this project, for her smiles and patience amid my distraction in finishing this book. My son, Miles, also continues to be a constant source of inspiration to me in his quest to understand the world, and I am grateful for his efforts as my very junior research assistant in Rio de Janeiro. In addition, I owe my ability to complete this project to my parents, Jim and Linda Donaghy, who have always served as my biggest cheerleaders and who continue to sacrifice their own time and energy—especially as babysitters—to allow me to pursue my goals. Finally, I thank all my friends, especially Kim Varzi and Beth LeNoach, and all my family, especially Jimi Donaghy, Bonnie Donaghy, Mary Alberti, and Evie Naranjo, for their endless encouragement.

Democratizing Urban Development

Introduction

In 2009, in Rio de Janeiro, the city government served notice to over five hundred families in the community of Vila Autódromo that they would be evicted to make room for a new stadium for the 2016 Olympic Games. A few years later, government officials advised the residents of the community of Buraco Quente in the city of São Paulo that they would be removed as an economic boom spurred construction and renovation (Buraco Quente Community Residents 2013). Thousands of miles away, in Washington, D.C., low-income residents of Chinatown's Museum Square apartment building faced displacement as the building went up for sale and residents feared they would be unable to find affordable housing elsewhere.[1] In Atlanta, too, low-income residents displaced by the demolition of public housing and rapid gentrification faced increasing difficulty in finding affordable housing, particularly in the historically black Old Fourth Ward neighborhood. These individual cases simply exemplify larger global trends. In all of these cities and many more around the world, the tenure of low-income residents is in peril, and rising housing costs prevent those at the bottom of the income ladder from attaining secure and decent housing in central urban neighborhoods.

The confluence of housing challenges in cities with diverse economic and political histories is certainly not coincidental. As cities strive to achieve "world city" status and attract international investment, the push for urban development tests the ability of cities to provide opportunities for all and to exhibit the ideal of "inclusive cities." As an ever-greater share of the world's population lives in cities, questions of inclusion increasingly matter for stability and sustainable development, and future trends to incorporate people of all income levels are critical for the practice of democracy and the legitimacy of the state.

In this environment, civil society plays a pivotal role in demanding accountability of the state to address the needs of low-income residents and support the goals of an inclusive city. But questions remain about how civil society organizations (CSOs) go about this task, the challenges they face, and the outcomes their efforts produce. We expect that the institutions of democracy dictate the avenues available to CSOs to influence public policies and programs, but we know less about why particular organizations seek to engage with various institutions or pursue alternate strategies at specific points in time. As much as democratic institutions define the possibilities for CSOs to engage in the political process, the activities of CSOs also indicate the extent to which these institutions are able to work in practice to incorporate diverse voices and interests. If institutions are not perceived as viable paths for reform, CSOs will instead seek other opportunities to achieve their goals. The locus of civil society engagement matters in that the actors who control decision making within institutions concerned with urban development likely shape the direction of policies and programs.

I argue that if cities are to be more inclusive, CSOs representing the interests of low-income residents need to be present at the decision-making table. But what we see is that the strategies CSOs undertake, constrained by their own agency and the environment in which they operate, largely determine the extent to which their role is transformational in democratizing urban development. The cases in this book provide evidence of how CSOs on the ground seek to influence official decision making through various means and the impact that ensues from these strategic choices. Through the lens of housing, the book details how and why CSOs engage in various strategies and how these strategies lead to achievements in housing policies, programs, and institutions. In particular, the book presents efforts by community organizations to secure housing for low-income residents across Rio de Janeiro; São Paulo; Washington, D.C.; and Atlanta. The physical location of a home is a primary determinant of whether residents are incorporated into the opportunities of the city, but the process by which affordable housing is preserved or achieved represents a broader indicator of how the needs of low-income residents as a group or class are integrated into urban governance.

Throughout the book, I assess how organizations representing the interests of low-income residents influence the direction of policies and programs to ensure access to affordable housing and the ability to stay put in the face of displacement. I use the term "community organization" rather than the broader term "civil society organization," to indicate that these are collective actors specifically focused on the preservation and promotion of inclusion at the community level. Across cities these types of organizations are diverse, ranging from social movement organizations, neighborhood associations, and nonprofit professional organizations.

Specifically, I address these main questions:

1. *How do community organizations working to preserve and promote affordable housing seek to be empowered through the strategies in which they engage?*

Given similarities in housing challenges across cities, we might also expect to see similarities in the strategies undertaken by community organizations concerned with these issues. Further, the global focus on inclusion and participatory governance among scholars, development practitioners, and global social movements should encourage community organizations to demand new forms of influence. However, many types of collective action exist in which organizations seek influence not only from the inside, through governmental institutions, but also from the outside, by persuading public officials, by electing allies to office, or by appealing to actors outside the local environment, such as international governmental organizations or philanthropic donors. This book serves to first document the strategies in which community organizations concerned with low-income housing engage. Though, as detailed in Chapter 2, previous literature on collective action tends to categorize the tactics of actors as either contentious or cooperative, I build on the classic "exit, voice, or loyalty" framework conceived of by Albert Hirschman to identify the source of empowerment that defines the strategy of contemporary community organizations (1970). I categorize strategies as "inclusionary," "indirect," "overhaul," or "exit-oriented."

2. What leads groups to take on certain strategies?

The factors behind why community organizations develop certain strategies are not well defined either through literature on collective action or participatory governance. This study seeks to remedy this gap by proposing two primary factors that should motivate the choice of strategies. In Chapter 2, I argue that the ideology of community organizations fighting for housing combined with the organization's relationship with the state strongly influences the choice of strategies. The ideology of an organization and its members shapes the goals and perception of the appropriateness of certain actions, while the relationship with the state establishes trust and expectations regarding responsiveness and accountability. This argument responds to the classic divide attributing the nature of collective action either to the agency of collective actors or to the structure of the environment in which they operate. What I argue is that both agency and structure matter for strategic decisions within organizations, but we need to know how these two elements combine to enable community organizations to shape public policies and programs. While I do find that the variables of political opportunities and resources also matter for shaping the strategies of community organizations, ideology and the relationship with the state play a particularly critical role in establishing an environment that is either conducive or detrimental to inclusion of civil society in decision making.

3. What are the outcomes of these strategies, both for ensuring housing for low-income residents and for democratic governance?

Finally, I ask what the outcomes of the efforts of community organizations are and whether the type of strategy they employ makes a difference in the outcomes we see. Literature on urban politics from the United States and Latin America has long warned that the power of the private sector in urban development drowns out the interests of community organizations seeking to preserve and expand property for social purposes. Recently, however, scholars including Clarence Stone (2015) find governments and private-sector interests more amenable to working with community organizations, recognizing equality and diversity as valuable tools to increase the benefits of urban development. I argue that strategies in which organizations seek influence within governmental institutions should promote housing outcomes that increase inclusion in the city and hold promise for transformation in the democratic governance of urban development through increased participation, accountability, and respect for diversity.

The Problem: Global Challenges to Housing and Inclusive Urban Development

Across the world, the United Nations warns that by 2030, 2 billion people will be in need of housing in cities (United Nations Preparatory Committee 2016). This includes the estimated 880 million people who currently live in inadequate housing in cities and the 1.8 billion projected population increase. The United Nations estimates $929 billion in investment is needed to improve housing for just the 880 million residents currently living in inadequate housing in cities.[2] The demand for secure and decent housing is only growing, even as the current supply and investment in affordable housing remains insufficient.

The confluence of low supply and increasing demand predictably leads to rising costs. The McKinsey Global Institute finds that an estimated 330 million households are currently financially stretched by housing costs, and they forecast that number to increase to 440 million by 2025 (Woetzel et al. 2014). In a study of two hundred cities around the world, a team of researchers from the Lincoln Institute, United Nations Habitat, and New York University found that the median house price to income ratio was 4.9, well above the 3.0 ratio generally considered affordable.[3] The study showed that affordability levels were not significantly different across developing and more developed countries. In fact, Beijing and Shanghai were two of the most unaffordable cities in the world. The team also found that rental prices were largely unaffordable, with the average renters across both developing and developed countries paying 31 percent of their income to housing.

Given rising costs and growing need, questions arise about what governments can and will do to address this gap and the difference interventions in housing will make for creating inclusive cities. Not only is affordable housing important for the physical comfort and security it provides to residents; it is also a key component of how low-income residents are perceived in the city and the opportunities for advancement that are available to them. As Peter Marcuse and David Madden write, "No other modern commodity is as important for organizing citizenship, work, identities, solidarities, and politics" (2016, 167). The effect of housing on well-being and participation in the life of the city cannot be understated. For example, Janice Perlman argues that despite increasing access to consumption goods and infrastructural upgrades, residents of Rio de Janeiro's favelas still lack respect from higher-income residents in the city, who view them as squatters or criminals who do not belong to the formal city rather than as citizens to be treated with dignity (Perlman 2010). Without this respect for people across class and across neighborhoods, Perlman argues, we can never have inclusive cities. In the United States, former president Obama argued that where one is born should not determine the limit of opportunities. During the Obama administration, Secretary of Housing and Urban Development Julian Castro reiterated this message at the 2016 United Nations Habitat III Conference in Quito and spoke about the need for "housing as a powerful platform to spark opportunities in people's lives" (Castro 2016). As Castro stated, housing is one link in a chain of social issues, including schools, food access, transit access, and employment opportunities, and should be prioritized as such.

The fact is, though, that the increasing cost of housing across cities removes the possibility for many to secure a decent place to live within the urban environment. Rising prices prevent new residents from finding affordable housing and also spur displacement, as long-time residents cannot afford increases in rent or property taxes. New construction for residential and commercial buildings as well as infrastructural development can bring new job opportunities and better provision of services to all residents. But the challenges to development are clear when low-income residents are either forced out or priced out of their existing communities in the process. Gentrification, in which new investment brings in middle- and upper-class residents to neighborhoods previously occupied by low-income households (Smith 1996), often means increasing revenue for the city, reduction in crime, new retail, and expanded options for entertainment, but frequently at the expense of existing residents. Empirically, there is still an ongoing debate about whether gentrification leads to displacement,[4] but as the case studies in this book demonstrate, many urban residents around the world do face upheaval related to development and gentrification, even if that is not always the rule. In addition, as neighborhoods gentrify and prices increase, evidence shows that first-time buyers and minorities in the United States and other developed countries are disproportionately affected by the challenges of attaining financing for homeownership (United Nations Habitat 2016, 13).

In response to these growing trends in inequality, the idea of creating more inclusive cities permeates current global discussions on housing and urban development. For instance, the New Urban Agenda, agreed upon in 2016 by United Nations member countries around the world, states:

> We share a vision of cities for all, referring to the equal use and enjoyment of cities and human settlements, seeking to promote inclusivity and ensure that all inhabitants, of present and future generations, without discrimination of any kind, are able to inhabit and produce just, safe, healthy, accessible, affordable, resilient, and sustainable cities and human settlements, to foster prosperity and quality of life for all. (United Nations Habitat 2016)

"Inclusive cities" are not simply achieved through the availability of affordable housing; rather the idea encompasses the broader goal of ensuring diversity. Nonetheless, officials from the United Nations call for housing to be at the center of the global urban agenda, suggesting that current patterns of housing production create cities of exclusion, through segregation and fragmentation of residents (Clos 2016). United Nations Sustainable Development Goal, Target 11.1, also calls for signatory nations to ensure access to adequate housing for all by 2030.

While the neoliberal approach to development suggests that governments should remove support from housing provision in favor of market incentives, continued gaps in adequate and affordable housing renew the call for government intervention. Though United Nations Habitat, the World Bank, and other international institutions once suggested that policies and programs should work toward "a world without slums," in which the primary goal was for the poor to have access to formal-sector housing, these institutions have now moved toward a world that integrates slum dwellers and low-income residents into the fabric of the city. This vision is encompassed by a number of policies and programs, including cooperative solutions, incremental housing, self-build schemes, upgrading of informal settlements, and new financing models (United Nations Habitat 2016, 14). The shift recognizes that neither the government nor the market can adequately generate formal-sector housing for all and that informality represents a necessary source of affordable housing. This new model promotes building on existing community strengths rather than disrupting social networks.

Further, current urban discourse acknowledges that housing interventions themselves are not the only key to the inclusive city; the means by which decisions are made also define inclusion. The New Urban Agenda calls for states to commit to broadening "inclusive platforms" that "allow meaningful participation in decision making, planning, and follow-up processes for all, as well as an enhanced civil engagement and co-provision and co-production" (United Nations Habitat 2016, 7).

At the global level, numerous initiatives increase the capacity of civil society to promote inclusive urban governance. For example, the Inclusive Cities Project, led by the global nongovernmental organization (NGO) WIEGO, argues that inclusive cities "ensure all residents . . . have a representative voice in governance, planning, and budgeting processes," as well as "access to secure and dignified livelihoods, affordable housing, and basic services," and its goal is to increase organizational capacity of CSOs for this purpose (WIEGO 2016). The World Bank views "spatial inclusion" as being the access to land, housing, and services, while "social inclusion" involves improving the terms of individuals and groups to participate in society, including participatory processes and rights-based approaches (Shah et al. 2015). In addition, for over a decade, United Nations Habitat has promoted inclusive cities as both a means and an end, in which the inclusive city is the outcome of good urban governance and inclusive decision-making processes are an essential means to achieving good urban governance (United Nations Habitat 2012). Inclusiveness in this regard can be achieved through a variety of policies and programs, including approaches that promote welfare, human development, the environment, institutions, and the right to development. For the purposes of this book, inclusion is defined by both the incorporation of community organizations in official decision making and the outcome of ensuring access to secure and decent housing for all residents. Access to government decision making is both the goal and the definition of inclusive cities. Enhancing the capacity and commitment of community organizations to participate in governance institutions—thereby democratizing urban development—is critical to this agenda.

The Role of Urban Mobilization

If we accept that civil society must play a significant role in creating inclusive cities, we then need to understand the incentives for civil society to participate in and demand new modes of governance rather than assuming the part these actors should want to play. We know community organizations fighting for low-income housing want spatial inclusion in the city, but the cases in this book also serve to elucidate the motivations and limitations of community organizations in working toward more inclusive governance.

In the 1980s and 1990s, mobilization around housing dissipated in cities around the world. In the developing world, and particularly in Latin America, scholars noted a number of challenges to widespread popular mobilization. First, neoliberal reforms limited the ability of cities to provide broad social benefits, which led demands for low-income housing to become more localized and less oriented toward reform of urban social policy (Roberts and Portes 2006). Second, popular movements faced co-optation by newly elected democratic regimes that could now claim to legitimately represent popular needs (Eckstein and Merino 2001; Foweraker 2005; Roberts 1997, 2002; Roberts and Portes 2006). And, third, regularization, urbanization, and state housing subsidy programs in cities such as Lima, Mexico City, Rio, and Santiago decreased the perceived need for widespread mobilization for housing (Roberts and Portes 2006). In the United States, the move toward privatization of services and investment in market mechanisms to provide housing across income levels reduced the funding provided directly by federal, state, and city governments. The move to dismantle public housing from the 1970s forward stirred little protest, in part because the federal one-for-one replacement rule limited numerical reduction of existing housing units and little changed quickly. It was not until the 1990s that housing authorities promised new mixed-income communities with greater amenities to residents and demolished public housing units in earnest.

Today, however, across cities low-income residents express a growing frustration with existing programs, policies, and institutions that do not adequately address their need for affordable, secure, and decent housing. In Latin America, low-income residents have found that democratic institutions are not enough to protect and promote the rights of citizens. In particular, regularization of titles to provide secure property rights and "urbanization projects" to improve the basic infrastructure of communities, including paved streets, sanitation systems, and electricity, among other amenities, have failed to guarantee inclusion and integration of the poor into the "formal" economy and politics of cities (McCann 2014; Perlman 2010). Across developing and developed nations, residents also increasingly decry close ties between the state and the private sector. Frustration over lack of consultation in development projects and protection of individual rights has motivated residents to again collectively mobilize. In the United States, the Occupy and Black Lives Matter movements distill the frustrations with inequality and discrimination that permeate cities. Following the financial crisis in 2008, Occupy protested the foreclosure of homes purchased with subprime loans and called on governments and private banks to assist rather than discard homeowners in trouble. Protesters called for the accountability of Wall Street to prevent deepening inequality, particularly based on homeownership. The Black Lives Matter movement has also taken to the streets to advocate for greater transparency and accountability of law enforcement, but more broadly members seek economic justice and structural change to combat discrimination against African Americans.

Mobilization of citizens around the world appears to be on the rise, and much of what we hear about in the news involves protest against gentrification and displacement. For instance, in 2015 a London group called Class War, organized through social media, vandalized a café they perceived to be a symbol of gentrification. One protestor interviewed stated, "We don't want luxury flats that no one can afford[;] we want genuinely affordable housing. We don't want pop-up gin bars or brioche buns[;] we want community" (Khomami and Halliday 2015). Several years earlier and across the hemisphere, in Ouagadougou, Burkina Faso, resident-organized groups, referred to as "crisis committees," protested residential displacement and threats to established neighborhoods over land title conflicts (Harsch 2009). After shutting down the protest, the government eventually made promises for more compensation and assistance for those being relocated. In Port-au-Prince, when the Haitian government threatened to clear slums in 2012, protestors erected flaming barricades and clashed with police in an effort to remain in place (*The Telegraph* 2012). In San Francisco, a group called the San Francisco Anti-Displacement Coalition (SFADC) is engaged in an ongoing fight against the consequences of gentrification, specifically a wave of evictions and landlord harassment forcing residents from their neighborhoods (Colomb and Novy 2016). The SFADC seeks to change city policy by proposing resolutions in the city council and ballot initiatives for voters, in addition to staging protests in public places.

These cities vary tremendously by socioeconomic characteristics and institutions, yet they all face backlash from residents frustrated that their interests and their physical place in the city are in jeopardy. In each of these cases reported by news outlets, residents took to the streets to influence government policies and programs that directly affected their lives. In fact, the most typical way that we view civil society impact is through its influence on public officials, either through disruptive protest, direct negotiation, or public advocacy campaigns. And yet, as the discussion of inclusive cities indicates, the expectation of activists, scholars, and global leaders is that civil society should also increasingly demand new opportunities for change from the *inside* of governmental institutions. Participatory governance institutions, including opportunities for managing official budgets, policies, programs, and planning processes, *could* provide civil society with a route for direct influence. These types of institutions are the means toward inclusive cities as well as the outcomes of demands for political inclusion.

In addition, the judicial system *could* provide an important outlet for housing conflicts and a direct voice in shaping housing outcomes for residents. Courts adjudicate the rights of residents as governments attempt to control land use. The extent to which community organizations access the court system to mediate conflicts and trust in the fairness of the courts demonstrates the viability of legal redress as an effective strategy. If organizations view the current administration or governmental system as inalterably controlled by real estate or other corporate interests, however, inside influence through participatory institutions or the justice system may not be viable options for redress. Instead, civil society may choose to replace public officials, seek influence from outside actors, or work autonomously to provide housing solutions.

Research Design

This study relies on a comparative case study approach to address the primary questions regarding strategies and outcomes of community organizations. The comparative case study approach allows for careful process tracing within individual cases as well as comparison across cases. By analyzing cities across the "developed-developing" divide, I show the similarities and differences that exist across diverse urban contexts. For years, comparative urban research has been limited by the assumption that the experiences of richer and poorer cities are not comparable. But the experiences we see in practice related to increasing costs and decreasing socioeconomic diversity in cities motivates the study across this divide. While clear differences exist across the United States and Brazil, we do not know how these differences matter until we conduct comparative research.

I selected the cases for this study primarily on the basis of similarities in the challenges of displacement and access to affordable housing. The United States and Brazil have some of the highest rates of urbanization in the world in addition to long-standing issues of inequality within cities. The cases under examination in this study exemplify the challenges of displacement and affordable housing while also demonstrating the variation in the approaches to respond to these challenges. The selection of cases across two countries allows for cross-national comparisons as well as cross-city comparisons.

More specifically, initially I selected Rio de Janeiro and Atlanta because both cities experienced significant displacement around preparation for Olympic Games. Rio de Janeiro hosted the Summer Olympic Games in 2016, the construction for which involved state-led removals of thousands of residents from informal settlements. In Atlanta, preparation for the Summer Olympic Games of 1996 also accelerated the demolition of downtown public housing buildings and the dispersal of low-income residents. In both cases, though the state initiated processes of removal, increasing real estate prices also provided the impetus for new developments that exacerbated the problems for newly displaced residents. During this time and well after, Atlanta experienced significant demographic change across neighborhoods long neglected for investment (U.S. Census Bureau 2011). In Rio, low-income residents traditionally crowd into centrally located favelas on steep hillsides, the wealthy preferring to live directly along the city's coastline. Leading up to the 2014 World Cup and 2016 Olympic Games, these favelas underwent drastic change as police interventions reduced the threat of violence and urbanization projects improved basic services in many of the favelas with the most desirable ocean views and central locations. In a sign of the changing times, both David Beckham and Madonna were rumored to have purchased homes in the city's central favelas (Williamson 2015a). True or not, the perception that favelas are now hot real estate reshapes the city's market. Locally, people refer to these forces of gentrification as "white removal" or "market removal" as opposed to forced evictions carried out by the municipal government.

I also initially selected the cases of São Paulo and Washington, D.C., because both cities had significant plans for city-center redevelopment that spurred rising prices and dislocation of residents. In São Paulo, the municipal government and then the state government made plans to revitalize the degraded city center, which threatened low-income residents who would be removed or priced out of the area. At the same time, the plans presented an opportunity to secure government-supported low-income housing in the city center. The city of São Paulo also experienced an increase in forced evictions in the 2010s. By 2012, 177 communities in the metropolitan region had either been removed or were notified of potential removal by the municipal government (Observatório das Remoções 2012). The justification for the vast majority of these cases was construction of public works projects, including upgrades to the subway system and a new highway (the "beltway") around the city. Many residents claimed that the city government largely ignored their rights to compensation and that many had no choice but to move far out of the city, removed from

employment opportunities and the communities they had once enjoyed.

In Washington, D.C., redevelopment of the Gallery Place/China-
town neighborhoods brought in new retail, dining, and entertainment, in addition to luxury condominiums and apartments. Tearing
down public housing and rising prices appear to have pushed low-income residents out of the area, even as advocates in the city mounted
protests to what they viewed as an affordable housing crisis (Sturtevant 2014). Redevelopment and gentrification have now touched all
areas of the city, and evidence of the threat of displacement is also seen
in the increasing number of landlord-tenant disputes in the remaining
low-income apartment rental buildings within and outside of the
downtown area.[5] Further, public housing residents face displacement
as their buildings are torn down and promises of replacement units
from the D.C. Housing Authority are not kept.

In each of the four case studies, fieldwork formed the basis of the
research. In each city, I met with leaders from a variety of community
organizations, other NGOs, the media, private-sector associations, and
government agencies related to housing and asked the same three main
questions regarding strategies and outcomes. These discussions led me
to focus more narrowly on specific organizations in each city that were
actively pursuing the goals of preserving or generating housing for low-
income residents and had made a significant impact during the time
period under study (2012–2016). Focusing on these specific cases allowed me to isolate how the strategies undertaken by organizations led
to certain outcomes. To understand the activities and motivations of
these organizations, I conducted interviews with leaders and attended
pertinent community and citywide meetings. In each city, I also spoke
with government officials regarding the effects of an organization's
strategies.

In Atlanta and Rio de Janeiro I selected the Historic District Development Corporation (HDDC) and the Residents' Association of Vila
Autódromo, respectively, as organizations that were both fighting to
preserve low-income housing in specific communities symbolic to the
future of inclusion in each city. In Washington, D.C., I chose the Housing for All Campaign, led by the Coalition for Nonprofit Housing and
Economic Development (CNHED), and in São Paulo, I selected the
União dos Movimentos de Moradia (Union of Housing Movements—

UMM) and the Frente de Luta por Moradia (Front for the Housing Struggle—FLM). These groups serve as umbrella organizations, mobilizing smaller organizations and residents for collective action while maintaining strong relationships with city government officials and institutions. The choice of different types of organizations across the cities—neighborhood-based versus citywide—allows for comparison of how each type of organization operates in different contexts.

To analyze the data for the case studies I used qualitative software to categorize thematic issues and key words. This process allowed me to note similarities and differences in the strategies undertaken by groups across cities and to link the demands and outcomes elicited by these strategies. The relatively long time frame from beginning to end of this study, from 2011 to 2017, meant that I needed to maintain continuous contact with key sources in each of the cities, make multiple site visits, and follow events as they unfolded through social media and news reports to ensure I captured the timeline of strategies and outcomes of these organizations' efforts.

Outline

The book begins with a comparative chapter on civil society, urban development, and housing across the United States and Brazil, the purpose of which is to orient the reader to the similarities and differences in the environment facing urban organizations across these two countries. In Chapter 2 I then present the main theoretical arguments regarding the typology of strategies, the factors behind the choices of strategies among community organizations, and the outcomes these strategies produce. I build on the variables behind strategic choices discussed by social movement and governance literature to explain both the factors internal and external to organizations that generate actions. Here I argue that ideology, the organization's relationship with the state, political opportunities, and resources shape the choice of inclusionary, indirect, overhaul, or exit strategies. Further, I argue that inclusionary strategies should lead to the most transformational changes in policies, programs, and institutions, but internal characteristics of the organization, the capacity of the city government, political shifts, and existing laws either enhance or limit the ability of community organizations to effect change.

In Chapter 3 I describe the resistance of Vila Autódromo in Rio, demonstrating that a radical ideology combined with a weak relationship with the state led to an exit strategy in which the community sought the support of international actors to pressure the city government to allow residents to remain in place. While the strategy produced limited victories for the community, the impact of their resistance on long-term structural change may be in providing a model rather than direct reform for those facing removal.[6] In Atlanta, a conservative ideology, a mixed relationship with the state, and limited resources produced the HHDC's indirect strategies for incremental change. New political leadership and increasing awareness of the growing crisis of affordability produced limited citywide reform, but little resolution to the challenge of long-term inclusion in the historic neighborhood.

In São Paulo, the UMM and the FLM wage a continuous struggle to hold the city government accountable for promises of investment in housing for low-income residents, often termed "social housing," and enforcement of zoning regulations. Of the four case studies, the housing movements in São Paulo are the only groups to have engaged in truly inclusionary strategies, but the existing participatory and legal institutions are far from sufficient as mechanisms of accountability. Influence of officials through disruptive tactics and bilateral negotiations also served to elicit promises and motivate implementation of programs. Government capacity in times of economic and political crisis, however, ultimately limited the movements' progress. Finally, in Washington, D.C., a relatively conservative ideology and a close relationship with the state encouraged indirect strategies to boost investment in a range of existing housing programs. Here, economic growth enabled the city government to increase investment, responding favorably to the Housing for All Campaign's long-term strategy. The campaign achieved their goal of increasing the budget for housing, though they did not prompt further institutional reforms that might provide for greater inclusion within policy making.

Though issues of tenure in the informal settlements of Brazil would seem to differentiate these two countries, the cases show that across cities residents struggle for the state to recognize their right to occupy space increasingly out of financial reach. Without organization, housing remains an individual challenge, but at the community level, residents realize their cases are strengthened by collectivizing the issue.

The cases reflect the importance of access to the legal system, direct negotiation with officials, and public consciousness of the residents' experiences. In addition, even though the victories for these communities are incomplete, they demonstrate a willingness from city governments to work with low-income residents collectively. Across cases, collective action pays off, but in different ways. At the heart of these conflicts is the desire of low-income residents to be recognized and treated as an integral part of the city. The cases demonstrate the similarities in insecurity facing low-income residents in cities experiencing rapid development and increasing costs of living, but they also show the importance of strategies for producing more favorable outcomes for residents.

Implications

How can the city be more inclusive and preserve existing diversity while improving the quality of life and promoting economic development? Often it may seem like development, as defined by increasing prosperity, services, profits, and revenues, is incompatible with development as defined by improving quality of life and increasing human capital. But every day we see community organizations around the world seeking to limit the power of profit to shape cities, insisting on a greater voice in urban development.

In the United States and Brazil, urban investment is reshaping cities at rapid speed. Though at first glance the issues across cities in the United States and Brazil differ significantly because of contrasting histories of urban development and the presence or absence of informal settlements, similarities exist in the processes by which gentrification, displacement, and the reduction of affordable housing take place. Community organizations across the world engage in various strategies to combat displacement and secure affordable housing, but we still have much to learn about why and when organizations choose the strategies they do to promote housing and the effect of these choices across diverse contexts.

This research suggests that today community organizations across the United States and Brazil still largely seek to influence policies and programs for housing from the *outside* rather than seeking opportunities for decision-making power from *within* government institutions. Their strategies demonstrate the traditional notion of separation between the state and civil society, but this indirect means of influence will not further the global agenda for inclusive cities. Community organizations face enormous challenges in garnering resources, mobilizing support, and counteracting the power of the private sector, but if we all desire more inclusive cities, community organizations may need to reflect on their own strategies and how they might change to achieve outcomes that promote incorporation, both spatially and politically. As the case studies demonstrate, organizations in the United States are more hesitant than those in Brazil to call for formal inclusion of civil society actors in government institutions if these representatives would be unelected by the people. But even in Brazil, where there is a longer tradition of incorporation of civil society into the state, newly created participatory institutions and legal instruments meant to protect the poor often fail to provide power to civil society and resolution to the significant challenges of housing. Of course, those who hold power in the environment in which civil society operates—including public-sector institutions and private-sector interests—also must see the value in including civil society in decision making and work toward that goal. The cases illustrate the long road ahead for civil society and government to fulfill the promise of inclusive cities, but the achievements of these organizations, regardless of their strategies, provide signs of hope for collective action as a means of preventing displacement and ensuring access to affordable housing.

1

The Role of Community Organizations in Urban Development and Housing across the United States and Brazil

The decision to study cities in both the United States and Brazil may at first appear to be an odd choice. And, in fact, the two countries and the cities therein do differ significantly in the length of time that democratic institutions have been in effect as well as many socio-economic variables. Brazil turned toward democracy only in the mid-1980s, after several decades of military rule, and the country still faces great challenges in prosecuting cases of corruption, forming political coalitions, and resisting clientelistic practices. Further, Brazil has had one of the highest rates of inequality in the world, with significant rates of extreme poverty across both cities and the countryside. But both the United States and Brazil have also confronted issues of marginalization by race, class, and geography, which have been exacerbated in recent decades by urbanization and global economic trends. In both countries, rising costs of urban living stretch the ability of residents at the bottom rungs of the economic ladder to remain in or secure decent housing, and these residents look to their governments for solutions.

In this chapter I explore a number of critical points of comparison regarding the politics of housing across Brazil and the United States that contribute to the activities of community organizations. I then turn to the question of whether we see a trend toward a new role for civil society across these two diverse nations. In particular, I note the influence of informality/formality, institutions, the role of the market versus the state, and geography as factors shaping the politics of housing and the environment in which community organizations operate. Though traditional U.S. urban politics literature has denied the impact of community organizations on urban development, more recently scholars, including Clarence Stone and his colleagues (2015), conclude that we are living in "a new era," in which collective actors at the community level matter more than ever for influencing the direction of urban policies and programs. In Latin America, too, scholars continue to debate the relative weight of low-income communities against the strength of the relationship between public officials and real estate and construction interests (see, e.g., Rubin and Bennett 2015; Sandbrook et al. 2007), generally finding that such connections are pervasive. The nature of low-income housing provision provides a test to the notion that businesses and government are more accepting of civil society influence now than in the past. Because social housing provision may not provide clear short-term returns to the local economy, while investment that leads to gentrification generates quicker profits, business interests need strong incentives to get behind the preservation or creation of low-income housing (Purcell 2008).

The debate about the influence of community organizations, particularly in the arena of housing, is far from settled and requires further exploration in cities across the globe. The brief review that follows demonstrates the similarities across cities in terms of challenges, solutions, and the proposals for reform of policies, programs, and institutions that will steer the future of urban development.

Comparing Housing Policies, Programs, and Institutions

We might expect that because poverty is more pervasive in Brazil that the scale of housing need would be greater than in the United States. Current statistics, however, do not straightforwardly confirm this conclusion. The official definition of "cost burdened" across both countries is a situation in which families spend more than 30 percent of their monthly income on housing, either in rental or mortgage payments (HUD 2017; IBGE 2014a). In the United States 36 percent of American households report spending more than 30 percent of their income on housing, while in Rio de Janeiro and São Paulo about 30 percent of renters are cost-burdened (IBGE 2014b). In the United States, among the 9.6 million lowest-income renters (earning less than $15,000 a year), 72 percent pay more than 50 percent of their income on rent, making them "severely cost-burdened" (Harvard University Joint Center 2016). Similarly, in Rio and São Paulo, about 72 percent of those earning less than half of the minimum wage in Brazil are considered to be cost-burdened by housing payments (IBGE 2014b). The challenges of meeting monthly housing expenses, especially among the lowest-income families, then, are quite similar across cities even if the quality of living conditions in the United States may be relatively higher. Merely by looking at pictures of the hillside favelas in Rio we can see the lack of sanitation, paved roads, and amenities that weaken the quality of life for residents and indicate government neglect as well as severe poverty. But in the individual lives of residents, the struggle to make ends meet affects residents across the North-South divide.

Important differences do exist, however, and these should not be ignored. In particular, significant points of comparison include the presence of informal settlements, the structure of governmental institutions, ideas about the role of the state and the market in housing policies and programs, and the geography of low-income housing.

Informality

Though "tent cities" in the United States have become more common since the 2008 financial crisis (Taylor 2016), informal settlements in Brazil operate at a much greater scale, containing over 20 percent of the urban population (IBGE 2014a). The term "informal settlements" generally refers to areas in which residents have built homes on land to which they do not have legal claim and includes the neighborhoods commonly known as favelas in Brazil. Informality in Brazil generates a greater number of conflicts over the right to stay in place and leads to ambiguities in the legal rights of residents, given provisions that guarantee "squatters' rights."[1] In addition, as James Holston (2008) points out, informality in Brazilian cities has generated a form of "insurgent citizenship" in which residents of informal settlements have long fought for basic rights and services from the government while at the same time developing communal bonds as they work to satisfy their local community needs.

Theoretically, compared to U.S. organizations, informality in Brazil creates a long-term organized community for collective action, greater knowledge of the policy-making system, and greater reliance on autonomous actions. But lack of traditional property rights still poses a particular hurdle for Brazilian organizations in persuading judges and government officials of the rights of residents to stay in place. Though laws in the United States can also be open to interpretation, generally speaking, contracts and formal titles provide residents with greater security.

The fact that informal settlements dominate Brazil as the primary source of affordable housing clearly influences issues of displacement and available policy options for creating more secure housing arrangements. Because land tenure is often ambiguous, but written protections for those who occupy the land are strong, community organizations in Brazil are likely to appeal to the courts in cases of displacement. But organizations also call for upgrading of existing informal settlements as a means of improving residents' quality of life and acknowledging that clearing residents is an untenable option. These goals are not so different from calls by public housing advocates in the United States to improve conditions for residents rather than uprooting residents to new, planned, mixed-income communities. The needs of people anywhere for safe and decent housing are the same, but the existing housing circumstances do create variation in the goals, activities, and policy options for organizations in each city.

Institutions

Institutions to promote access to housing for low-income residents are on the surface quite similar across cities in the United States and Brazil. At the federal level, both countries have large bureaucratic agencies—the Department of Housing and Urban Development (HUD) in the United States and the Ministry of Cities in Brazil—tasked with distributing money to the state and city levels to enable access to housing for low-income citizens. At the city level, each of the case study sites also maintains a central housing agency tasked with managing the creation and maintenance of low-income housing and distributing federal and state funding. D.C. and Atlanta both have Housing Authorities, which administer rental voucher and rental subsidy programs as well, and municipal-level departments that administer other local programs. In Rio and São Paulo, municipal housing secretariats manage contracts from the federal Minha Casa Minha Vida (My House My Life) Program (MCMV) in addition to programs for regularization, urbanization, and land-use permitting. The secretariats also create housing plans with the participation of local CSOs.

In the United States, HUD states its mission as "to create strong, sustainable, inclusive communities and quality affordable homes for all" through programs that support the acquisition of mortgages, provide rental assistance, deliver grants for community assistance, protect people from discrimination, and enact regulations in the housing market.[2] HUD was created by Congress as a cabinet-level agency in 1965. Though overall federal funding for housing programs in the United States has declined sharply since the mid-2000s, Congress did allocate budget increases in the past decade for rental assistance programs, public housing operating assistance, homeless assistance grants, and housing counseling (Schwartz 2015, 57). Since 2011, programs to improve public housing, housing for the elderly, and housing for the disabled experienced severe cuts by a more fiscally conservative Congress.

In Brazil, the Ministry of Cities was created in 2001 to fill a vacuum in housing assistance left by the dissolution of the Banco Nacional de Habitação (National Housing Bank) during the country's democratization process in 1985. The Brazilian Constitution of 1988 enshrined the right to housing, but the institutional framework for housing was not constructed until the passage of the Estatuto da Cidade (Statute of the City, or City Charter) in 2001. The Ministry of Cities contains secretariats for housing, sanitation, and transportation. Under the Secretariat for Housing there are separate departments for housing production, institutional development, technical cooperation, and urbanization of precarious settlements. The secretariat is responsible for implementing the National System for Housing in the Social Interest, with an accompanying Fund for Social Housing, through a participatory council that includes representatives from national housing movements, private-sector associations, and government agencies.

Compared to the United States, the institutional structure for housing assistance in Brazil appears, at least on paper, to be more inclusive of CSOs. Brazil is well known for its use of participatory governance institutions—often mandated by law—to promote citizen inclusion in official decision making (see, e.g., Avritzer 2009; Wampler 2015). Though a number of cities in the United States have begun to implement participatory budgeting processes, citizen engagement within government institutions has generally been more ad-hoc through advisory councils or planning processes for specific projects. In Brazil, all cities with over twenty thousand residents are required to have a participatory housing council, composed of government officials, CSOs, and social movements, to manage transfers from the federal Fund for Housing in the Social Interest (Donaghy 2013). Members from civil society and social movements are elected to two-year terms, though the frequency of meetings and responsibilities afforded to the councils varies considerably by city.

Aside from legislative institutions, judicial institutions in both Brazil and the United States provide protection for residents, particularly those facing displacement. The Statute of the City in Brazil builds on the constitutional provision that all property must fulfill a social function. One legal right specified by the Statute of the City is *usucapião urbana*, or "adverse possession of urban property," which allows residents of small lots to gain title of ownership if they can prove they have lived continuously on the property for five years (Friendly 2013). In negotiating indemnity payments or contesting eviction notices, residents use this legal right to make their cases for greater benefits and the right to stay in place. In both Rio and São Paulo, the Defensoria Pública, or Public Defender's office, assists residents in filing claims and negotiating with government officials. In U.S. cities, legal aid organizations assist low-income residents with landlord-tenant disputes and incidences of foreclosure, though there is not a dedicated institution like Brazil's Defensoria Pública to mediate housing conflicts from the perspective of the resident.

Institutions provide the outlet for grievances and the targets for reform. In Brazil, the increase in federal funding for housing in contrast with the decrease in funding in the United States may make the federal level a greater target within organizational strategies, but this is not necessarily the case in the United States even if organizations continue to view the federal government as the ultimate source of housing aid. Given the presence of formal participatory institutions, we might also expect community organizations to take advantage of these deliberative spaces rather than taking to the streets or exiting the chain of governance. In the United States, though, even without many formalized participatory institutions, opportunities at the local level likely do exist for insider participation, and we need to know what these are before we can genuinely reflect on the impact of these institutional differences. The presence of the Defensoria Pública, too, may elicit greater investment of effort by community organizations in the judicial system in Brazil compared to the United States, where this type of public defense does not exist, but again, local variation in courts means organizations in some U.S. cities choose to access the legal system more than in others. The effects of institutions are always complex in any context, and here the direction of influence of housing agencies and the judicial actors becomes an empirical question for evaluation in the case studies.

The State versus the Market

In both the United States and Brazil, there is a tension regarding the role of government in ensuring affordable housing. On the one hand, the idea that the state should intervene only through the use of market mechanisms guides the provision of rental housing vouchers, tax credits, and incentives for construction of properties targeted to low-income residents. On the other hand, the vision of housing as a social right steers the demands of advocates seeking further public investment and the use of legal mechanisms to prevent displacement. This sets up a clash between the market and the right to housing across cities and countries.

In Brazil, the federal government continues to take on a primary role in financing construction for low-income housing, while in the last two decades in the United States almost no money from HUD has gone toward new construction for public housing (Schwartz 2015). In the United States, the federal government still provides some money for the preservation and replacement of public housing, and the Low-Income Tax Credit does incentivize private development of designated low-income units, but the majority of HUD funding for low-income housing goes toward rental vouchers and block grants to states to conduct their own programs (Schwartz 2015, 7). The move away from construction of public housing came after a report commissioned during the Nixon administration cited the deteriorating physical conditions and widespread crime associated with inner-city projects. In contrast, the Brazilian federal government invests heavily in new construction of housing targeted toward very low-income families, primarily through the MCMV Program. Unlike U.S. public housing, the Brazilian government offers low-rate financing to purchase these units. For families who earn less than approximately US$800 per month, the federal government offers financing for ten years, with payments as low as the equivalent of $8 a month.[3] In April 2014, the Ministry of Cities announced that 2.4 million units had been constructed as part of the program since 2009, with 400,000 more to be completed in 2015.[4]

Through the MCMV Program, the government of Brazil supports the ideal of home ownership, which the U.S. government chooses to support mainly through tax incentives. The U.S. government provides tax incentives in the form of deductions for mortgage interest and property taxes, which critics point out mainly benefit affluent households that can afford to purchase homes without assistance (Schwartz 2015). Some cities, including D.C., provide tax credits for first-time homebuyers, though the credit is not income specific. The Federal Housing Administration also offers mortgage insurance to low-income buyers to be able to qualify for market-rate loans, but the federal government does not directly subsidize mortgage payments in any way resembling the Brazilian program.

As noted, since the 1970s rental vouchers have been a growing form of assisting low-income residents with housing needs in the United States. Approximately 2.4 million households received rental vouchers in the United States as of 2014 (Schwartz 2015). Brazil has also recently adopted the use of rental vouchers as a means of housing the poor, but the idea is generally that rental vouchers should be used for short-term emergencies until residents can secure a unit in a public housing complex. In São Paulo, rental vouchers are often granted to residents displaced from favelas, but the time is generally limited and the amount is well below market rate for rental accommodations in the city. Finally, in a limited number of states in the United States, rent controls assist low-income renters—a policy idea that has not yet been adopted by Brazilian states or cities.

Geography of Low-Income Housing

Unlike in U.S. cities, whose rich left the city centers for the suburbs in the second half of the twentieth century, in Brazil the wealthy have always occupied the urban core, while the poor have been pushed toward the periphery. Recently, though, trends in both countries have shifted. In the United States, a movement among baby boomers and millennials to "return to the city" drives up prices within the urban core, as developers seek to meet market demand for luxury condos, retail, entertainment venues, and upscale restaurants. In cities like Atlanta and D.C., lower-income residents increasingly find affordable housing in the suburbs, such as Clayton County, Georgia, and Prince George's County, Maryland, respectively (Sturtevant 2014, on D.C.). Relatively good public transportation systems, cheap access to cars, and jobs that are spread out beyond the city's urban core all encourage moving to the suburbs.

In contrast, in Rio and São Paulo, the majority of jobs continue to be concentrated in the city centers, connected to the neighborhoods in which the wealthy live. Public services, jobs, and amenities remain less plentiful in the suburbs of Brazilian cities than in the U.S. suburbs. Nonetheless, gated communities, often on the peripheries of Brazilian cities, provide a measure of security away from the perceived and real dangers of the city and motivate sprawl of the wealthy outside the urban core (see, e.g., Caldeira 2001). Development of these enclaves for the wealthy tends to lead to displacement of residents living informally on newly valuable land and drives up prices across the periphery, even without large-scale improvements in infrastructure and transportation beyond community gates. In general, solutions to ensuring that residents are able to secure affordable housing varies locally across the United States and Brazil, with more options available outside of the urban core in the United States and greater need for center-city housing in Brazil.

Another source of divergence in U.S. and Brazilian housing policy is the goal to deconcentrate poverty. Through the dismantling of public housing and the use of rental vouchers, the aim of U.S. housing policy is to allow people to choose where to live instead of confining "the poor to poor communities." Given the rising cost of rents in cities, however, the extent to which the poor can "choose" where to live is still limited. In Brazil, where favelas have been the primary source of affordable housing options, in the 1990s and 2000s the federal government recognized the reality that, given their scale, improving the favelas through infrastructural and service upgrades would be far more efficient than removing and relocating residents. The federal government provides funding for upgrading primarily through the Programa de Aceleração do Crescimento (Program for Accelerated Growth—PAC), launched in 2007, which contracts private firms to undertake various types of development projects across the country. Generally, the process of upgrading favelas goes hand in hand with regularization, or land titling, programs.

Forced removals of favela residents in the past decade, discussed further in the Rio de Janeiro and São Paulo case studies, contradict the Brazilian government's investments in upgrading and regularization of tenure, though unlike in the case of removals related to the demolition of public housing in the United States, removals in Brazil do not generally signal concern over the geographic concentration of poverty. In Brazil, the policy solution for residents displaced from favelas is often resettlement in public housing units, thereby further concentrating poverty, while in the United States it is the public housing residents who are forced to relocate, often with the assistance of rental vouchers. Displacement across cases is not simply due to the unfortunate rise in the cost of living that pushes people out of the city, but also results from government policies that shape the landscape for affordable housing in the city's core.

The Demands of Community Organizations

Given these similarities and differences in the urban environment across the United States and Brazil, the goals of community organizations might be expected to vary according to local circumstances, but I also identified many similarities in the programs, policies, and institutional changes groups seek across contexts. In all cities, community organizations concerned with housing seek increases in resources allocated to housing; protections for residents facing displacement; opportunities to allow those facing displacement to stay in place; centrally located, safe, and decent government-subsidized or regulated housing; a judicial system that upholds existing laws and regulations; and more opportunities to participate in planning and development processes.

Preventing Displacement

In São Paulo and Rio, the first demand of community organizations in response to state-led displacement (involuntary evictions) is generally for the community facing eviction to have the right to stay in place. The tenure status of residents comes into play, and Brazil's legal system offers strong protections for "squatters"; the Estatuto da Cidade states that those who have lived on a publicly owned property for at least five years have the right to adverse possession.[5] Social movements also call for the implementation of the constitutional provision that all property must be used for a social purpose. Such movements in Brazilian cities often occupy abandoned buildings or properties whose owner is behind in paying taxes, claiming possession on the basis of this constitutional provision. Along with the right to stay in place, communities also call for regularization of land titles to prevent future eviction and for urbanization projects to improve living conditions. If communities are not allowed to stay in place, then calls for fair-market indemnity payments or resettlement to nearby social housing come into play.

More recently, gentrification has become a larger issue in both São Paulo and Rio as the properties of residents within favelas and other areas take on higher market values (Williamson 2015b; Torres et al. 2003). Theresa Williamson, director of the Rio-based NGO Catalytic Communities, has called for collective land titling or community land trusts in order to prevent favelas from being bought by the rich, thereby removing the current source of affordable housing in the city. In São Paulo, rising rents have led to increasing numbers of long-term occupations of abandoned buildings, the majority led by the main social movements in the city. These occupations provide a critical source of affordable housing in the city center. Residents of *cortiços* (tenement houses) in the city center also face increasing financial pressure to move far out to the periphery (Barbosa 2015). In response, social movements in São Paulo call for renovation of abandoned properties, some of which are currently occupied by movement members, as well as construction of new social housing in the city center. Social movements argued that financing for these projects should be available through the federal MCMV Program, with smaller contributions from the city government.

Over the last decade, responding to the challenges of gentrification has been one of the most confounding issues in urban planning and politics in U.S. cities. Planners, city officials, and community organizations struggle with the question of how to generate economic growth, reduce crime, and create attractive, livable neighborhoods without generating displacement among current residents. For renters, possible solutions include expanding rent control, which limits the percentage increase in rent per year for current residents, and extending the time limits for units subsidized through the Low-Income Housing Tax Credit program.[6] In addition, since one of the main problems for renters is that landlords in up-and-coming neighborhoods wish to sell properties in order to profit from their investment, community organizations often call for laws that give tenants the right of first refusal to purchase the property at market value, and also funding to enable incumbent residents to purchase the property. Housing trust funds, operated at the municipal level, often are the primary source of funding for tenant purchase programs (Schwartz 2015, 279). For homeowners, tax abatements to offset increases in property taxes and foreclosure assistance may help to prevent displacement.

In terms of displacement related to the demolition of public housing complexes in the United States, residents can choose to fight for the right to stay in place and/or for the renovation of existing units rather than demolition. Alternatively, residents can accept the provision of rental vouchers to move elsewhere, or if they perceive these opportunities to provide them with a better quality of life, the promise of a unit within a newly constructed mixed-income complex.

In sum, across cities of Brazil and the United States, community organizations seek several common remedies to the problem of displacement. Organizations call for legal protections of residents, efforts to improve property conditions, and financial subsidies for residents to be able to remain in place. Alternatively, if displacement is inevitable, organizations seek new options in public housing and rental vouchers to allow residents to secure decent living conditions. Though the context of displacement varies across cities, the means of resolving these conflicts are often very similar.

Creating Affordable Housing

Whereas direct government intervention is almost always necessary to address issues of displacement, the creation of affordable housing comes about either through direct public provision or the result of market incentives. As previously mentioned, in Brazil, the Minha Casa Minha Vida Program has been the largest source of formal-sector affordable housing since it began in 2009.[7] As is discussed in the case study of São Paulo, the main issue with the program for meeting urban demand has been the rising price of land in city centers, which reduces the profit motive for private-sector development. To ensure building for the low-income market in the city center, community organizations call for inclusionary zoning laws that state the percentage of new units that must be reserved for low-income residents.

In the United States, community organizations also recommend inclusionary zoning laws as an important policy remedy, but in practice these laws have so far had limited effect in major cities (Schwartz 2015, 283). Organizations also call for the expansion of the Low-Income Housing Tax Credit, which incentivizes builders to set aside affordable units in new construction, but because the credit is generally time limited, organizations also call for the federal government to make these subsidies permanent. Community organizations petition the federal government agencies to extend tax and voucher programs while also recognizing the need for city governments to extend inclusionary zoning provisions, homeownership programs, and municipally funded rental voucher programs.

Institutional Change

The development of housing agencies, participatory mechanisms, and judicial bodies that address issues of housing are important institutional outcomes. Not all community organizations will demand change in institutions, either because they are satisfied with existing institutions or believe targeting institutional change to be an ineffective strategy for achieving their goals, but without bottom-up participation in institutions, the type of change that top-down reform elicits is at issue. Potential outcomes regarding institutions differ based on the existing institutional environment, but in general, outcomes in which institutions are strengthened or created to promote a greater voice for low-income residents and greater accountability to their needs should be key to changing the course of housing and urban development. While institutions evolve over time, the differences in housing outcomes produced by stronger, more responsive, transparent, and accountable institutions should provide long-term effects in the prevention of displacement and the provision of affordable housing.

Evolution of the Influence of Civil Society on Urban Development

Community organizations may have explicit, well-developed goals, such as those described above, but what impact do they actually have in making these goals reality? The consensus of previous literature on urban politics, particularly from the United States, was "not much." Writing about Atlanta in *Economic Growth and Neighborhood Discontent* (1976), Stone argues that low-income neighborhoods might win small victories but will never affect long-term agendas as long as government officials were most concerned with development of central business districts and had money to make their goals happen. John Logan and Harvey Luskin Molotch subsequently argue that the city functions as a growth machine, with public officials, the media, and labor union leaders acting in coalition to support projects of accumulation (Logan and Molotch 1987; Molotch 1976, 1979). John Mollenkopf (1983) argues that growth machines vary historically as the resources of coalition members shift, but the bottom line remains that coalitions, which exclude low-income community organizations, are key for the path of urban development. Further negating the role of community-level voices, scholars in the 1980s and 1990s argue that global competition reinforces the power of well-connected elites to shape the agenda of urban governments (Sassen 1988, 1991). According to Manuel Castells (2009), transnational networks wield power, while urban dwellers are largely excluded from the functioning of the city and the international business arena. A related line of analysis, urban regime theory, provides a tool for explaining public- and private-sector relationships. Stone's work came to dominate U.S. urban politics literature, though its applicability to Latin America, and Brazil in particular, has never really been systematically tested (Mossberger and Stoker 2001). Like other observers in the early post–World War II era, Stone argues that a coalition of city officials and business elites form around mutual interests in the generation of revenues and profits, limiting the ability of civil society to shape policy outcomes. The approach forges a middle ground between pluralists, who view political outcomes as the result of the influence of various interests, and structuralists, who argue for the primacy of economic power in policy making (Stone 1993, 2).

Over time, however, we have seen significant cracks in the hegemony of the urban regime in practice and in theory. As Peter Evans (2002) argues, differences across cities, particularly in terms of livability and amenities, indicate that local political logics, including the role of civil society, make a substantial difference in the lives of city residents. We do not see pure uniformity in the responsiveness of government officials to the needs and desires of residents any more than we see uniformity in the platforms, resources, and goals of city governments across one country or around the world. As any series of case studies demonstrate, there are always instances where community organizations appear to make a difference and moments when we can conclude that the public-sector agenda or private-sector interests won the day. To cite just one example, in their review of movements for housing in New York City, labor rights in Los Angeles, and education in Detroit, Michael Jones-Correa and Diane Wong (2015) find that community actors have the ability to mobilize resources and carry out sustained agendas, thereby challenging the notion of elitist control conceptualized by regime politics.

In addition, though urban scholars since the 1990s have argued that the future of cities rests on the city government's ability to attract international capital to become "global cities," thereby reducing the power of local communities (see, e.g., Sassen 2011), in the past decade urban scholars and practitioners have also recognized that to be effective in creating not just "global cities" but prosperous cities across socioeconomic divides, development must come from the ground up as well as through international connections and investment (Goldman 2014). Further, scholars such as Judith Tendler (1998) argue that good governance, which involves the institutionalized inclusion of civil society, is key to greater transparency and accountability in policies and programs. Broadly speaking, then, thinking in development policy has trended toward the inclusion of CSOs in policy making and program implementation.

More recently, in *Urban Neighborhoods in a New Era*, Stone and his colleagues acknowledge that relationships and policy making are more fluid now than in the past, fueled by new actors, issues, and institutional arrangements. They argue that both community organizations and business interests have changed, which in turn has provided more openings for the influence of civil society. Stone et al. write:

> The current period allows for some mixing of economic development aims with community-based concerns. The terms of this mix are negotiable, and the line between what favors economic development and what attends to community concerns has become increasingly fuzzy. Power is less and less a showdown between clearly differentiated antagonists and more a matter of how policy issues are framed, albeit accommodations are sometimes far from amicable. (2015, x)

No longer is development a zero-sum game of winners and losers; rather, the authors suggest that neighborhood politics involves a "contingency-filled outlook," in which actors negotiate the best possible outcomes. Through their case studies in the United States, Stone et al. identify displacement as a key area of friction across communities and provide evidence of incremental, piecemeal change rather than quick shifts brought about by specific events or single decisions. This finding coincides with Martin Horak's argument that institutional change does not happen from one single decision or event but rather evolves from "a *series* of non-simultaneous critical decision points, whose cumulative resolution results in the construction of a new political order" (2007, 24). Karen Orren and Stephen Skowronek (1994) also find that in the American context the development of institutions is typically "asynchronous." In looking at outcomes of the efforts of community organizations, particularly related to institutional development, change may appear gradual rather than instantaneous.

Just as important as a change in the outlook of government actors and private-sector interests toward urban development may be a shift in the strategies of community organizations. In Stone et al.'s conception, government and business interests are now more aware of the connectedness between economic and social conditions, but at the same time community actors have also become more willing to bargain than protest. Moderation of positions on both sides in the United States has opened the possibilities for community influence and change that did not exist in the past.

In Latin America, a similar phenomenon to that in U.S. cities has taken place. Sandbrook et al. (2007) argue that social democracies provide a new model for states to promote economic growth while also tending to the social welfare needs of low-income citizens. Members of the private sector will accept the rise of social democracies because they believe they also benefit from human capital development, stability, and the mitigation of conflicts that come from a lower class receiving assistance from the state (Rubin and Bennett 2015). Within this model, civil society should have a greater voice in policies and programs, no longer marginalized by alliances between business and the state. Ann Helwege (2015) argues that business leaders have been more open to civil society–initiated reforms as a result of a realization that reducing poverty and inequality has positive consequences for all. Wendy Wolford (2015) also describes the ways in which social movement strategies have moderated since democratization, as leftist groups no longer call for the downfall of the regime but rather express willingness to negotiate within the capitalist system. Left-leaning movements now have both the opportunity and the will to engage with the state.

At the same time, other scholars in Brazil argue that the weight of the private sector and the coalition formed with public-sector interests is growing rather than diminishing. For instance, Eduardo Marques (2013) describes the ways in which donations from private companies are critical for campaign financing and forming relationships once new administrations take office. Officials form strong relationships with private contractors of public services and public works projects, generating coalitions based on land production, urban renewal, and large-scale construction projects. In the 2014 municipal, state, and federal elections, each of the six major real estate and construction firms in the country were on the top ten list of donors (Tribunal Superior Eleitoral 2014). Traditional clientelistic relationships are now made more complicated by the need for officials to court the interests of these large companies in order to stage campaigns. Though clientelism surely still exists, government officials also face pressures from multiple actors in generating urban development in order to compete for global investment and tourism dollars. Hosting mega-events, as Brazil did with the World Cup in 2014 and the Olympic Games in 2016, sharpens the focus of government officials to reshape the image of the city for the international stage and creates new interests around development, not all of which have the welfare of low-income residents at heart (Andranovich, Burbank, and Heying 2002).

But, as previously noted, within the urban development environment Brazil is widely known for its innovative democratic institutions and incorporation of civil society into official decision making. Scholars often cite the importance of the Workers' Party (Partido dos Trabalhadores, PT) for implementing social programs and participatory institutions (Abers 1996; Baiocchi 2001; Baiocchi, Heller, and Silva 2011). Previous research finds that participatory institutions are associated with an increase in the probability of municipalities adopting a wide range of housing programs and policies (Donaghy 2013), and participatory budgeting processes have been associated with improvements in metrics of residents' well-being (Touchton and Wampler 2014). The strength of the impact of these institutions may sometimes be in doubt, but their existence indicates a greater willingness in the present than in the past to provide community organizations with the opportunity to influence urban development. Together, though, the contradictory effects of participatory institutions and the influence of the private sector continue to provide an uncertain outlook for the role of community organizations.

At the global level, a recent, broadly conducted study by United Nations Habitat; the Global Network of Cities, Local, and Regional Governments; and the London School of Economics provides more precise—and largely positive—evidence of the effect of CSOs on urban development. The survey questioned municipal government officials from cities around the world to understand the major influences on urban policy (London School of Economics 2016). In response to a question on citizens' influence on local policies, sixty-four out of seventy-five respondents cited "elections" as having significant influence. In ranked order, officials then cited local referenda, public consultations, protests/demonstrations, neighborhood advisory committees, social media campaigns, and public hearings as wielding significant influence.[8] The survey confirms the importance of representative forms of democracy for influencing local policies, but according to city officials, many other forms of participation are also significant for impacting the decisions of public officials.

CSOs certainly appear to fight an uphill battle in securing policies, programs, and institutions that serve the interests of those who have traditionally been politically marginalized, but the benefits of housing for low-income residents serve the interests of a wide variety of residents who wish to see cities thrive socially and economically. To influence urban development, community organizations must counteract the economic weight of the private sector as well as opposition from government officials concerned with economic growth. The private sector across countries does still play a significant role in decisions regarding development decisions and the influence that community organizations have on policy outcomes. The question, now, is how community organizations are able to negotiate with or circumvent the power of the private sector to persuade governments to enact housing policies and programs favorable to the poor rather than the wealthy.

Conclusions

Cities across the United States and Brazil need dramatic change to meet the growing needs of low-income residents to secure decent, affordable housing. Though cities in the United States and Brazil differ in terms of existing levels of informality, ideas about the role of the market and the state in housing policy, institutions, and geography, the need for interventions, government or otherwise, increase the urgency for governments to address the challenges of displacement and access to affordable housing. The scale of informality, a reliance on the state to provide housing benefits, and the presence of participatory institutions in Brazil might suggest that community organizations play a greater role in housing policy and programs than in the United States, but the growing need for affordable housing across these two countries also suggests the need for changing modes of governance to address increasing housing challenges. The proposed solutions of community organizations across these two countries differ in the details, but not in the primary goals of preserving and expanding access to decent housing for low-income residents. The case study chapters demonstrate the extent of both convergence and divergence of strategies and outcomes in U.S. and Brazilian cities.

2

Strategies and Outcomes
of Community Organizations

In practice, how do we see civil society organizations (CSOs) maintaining pressure for inclusion in cities where *exclusion* of residents appears to be unrelenting, particularly as the cost of urban living soars? Do the strategies of CSOs at the ground level reflect the momentum to create more inclusive cities suggested by global rhetoric and institutions? The adoption of strategies by CSOs to amplify inclusion, in both the political and spatial sense, is critical for creating an urban future in which cities thrive on the diversity of residents rather than catering to a wealthy few.[1]

In this chapter I first develop a typology of strategies based on the means by which CSOs seek influence. I argue that community organizations fighting for low-income, affordable housing will undertake an array of strategies in different moments, but we need to define and understand why these organizations engage in the strategies they do in order to gauge whether these efforts will bring about more democratic urban development. I begin with the hypothesis that organizations seeking to prevent displacement and generate more affordable housing strive for greater inclusion in formal decision-making institutions in order to achieve their demands. The extent to which organizations seek institutional inclusion, however, varies based on a number of contextual factors specific to the organization and the external environment. Primarily, the ideology of the organization's members and the organization's relationship with the state affect whether the CSO engages in inclusionary strategies or follows what I term "indirect," "overhaul," or "exit" strategies. Resources and political opportunities also significantly influence the strategic choices of organizations, though the direction of that influence may be highly contextual.

Long ago Albert Hirschman argued that dissatisfied individuals would choose either "exit, voice, or loyalty" (1970). While my conception of strategic choices builds on Hirschman's work, I find that, in many contexts around the world, there are now more choices about how to convey one's voice in order to influence policy and program outcomes than in the era in which Hirschman wrote. Therefore, I've refined my categorization and understanding of when and where CSOs choose to assert their "voice." The categorization here adds the dimension of collective action and further specifies how organizations choose to use their voices, influence key officials, select new leadership, and/or seek autonomous solutions by exiting the existing power structure.

After establishing a typology of strategies and identifying the factors behind strategic choices, the next question is, "So what?" The answer to this famous "So what?" question is that strategic choices matter for outcomes: whether community organizations achieve the goals they desire, and further, whether these achievements enhance democratic urban development. I argue that more inclusive strategies lead to transformation in the practice and benefits of democracy, while indirect strategies maintain the status quo in policies, programs, and institutions. Overhaul strategies can lead to immediate political change, while exit strategies indicate a removal from, and thus little impact on, local politics.

I begin the chapter with a discussion of how scholars have defined collective participation and then turn to my categorization of strategies. The next section then presents the theoretical framework around why community organizations engage in certain strategies, and the final section proposes a framework for understanding how different strategies lead to different outcomes and the variables that influence these relationships.

This chapter contributes to the literature on collective action in three ways. First, by developing a typology of strategies undertaken by organizations working on similar issues across cities that vary by political and economic history, I provide a valuable framework for comparison. Second, I combine previous findings regarding the factors behind organizational strategies to develop a cohesive argument about the dynamics at work. It is this dynamic between variables involving ideology and the political environment, reflecting whether community organizations have both changed their rhetoric and are able to respond to a changed political and economic environment, that suggests the new role they play in urban governance. Third, the logic of the influence of various strategies on outcomes contributes to our knowledge about what works in ensuring multiplicity of voices in democratic decision making.

Defining Modes of Collective Action

Previous literature suggests great diversity in collective action and group activities that seek to influence policy making. For instance, classic literature on social movements often focuses on whether groups pursue contentious or cooperative activities. Charles Tilly (1978) identified the "repertoires of contention" as the range of tactics in which movements engage. Sidney Tarrow then referred to contentious politics as "disruptive direct action against elites, authorities, other groups, or cultural groups" (1994, 9), while cooperative actions involved negotiating directly with public officials, participation in elections, and other nonconfrontational activities. Past research on informal settlements in Latin America often identified cooperative strategies as clientelistic, such as neighborhood associations trading particularistic benefits for votes (Gay 1994). Across categories, the repertoires of contention perspective generally assume that groups carry out certain activities at various points in time to maximize their influence on those in power.

The contentious versus cooperative dichotomy, however, no longer accurately describes the wide range of activities undertaken by social movements. If we focus on the nature of tactics alone, we fail to capture a complete picture of the strategies groups adopt in order to achieve their demands. Participation in government institutions may be considered cooperative, but when organizations have the opportunity to deliberate on, disagree on, and cast votes against government proposals within participatory institutions, their actions may in fact lead to radical change. The dichotomy of cooperation versus contention also assumes that CSOs exist outside of official state institutions, when in reality the line is often blurred by overlapping memberships, formal partnerships, and institutions that incorporate government and civil society.

More recently, governance scholars propose that participation from *within* public institutions provides a stronger means of influence than traditional advocacy, bilateral meetings, or disruptive tactics (for example, Wampler 2010; Avritzer 2009). Scholars have favored participatory institutions as remedies to traditional inequalities in power and decision making. Carole Pateman outlines the distinction between deliberative and participatory forms of democracy. While deliberative democracy provides citizens with the ability to voice opinions, come to consensus, and make decisions, Pateman argues that it still "leaves intact the conventional institutional structures and political meaning of 'democracy'" (2012, 10). Participatory democracy, in contrast, requires "reform of undemocratic authority structures" in order to "provide opportunities for individuals to participate in decision making in their everyday lives as well as the wider political system" (10). Pateman uses the example of participatory budgeting in Porto Alegre, Brazil, to demonstrate the ways in which participation can become institutionalized and come to be viewed as a right of citizens. Numerous studies on participatory budgeting attempt to explain why and how the process developed in this one city and the ensuing effects on democratic citizenship in Brazil (see, e.g., Abers 1996; Avritzer 2009; Baiocchi 2005; Wampler 2010). Since these early studies, researchers have begun to assess in greater depth the impact of participatory institutions, not just in terms of democratic citizenship but in the redistributive outcomes they produce for citizens (Touchton and Wampler 2014; Donaghy 2013). As participatory budgeting and other participatory institutions are replicated in cities around the world, researchers have also tried to refine the parameters around which participatory democracy arises and is sustained.

Reforms that institutionalize participatory practices are meant to reshape existing relationships between the state and civil society. In an era in which trust in government and disaffection among voters appear to be growing in not only Western democracies but also newer democracies, such as Brazil, Chile, and Mexico, participatory democracy should have the power to reengage citizens, but only if they see the value in participating. For participation to be worthwhile, institutions must have real power devolved from the state and produce significant policies and programs that improve the lives of citizens.

CSOs around the world, but particularly in Brazil, have fought for the creation and implementation of participatory institutions and a legal framework that prioritizes the rights of low-income citizens. As such, we might expect CSOs in Brazil to adapt strategies to seek change from *within* the state, in line with the participatory governance model. In Brazil, Orlando dos Santos argues that governance entails "more accountability from municipal governments concerning social policies and the demands of their citizens; opening channels for ample civic participation of society" (2002, 88). Studies on urban participatory governance in Brazil often view the state with suspicion and argue that social control through institutionalized participation is the answer (for example, see Ribeiro 2012; Santos et al. 2004; Frey 2007; Cardoso and Valle 2000; Abers and Keck 2009). In reality, however, various factors limit the effectiveness or viability of inside participation and instead motivate a continuation or renewal of strategies meant to influence officials from the outside (Acharya, Houtzager, and Lavalle 2004; Tatagiba 2010; Dowbor 2012). Reliance by CSOs on new institutions should therefore not be taken for granted; rather, we should continue to ask when institutional strategies provide the best perceived outlet for civil society demands.

In the United States, ideas about the role of community organizations participating within the state also have a long history. Literature on community development stemming from activism in the 1970s provides two important models of organizing that emphasize differences in contentious versus cooperative actions and the goals for community change. Scholars argue that advocacy around urban issues in the United States tends to represent either a community "building" or a community "organizing" model. As Susan Saegert notes, community builders "emphasize bonding and bridging social capital," while organizers "work with disenfranchised communities to make demands on the existing power structure through confrontational actions" (2006, 275). Community builders tend to work cooperatively with the institutions and actors who control resources in order to achieve community goals (Gittell and Vidal 1998; Saegert 2006). Community organizers, alternatively, mobilize residents to engage in protest, marches, and occupations to demand that governments provide needed services, jobs, and housing (Stoecker 1997; Saegert 2006). Similar to the builder/organizer models, literature on community activism also provides a distinction between "insider" and "outsider" strategies. Insiders tend to work for reform within the system, such as through lobbying, accessing resources and elites, and by way of paid staff, while outsiders generally challenge institutions and participate in contentious activities (Tilly 1978; Gamson 1990). Neither of these categorizations, however, implies direct influence in decision making, unmediated by public officials.

Much like in Brazil, in the last few decades, U.S. scholars, such as Archon Fung and Erik Olin Wright (2003), have moved the conversation in urban development toward implementing practices of participatory democracy. For instance, Fung (2009) argues that participation is becoming more empowered as mechanisms such as advisory panels, public hearings, and discussion groups actually determine the actions taken by officials. Further, Fung finds through his research that decision making, particularly around education and policing, has become more deliberative as community members and officials debate together the merits and challenges of proposed reforms (2009).

Organizations that seek to shape the future of low-income housing across the United States and Brazil increasingly rely on the ideal of inclusion in the city as the foundation for arguments about preserving affordable housing as well as generating increasing opportunities for low-income residents to live and be included in the fabric of the city. The question now is whether and how CSOs have also adopted the means of participatory democracy to influence politics and policy from the inside. As Pateman noted, participatory democracy entails not only inclusion within government but also the ability to make decisions that directly affect one's life. The objective of community organizations fighting against displacement and for affordable housing, then, should be institutions that incorporate their voices as well as the ability to make decisions that enable low-income residents to choose where to live.

Defining Strategies by the Means of Empowerment

As the previous discussion demonstrates, the means by which community organizations interact with the state and act autonomously to voice their demands are far from predetermined. "Strategy" is a term often associated with business or military planning, but any kind of organization needs a strategy, a plan of action, in order to succeed in achieving its goals. Along these lines, in *Strategies for Social Change*, Gregory Maney et al. write, "We define strategy as a plan of collective action intended to accomplish goals within a particular context. Strategy . . . entails defining, interpreting, communicating, and implementing a plan of action that is believed to be a promising way to achieve a desired alternative future in light of circumstances" (2012, xvii–xviii). This definition highlights several key points: (1) Strategy must be purposive. Organizational leaders and members intentionally devise a plan of action rather than simply acting in an ad hoc, piecemeal fashion. (2) Strategy involves collective action—that is, citizens do not act individually; rather, their combined efforts are perceived to be necessary to reach common goals. (3) Strategy must be context specific. The same one-size-fits-all strategy cannot work across issue areas and arenas; rather, organizations must design a plan of action that expressly responds to the political, economic, and legal environment in which they operate.

Strategies also involve three components: goals, targets, and tactics. In an influential activist manual used by community organizations in the United States, the authors recommend that organizations map out their strategies by identifying these three categories as well as the potential allies, opportunities, and threats that shape each one (Bobo, Kendall, and Max 2001, 30). Here, a strategy is more than a plan to get things done. Members must also consider the power relationships among relevant actors. Looking at the goals, targets, and tactics together provides a holistic understanding of the plans organizations create to achieve their demands.

Across cities with distinct democratic paths we would expect to see variation in the ways in which citizens organize to petition their governments to address social grievances. But as cities experience similar issues related to the need for affordable housing, we might also expect that the similarities in grievances lead to similarities in calls for redress. Where democratic institutions have been perceived as weak, particularly in the developing world, we may expect citizens to be more likely to engage in contentious tactics rather than cooperation with the state. In the past few decades, however, as democratic institutions deepen in Latin America, we increasingly see citizens taking advantage of institutionalized channels to bring about results. Conversely, in the United States, we also see instances of contentious activities, such as the Occupy protests or Black Lives Matter, in which citizens voice their frustration with the promise of the democratic system to provide equal opportunities for all.

Developing a typology of strategies allows us to differentiate between strategies among groups and across time. As Maney et al. (2012, xiii) argue, developing strategies involves difficult choices about which path will lead to the outcomes groups desire. These choices reflect differences among groups in the path they will pursue, yet to date little scholarship addresses how to categorize these diverse paths (Goodwin and Jasper 2004, 16). Where scholars do evaluate strategies, they tend to prioritize one variable without providing a dynamic picture of the factors that influence activities. Identifying the forces that shape the strategies of community organizations helps us to understand when and how groups eventually succeed in achieving their goals and the ways in which democratic institutions promote or impede diverse voices in urban development.

Across the social movement and participatory democracy literatures a key difference is clearly in the mechanisms, or strategies, by which organizations seek to be empowered. Moving forward, categorizations of strategies should reflect the locus of collective efforts and the nature of the desired change. Here, I label the strategies of housing movements as "inclusionary" (those that attempt to influence public decision making from within government institutions and enable citizen choice) and as "indirect" (those through which influence is mediated through persuasion of government officials, voters, or other actors). "Overhaul" strategies seek to change leadership and institutions to represent organizational interests, and "exit" strategies involve developing autonomous solutions or seeking redress from outside authorities. Different types of organizations will engage in different activities, but the key point of comparison is the way in which they seek to be empowered.

Inclusionary Strategies. Organizations that seek influence through institutions by exercising greater voice in official decision making and formal protection of rights are engaging in what I term inclusionary strategies. The goals of these strategies involve giving concerned organizations and low-income residents most affected by the challenges of affordable housing a direct voice in democratic institutions across the executive, judicial, and legislative branches of government. The protection of rights also enables residents to securely make their own decisions about where to live. The goals may include new programs to generate affordable housing, new legal protections to enable low-income residents to remain in the city, or greater access to the court system to adjudicate claims. The targets of inclusionary strategies are the agents directly responsible for housing, the mayoral administration, and possibly other levels of government with direct influence on city housing, but the means of influence is through institutional rather than bilateral channels with government officials. Tactics involve participation in institutions that enable direct influence on government decision making, fighting for housing rights through the judicial system, and training of members to participate in government decision-making processes.

Indirect Strategies. These strategies rely on the organization's ability to influence the decisions of public officials through existing relationships and institutions. They may rely on personal connections and clientelistic relationships rather than seeking to influence decision making through participatory mechanisms or adjudication through the legal system. The goals are to persuade public officials to satisfy the organization's demands or to provide loyalty in exchange for benefits. Targets are the public officials most directly responsible for housing decisions, and tactics focus on face-to-face meetings with public officials, lobbying efforts, mobilizing support among local voters, and creating networks among similar organizations.

Overhaul Strategies. Rather than working within the current administration or regime, some organizations work toward electing a new mayor and city council or reshaping government institutions. The mechanism of change is the electoral process, though this strategy is closely related to indirect strategies in that the ultimate means of influence is through relationships with public officials. The goal may be to elect leaders who are more sympathetic to the cause or to change the leadership institutions in which housing decisions are made, but not necessarily to reshape the ways in which decisions are made within institutions. The targets will be voters who can elect allies to public office. Tactics might involve organizational leaders running for office themselves or endorsing sympathetic candidates for office.

Exit Strategies. Instead of engaging with local political or financial interests, organizations concerned with housing may choose more autonomous solutions or seek influence at higher levels of government or among global actors. Goals may involve developing autonomous governance structures and communities that exist outside of the formal market. The targets of these strategies are underserved populations in need of housing solutions and potentially nongovernmental sources of funding. Tactics include self-built housing, cooperatives, and greater reliance on informal settlements. Alternatively, groups may choose to appeal to federal or state authorities or to international governmental organizations, such as the United Nations, for redress and assistance, therefore bypassing the perceived and real difficulties of negotiating at the local level. Finally, the global media may be an effective means of extending voice when domestic options have failed. By publicizing issues internationally, organizations indirectly exert pressure on local government officials wary of negative press.

It is important to note that quite often groups use multiple strategies in tandem rather than choosing a single course of action. The key is to discern when and why organizations choose certain strategies at different moments in time. Just as social movement and community development scholars acknowledge that contentiousness and cooperation are not necessarily opposites, but rather reflect choices within an ever-changing political environment,[2] so are the strategies I have defined a response to evolving circumstances.

In addition, though this typology draws neat boundaries across strategies, reality is always messy, and at times the categorization of strategies is not obvious. Any categorization has to differentiate among strategies while also recognizing the extent to which each might complement the other. For the purposes of analysis, I begin with this typology and view the case-study chapters that follow as tests of whether and how it reflects reality.

The Choice of Strategies

Previous literature finds several key variables that influence the strategic decisions of organizations: ideology (Melucci 1995), the relationship of the group to the state (Banaszak 2010), political opportunities (McAdam, Tarrow, and Tilly 2001), and resources (McCarthy and Zald 1977). I argue that the ideological orientation of groups and their relationship with the state, in particular, substantially influence the strategies they adopt. Prioritizing these two variables recognizes that CSOs have both expressive and instrumental goals, the dynamics of which have not been well studied.

In addition, however, while I find the two variables of ideology and the relationship of the organization with the state particularly salient for determining the nature of strategies, other factors related to political opportunities and resources also play significant roles and are addressed in the following discussion. These two variables are derived from traditional social movement literature regarding the choice of tactics, which, as I argue, are part of organizational strategies but do not alone define strategies. In addition, the direction of the impact of these variables on strategies may be very context specific, but the case-study analysis to follow reveals some characteristic chains of causality.

The Dynamic between Ideology and the Relationship with the State

As James Jasper (2004) suggests, we need to understand how agency and not just structure determines the decisions of movements. Jasper conceives of strategies as the result of a number of dilemmas facing leaders about the path they should take. These dilemmas not only include how organizations adapt to the political context in which they seek to achieve goals; they also reflect the beliefs and feelings of those choosing courses of action. Though game-theoretical approaches have been used to analyze strategic choices (Schelling 1960; Lichbach 1987; Axelrod 1997; Oliver and Myers 2002), Jasper (2004) argues that a focus on a narrow set of decision games understates the complex dynamics between agency and structure. David Meyer (2014, chap. 5) also argues that both collective identity, similar to the concept of ideology, and instrumental concerns shape strategies. Activists pick tactics that they think are effective and not overly risky, but they also consider how they view themselves in the world, which is shaped by beliefs. As Aidan McGarry and Jasper write, "Rather than neutrally selecting whatev' tactics seem most likely to attain stated goals, protesters feel moral a emotional attachments to certain tactics and are repulsed by others" (2015, 10). Tactics may even become an end in themselves, including the use of nonviolence and participatory institutions.

The ideological position of community organizations, based on the convictions of individual members and leaders, orients the goals they strive to achieve and ideas about the appropriateness of certain actions. Pamela Oliver and Hank Johnston define ideology as "a system of meaning that couples assertions and theories about the nature of social life with values and norms relevant to promoting or resisting social change" (2005, 192). Ideology motivates personal and collective action and sets the limits for the actions individuals believe are just.

The concept of collective identity is closely related to that of ideology. The collective identity of a group is generally based on the shared belief of how the world does or should function. As Alberto Melucci writes, "collective identity is an interactive and shared definition produced by several individuals (or groups at a more complex level) concerned with the orientation of action and the field of opportunities and constraints in which the actions take place" (1995, 44). Collective identity, then, as an expression of ideology is not separate from rationality as some might suggest, but rather reflects the understanding of groups as they exist within the world. The concept, Melucci argues, can be studied through the analysis of documents generated by collective actors to assess the ideologies of the group (1995). The identity of groups, based on how members view their role in the world, is expressed through the written materials they produce as well as the ctions they undertake. For the purposes of simplicity, I refer to the luence of "ideology" rather than both ideology and collective iden- with the understanding that collective identity is also a compo- f the broad ideology projected by community organizations.

atin America, Susan Stokes's seminal work on Lima (1991) pro- idence to confirm the centrality of ideology to the strategies ommunities. Stokes found that the strategies of shantytown secure benefits were not based on a rational-actor model residents' worldviews, which were either more conserva- e more clientelistic, or more radical, and hence more adicals saw the need to confront the rich to reshape e, while clientelists in some way identified with the d to avoid confrontation. Residents chose their strategies on the basis of their understanding of their place in the world rather than solely on a cost-benefit calculation regarding effectiveness. Over the last few decades scholars have suggested that the "right to the city," as originally envisioned by Henri Lefebvre in the 1960s, provides a common ideology across urban movements in diverse contexts (Brenner, Marcuse, and Mayer 2012; Harvey 2003; Marcuse 2009; Mitchell 2003; Nicholls and Beaumont 2004; Purcell 2002, 2014; Smith and McQuarrie 2011). The right to the city approach argues for restructuring urban power relations, implementing resident-oriented planning, rejecting the capitalist profit motive, and promoting political learning as a process (Belda-Miquel, Peris, and Frediani 2016). Margit Mayer argues that similarities in issues across cities unite residents around the call for the right to the city:

> Connections between struggles in so-called first world metropoles and those in cities of the global South, where the fight against privatization, speculation, eviction and displacement is even more existential, have become quite tangible and real: it is frequently even the same real estate developers and the same global corporations that are responsible for the displacement, eviction or the privatization of public goods. (2009, 367)

The struggle for the right to the city is not restricted to cities with a particular political or economic history because it is quite clear that common challenges to the inclusion of low-income residents exist across these divides.

David Harvey argues that the right to the city is a moral imperative, compelling citizens to not merely legitimate the actions of city governments through elections but to seek to constantly reshape the nature of the city to be more inclusive and responsive to citizen needs (2003). The focus on rights frames the issue of housing as a battle for possession of the physical space of the city. Though Lefebvre did not originally conceive of the right to the city as a juridical right, in practice, claims to the right to the city often invoke a reliance on judicial actions as a means to achieving rights (Lefebvre [1968] 1995). In addition, organizers calling for the right to the city appeal for greater inclusion in participatory decision-making spaces in order to be part of the process. Communities that align with local, national, and international movements promoting the right to the city frame their fight in terms of human rights violations and a collective class-based struggle rather than individual cases.

Organizations concerned with housing in Brazil have increasingly adopted a more radical view of their role in seeking to secure the place of low-income residents in the city. In the 1970s, Ecclesiastical Base Communities (CEBs) formed around the notion that poor residents had the right to inclusion in the city and in the country. According to James Holston (2008), residents of Brazilian cities came to see their goal as the generation of new rights, not just the claiming of existing rights. Holston states that rights-based arguments provided the poor with a strategy to fight inequalities and the ability to reject "illegality and marginalization through the demonstration of competence ('know your rights') and negating humiliation through the dignity of participating in the public sphere as bearers of rights" (2008, 241). Holston provides the ideological basis for strategic actions, but he does not detail the current strategies used by neighborhood associations or social movements to lay claim to their rights. Even so, his work is fundamental to understanding how informality motivates a rights-based set of activities through which residents are fighting for basic recognition that they belong in the city. Informality generates an ideology of social justice and a collective identity around the common cause of inclusion. On the basis of Holston's work and the proliferation of informal settlements in Brazil, I would expect community organizations throughout the country to take on radical strategies toward inclusion.

In the United States, claims to belonging are tied more to class or race than to property rights and marginality. Much of the ideological motivation behind the idea that poor communities must be involved in solving their own problems comes from the United States in the 1960s, in particular through the work of Saul Alinsky (1969). As mentioned above, community-organizing efforts attempt to address the problems that arise from structural relationships that have often excluded inner-city communities from resources and power in decision making (DeFilippis 2001; Saegert, Thompson, and Warren 2002). Randy Stoecker (2003) argues that the view that cities are divided into "haves" and "have-nots" motivates confrontation. Community organizers emphasize the importance of building political power to achieve goals and understand that conflict is an inherent part of this process. Organizers hold the worldview that progress is achieved only by disrupting the societal structure. Community builders, on the other hand, generally follow a more conservative path in which goals are achieved through consensus building, partnerships, and social capital (Gittell and Vidal 1998). While neither of these positions approximate the conservative bent toward clientelism documented by Stokes, the organizer's view more closely resembles the ideology of claiming one's rights than the community builder's position. Regardless, the model of involving poor communities in solving their own problems, long established in the United States, may also motivate community organizations to adopt an ideology based on the notion of inclusion and social justice in fighting marginalization within the city.

Organizations in the United States specifically incorporating ideals of the right to the city came out of protests against neoliberal reforms promoted by international institutions in the 1990s, shifting the locus of contention from the global to the urban (Mayer 2009). The Right to the City Alliance seeks to incorporate this ideology into urban activism (2015), though they are perhaps not as organized across the United States as movements promoting the right to the city in the developing world. In Latin America, movements explicitly incorporate the language of the right to the city into their discourse to claim inclusion in urban planning and policy. In Brazil, right to the city concepts are incorporated into the Estatuto da Cidade, the Statute of the City, which regulates portions of the national constitution related to cities, mandating the implementation of a participatory council for urban development and detailing land rights based on length of possession that are critical for residents considered long-term "squatters" in informal settlements. Though in practice the implementation of the Statute of the City has been uneven, the document has moved the country substantially forward in recognizing the rights of low-income urban dwellers (Friendly 2013). The National Forum for Urban Reform, the main umbrella organization coordinating urban movements across the country, also adopts the language of the right to the city and encourages citizens to know their rights in order to achieve their own victories.

The right to the city represents an alternative ideology to the Marxist, revolutionary calls of the past as well as a move away from the clientelistic politics characteristic of Latin America. In the United States, the right to the city also signifies a shift away from politics "as usual" around development policy toward demands for less corporate influence and greater fairness in the allocation of resources. Adoption of the right to the city ideology across cities should be a signal that organizations today have broken with past ideological orientations.

On the basis of this discussion, I would expect organizations across the United States and Brazil adopting the language of the right to the city to engage in strategies that promote inclusion in institutions and in the city through rights that protect and promote access to affordable housing in central areas of the city. While the right to the city ideology motivates citizens to call for radical transformation, in practice, the focus on rights and inclusion should prompt groups to use the force of law to generate and uphold their rights and participatory institutions to increase their direct influence on policy. The extent to which the activities of community organizations across cities actually reflect the goals of the right to the city in practice remains in question, however, and the cases in this book provide evidence of how the right to the city ideology plays out across contexts.

At the same time that organizations worldwide have adopted the language of the right to the city and of housing as a fundamental right of citizens, Jon Pierre and Guy Peters (2012) argue that there has been a fundamental change in the role of government in the practice of governance. The formal institutions of government increasingly seek to balance societal influence with the control they themselves exert over society. A defining factor in the exercise of governance is the relationship between civil society and the state. Without formal institutions to facilitate relationships between civil society and the state, these relationships are largely determined by personal connections among actors and publicly held alliances. The relationship of organizations with the state, in turn, determines access to decision making and the extent to which public officials view community organizations as legitimate partners in urban development. This relationship further shapes the strategies organizations pursue to achieve their demands.

This relationship between community organizations and the state is formed by a number of factors, including the employment of organizational members within the government, insider access to officials forged through personal relationships, working together in formal institutions, and general trust in the judicial system and the government bureaucracy. Generally, organizations see themselves as either allies or opponents of the city administration based on their relationship with the ruling political party, their perception that the mayor or legislators are or are not on their side, and the extent to which they have easy access to officials, both elected members and nonelected bureaucrats.

A *strong* relationship with the state may be defined as one in which organizational leaders maintain close contact with relevant officials and generally trust officials to take their requests into account and act on their promises. Leaders also largely trust in the power of the judicial system to uphold the rights of all citizens. A *weak* relationship, in contrast, is one in which organizational leaders have minimal respect and trust for public officials and do not view the administration as generally acting in the interests of low-income residents, particularly in regard to housing. Organizational leaders may also view the judicial system as corrupt or biased against the rights of low-income residents.

Though literature on civil society often assumes organizations exist outside of official state institutions, in reality the line is often blurred by overlapping memberships, formal partnerships, and institutions that incorporate government and civil society (Stoker 1998; Abers and Keck 2009; Hochstetler and Keck 2007). For example, in the case of São Paulo, Eduardo Marques argues that organizational ties are often personal, and informal relationships significantly affect the policy process (2013). As Salo Coslovsky finds regarding the relationship between civil society and the state in São Paulo, "Channels of mutual influence go beyond formal complaints, official policy councils, and public hearings to include a number of informal connections between public officials and outside agents that can be quite consequential even if not readily visible to outsiders" (2015, 1112). In the case of the United States, Lee Ann Banaszak (2010) forcefully argues that failure to acknowledge the insider roles of movement activists weakens our understanding of how government officials and civil society organizations interact in policy decision making and the effect these insiders have on the strategic decisions of organizations. Examining the women's movement in the United States, she finds that groups that had more interaction with the state tended to be more likely to use insider connections as part of their strategies to generate change than groups that did not have these connections.

Personal relationships based on party or other alliances strongly influence how organizations view the effectiveness of various strategies. In fact, much of the literature on the relationship of civil society organizations with the state focuses on the effect of alliances on tactical choices. It is also the case that this research has yielded very disparate findings. For instance, scholars have asked whether organizations are more likely to negotiate rather than protest under a friendly administration. In São Paulo, Kathleen Bruhn (2008) found this to be true during several administrations of the Workers' Party (PT) in which the housing movements felt they had adequate access to officials through institutional channels and hence no need to protest. Other scholars have found that cooptation by the state in a friendly administration reduces the independence of organizations and hence the likelihood that they will protest (Auyero, Lapegna, and Poma 2009; Eckstein and Merino 2001; Foweraker 2005; Roberts 1997, 2002). Under an administration viewed as the opposition, the argument is that those that are shut out of closed-door meetings with administration officials may be more likely to protest. But as Bruhn found in São Paulo, under a strongly conservative administration the housing movements there chose not to protest, believing that it would have no effect on officials' decisions (2008, 151). The debate may still be open, then, about the effect of the relationship with the state on tactical decisions.

The presence and character of institutions meant to incorporate civil society are also central to strategic direction and reflect the existing relationship of civil society with the state. Organizations need the opportunities to participate in decision making to directly influence policies and programs, but trust in the fairness of the process is key to whether these institutions function to increase direct voice. Judicial institutions secure property rights, enforce housing regulations, and implement inclusionary zoning laws, but the perception of fairness within these institutions matters for whether groups consider them viable mechanisms for achieving goals.

The interaction between ideology and the relationship with the state propels organizations to either seek greater influence within the state or view other strategies as more effective means toward achieving demands. Organizational leaders have to first view their role in the world as agents of structural reform, such as called for by the right to the city, rather than as simply defenders of public benefit distributions to ameliorate the challenges of housing costs. To be transformational, however, organizations not only must embrace the goals of the right to the city or the right to housing, more broadly; they also require the means of inside influence through strong personal relationships with public officials, participatory institutions, and trust in the judicial system.

The previous discussion generates the following hypotheses, also summarized in Table 2.1:

1. An ideology based on the ideals of the right to the city or the right to housing, in combination with a close relationship with the state, motivates community organizations to pursue inclusionary strategies. Organizers calling for the right to the city should rely on judicial institutions as well as participatory decision-making spaces in order to be part of state processes. As Lefebvre theorized, inclusion is gained through social transformation of power relations and cannot be granted by the state (Lefebvre [1968] 1995). Direct strategies in which organizations seek influence from the inside reflect the goal of taking power for themselves. But leaders will not engage in inclusionary strategies if they do not believe the city administration will make good on promises or if judges are biased. A strong relationship with the state is therefore also key to strategies promoting inclusion.

2. Where organizations adopt a more radical ideology in terms of rights, but experience a weak relationship with the state, leaders will find it necessary to exit local governance and appeal to higher-level government authorities or engage in autonomous solutions. These organizations seek transformational change but do not view the city administration or the justice system as effective partners for generating reforms.

TABLE 2.1. INTERACTION BETWEEN IDEOLOGY AND RELATIONSHIP WITH THE STATE: EFFECT ON STRATEGIES			
		Ideology	
		Rights-based	*Conservative*
Relationship with the state	Strong	Direct	Indirect
	Weak	Exit	Overhaul

3. Where organizations have a strong relationship with the state as defined by insider access to the administration, alignment of party goals, and trust in the regime, but a more conservative ideology, they will likely seek strategies to influence the decisions of policy makers rather than inclusionary strategies. Without the explicit goal of transformational change through inclusion, organizations will not push for direct influence, but rather rely on traditional modes of advocacy through indirect strategies.

4. A weak relationship combined with a conservative ideology that does not prioritize structural change leads organizations to seek complete overhaul of the administration to elect officials who more closely identify with the organization's goals, without pursuing inclusionary means of influence within the current system. When the relationship is weak and community organizations do not feel city administrators view them as legitimate partners in governance or respond negatively to their requests, inclusionary strategies may be perceived as ineffective. These organizations do not necessarily seek greater inclusion, but believe the primary means to achieving demands is through the election of allies into office.

Political Opportunities

Political opportunities, in the form of new institutional leadership, new governmental allies, or new policy options offered by state officials reshape strategic decisions (Tarrow 1994; McAdam, Tarrow, and Tilly 2001; McAdam, McCarthy, and Zald 1996). Through political process theory, Charles Tilly (1995) argues that the repertoires of social movements develop appropriate to the political arena and therefore shift over time as the incentives of actors and political institutions evolve. The ability of groups to mobilize citizens to action also depends on particular political events or trends (McAdam and Boudet 2012).

An ideologically aligned or unaligned administration shapes the relationships of civil society organizations with the state, but political or economic events may also reshape political opportunities. For example, when an election is at hand, strategy may shift toward changing the political regime or a more clientelistic form of securing benefits for votes (Rivadulla 2012). Assuming a positive opportunity arises, such as the election of an allied mayoral administration, community organizations will view inclusionary strategies as more productive than under an adversarial administration. Previous work on interpreting the effect of electoral cycles focuses on whether civil society organizations engage in contentious activities or utilize institutional channels before and after elections. For instance, while protest may be effective in bringing attention to an issue before election time, direct negotiation may be more appropriate for presenting proposals for urbanization and soliciting promises from recently elected government officials. María José Álvarez Rivadulla (2012) finds evidence of squatters in Montevideo capitalizing on clientelistic methods to gain services and goods when their votes were greatly sought after but reformulating their strategies once they perceived politicians did not view them as an important voting bloc. Looking at São Paulo, Bruhn argues that electoral cycles matter for protest activity. She finds that protest activity is concentrated around "either the election year (to secure candidates) or the honeymoon year (to secure favors)" (2008, 161).

Stages in the policy process may further influence the timing of strategic choices of organizations. On the basis of case studies from around the world, Hilary Silver, Alan Scott, and Yuri Kazepov (2010) find that the policy-initiation phase brought out conflict and antagonism, while the decision-making stage elicited deliberation and compromise. Their argument provides temporal specificity to the understanding of civil society strategies; the choices of groups reflect the nature of what is possible to achieve in the moment. To take the argument further, when the policies and programs demanded by organizations are stalled within the bureaucratic or legislative process, groups may also change strategy in order to generate attention to the delay or to seek redress through other avenues.

In sum, changes in the political environment, brought about by elections, policy cycles, or other major events lead organizations to recalculate the effectiveness of one strategy over another or to engage in multiple strategies at the same time. Elections and policy cycles add a relatively predictable timeline for organizations to plan activities when they will be most effective. For instance, inclusionary strategies may be most effective when legislation or program criteria are proposed by state actors, and community organizations want to ensure they are involved in the debate and implementation of proposed changes. Overhaul strategies are appropriate when elections are near, but exit strategies might be more effective to address immediate problems in a contentious political environment when the opportunity for administrative change is many years in the future. Finally, unexpected or nonroutine events, such as hosting mega-events or the occurrence of natural disasters, may shift the calculus of organizations in how they frame problems in the city and the expectations they have for the capacity of the government to respond to their demands.

Resources

The availability of resources, in terms of money, the number and capacity of members, and connections should also shape the decisions of community organizations. Resource mobilization theory suggests that organizations are able to mobilize people to their cause on the basis of available resources and that the capabilities of members shape the goals and tactical choices of the organization (McCarthy and Zald 1977). Professional NGOs with large staff may be able to better navigate institutional channels and provide advocacy training for community residents than neighborhood associations that comprise only local residents (Evans 2002). Where legal service personnel are willing to help, or are on staff, community organizations are also far more likely to use the force of law. When organizations have fewer resources, however, scholars have argued that they may be more likely to form stronger networks (Arias 2006). Establishing networks across communities, cities, and countries allows organizations to overcome the difficulties of local participation and resource constraints. Brazilian cities tend to be highly segregated by income, and low-income residents tend to have the least contact with other income groups as a result of territorial segregation (Netto, Pinheiro, and Paschoalino 2015). Networking, because it enables communities with little experience navigating policy channels access to the capacity of other organizations, may lead to greater investment in the strategies of the wider network.

Across contexts, collective action may be particularly difficult to cultivate among the poor, and when they do participate, low-income residents may have little in the way of financial resources to support the group. Again, scholars argue that organizations with fewer resources will form strong networks. For example, Enrique Desmond Arias suggests that when groups act in concert, it raises the costs of silencing individual groups while making officials aware of problems across communities (2004).

In the informal settlements of Brazil, resources in terms of numbers of participants may be generated by a common identity formation, contradicting the notion that there is inherent difficulty eliciting participation. In this regard, the age of the community and the community's history of mobilization may be a factor. As stated above, Holston (2008) argues that the self-building process typical of informal settlements leads residents to band together to make demands of the government for inclusion in the services of the city. Theoretically, the more recently residents have gone through this process of making communal demands, the more likely they will be able to pull together to make further demands. Informal settlements that have faced constant threats of eviction over the years may also enjoy more group cohesion and capacity than those that have not had to previously negotiate with government officials. In the United States, communities that have long been involved in struggle, whether it be directed toward improving schools, reducing violence, combating racism, or other challenges, also benefit from the experience and cohesion that come from long-term mobilization, but they also may be more likely to engage with large nonprofit organizations to address big issues rather than remain rooted at the community level.

In general, though, given the less-professionalized, under-resourced environments in which community organizations in Brazil operate, I expect there may be a greater tendency toward networking and coalition building than in the United States, where organizational staff tend to be better paid through private foundations or government grants and therefore are more able to lobby policy officials for change.

Outcomes: *When* Do Community Organizations Matter?

The outcomes of civil society efforts can be measured in myriad ways, from the longevity of organized activity and changes in public opinion and practices to changes in government authorities' positions or policies, shifts in resource allocation, and creation of deliberative bodies that include civil society voices (Maney et al. 2012, xxiv). All of these indicators are critical for understanding the full dynamic impact of organizational activities, as we would expect that in a democracy shifts among the public should lead to shifts in government responses. Without sustained actions and changes in the public's perception of a problem, changes in policies, programs, and institutions are unlikely, particularly if officials are accountable to the electorate. Here, I focus on the concrete shifts in the responses of public officials to preventing displacement and promoting the availability of affordable housing for low-income residents. In addition, changes in institutions, including deliberative mechanisms as well as traditional bureaucratic agencies, indicate the willingness if not the capacity of governments to address housing needs and represent important outcome variables.

At the most basic level, to effect change, strategies of community organizations must reduce opposition. Various factors shape the impact of different types of strategies and the overall effect that community organizations may have on policies, programs, and institutions, but strategies are critical to the way in which opposition is mediated or overcome. I argue that to generate change, strategies must shift who has the power to achieve development goals. The ways in which community organizations seek to be empowered through their chosen strategies should matter for whether and how their voices affect policies, programs, and institutions. Different types of strategies—inclusionary, indirect, overhaul, or exit—shape the direction of democracy in urban development. On the one hand, inclusionary strategies most strongly upset the balance of power, and as such are the most difficult path to reform. Inclusionary strategies, though, should have the greatest power for transformational change in how urban development plans are conceived and implemented. On the other hand, indirect strategies are the easiest to implement and achieve results, but the results will not be transformational. Overhaul strategies remove the obstacle of political will, but lead to political rather than necessarily structural change in policy making. Last, exit strategies enable independence from local politics, which may mean more power for community organizations in the long run, but does not immediately transform the local political structure.

These arguments are detailed below and summarized in Table 2.2:

Inclusionary. The goals of inclusionary strategies are oriented toward deeper structural change through the imposition of new or strengthened institutions that incorporate civil society. The targets of this type of strategy are likely to be government institutions, rather than a broader audience, including private-sector interests. Though private-sector actors may also be involved in participatory governance, the goal of inclusionary strategies is to overcome rather than compromise with the private sector. Successful outcomes for inclusionary strategies include decisions to allow residents facing eviction to stay in place and resources to provide additional low-income housing, but of great importance will be reinforcing direct influence and strengthening or creating institutions to promote these goals. In addition, inclusionary strategies should lead to significant reform of existing programs or the adoption of new programs proposed directly by community organizations themselves. The outcome for democracy is transformational in that community organizations achieve real decision-making power and ensure accountability of public officials.

Indirect. The expected outcomes of indirect strategies through which community organizations seek to influence government officials, include increasing resources dedicated to housing issues or expansion of policies and programs. In general, the outcomes of these strategies are more likely to increase existing programs rather than bring about novel interventions. The impact on democracy is to reinforce the status quo, that is, the current distribution of influence regarding the power of community organizations in urban development.

Overhaul. Community organizations may seek to overhaul the administration in order to bring in allies or run candidates from their

TABLE 2.2. TYPES OF STRATEGIES: IMPACT ON OUTCOMES

Type of strategy	Instrumental goals	Outcome for democracy
Inclusionary ➡	Structural change, direct decision making	➡ Transformational
Indirect ➡	Additional resources, implementation of programs	➡ Status quo
Overhaul ➡	Allies in power	➡ Political change
Exit ➡	Outside influence, autonomy	➡ Independence from local politics

own ranks. Outcomes include the successful election of candidates, and, in terms of housing, outcomes should match the stated demands of the organizations that supported the administration in achieving office, which are likely contrary to the policies and programs of the previous administration. Overhaul should provide a greater role for housing and low-income interests in the exercise of political power.

Exit. Through exit strategies community organizations seek autonomous solutions to problems or assistance from outside actors. In the short term, the outcome of these strategies should be a remedy for the immediate problem at hand, for instance, an eviction or need for affordable housing in a particular area. In the long term, the outcomes of exit strategies may be less clear. Whether the political environment changes as a result of exit or whether current conditions that did not allow for effective local advocacy prevail depends on alliances formed and the permanency of the immediate decision. Autonomy shifts the power to solve collective problems to the people, but appeal to outside actors shifts the power to shape local urban development to external control.

Intervening Variables in Outcomes

A number of factors influence these predicted relationships. The factors that Stone et al. conclude contributed to changes in neighborhood politics in the United States include alliances, resources, and elections, which previous literature also indicates are important for shaping the impact of civil society (for example, Tilly 2004; McAdam, Tarrow, and Tilly 2001). Given that current literature suggests dynamics between the private sector, civil society, and government may be similar in Latin America, I investigate whether these same factors matter across the hemisphere. Specifically, I assess how internal characteristics, alliances, money, and existing laws shape the impact that community organizations may have through their activities.

Internal Characteristics

First, the internal characteristics of an organization should matter for its efficacy no matter the strategy. Scholars have argued that bottom-up organizations, rather than short-term movements, are necessary for mobilizing and sustaining claims over time (Morris 1984; Rupp and Taylor 1987). In the case of Rio de Janeiro, Robert Gay (1994) found that the unified organization of residents mattered for long-term benefits and permanence in one favela, while top-down leadership produced clientelism in another favela and brought only short-term benefits. Tilly (2004) also argued that the success of movements depends on not only their numbers but also their ability to sustain contention over time.

To be sustainable and effective, organizations need the practical ability to implement strategies, and in this regard unity based on social capital and civic capacity to engage government officials are keys to success. Scholars claim that development of social capital enables communities to organize for a common purpose and hold governments accountable for the provision of rights and public benefits (Ackerman 2004; Fox 1996; Putnam 1993). In instances of evictions, for example, social capital is critical for residents to trust each other and their representatives to present demands. Similarly, Stone (2001) finds that civic capacity, involving a high degree of consensus and commitment to a common goal, enhances the ability of a community to solve problems. Certain communities may exhibit greater civic capacity through strong leadership and connection to other organizations, which may be particularly important when officials lead from the top down rather than incorporating civil society (Briggs 2008). The power to mobilize supporters, the leadership to direct collective action over time, and the ability to maintain common goals, then, should influence the effectiveness of organizations in achieving their demands.

Further, as Stone et al. (2015) argue, access to resources matters for the ability of organizations to impact power relations. In the U.S. context, these authors argue that philanthropic organizations and educational and medical institutions provide needed resources to community organizations. In the case of Brazil, I would argue that the same applies; access to university partners, research institutions, and international funding from NGOs often enables community organizations to operate and achieve their missions. The greater the access to nongovernmental funding and resources, the better able organizations should be to achieve their goals.

Along these lines, scholars also argue that alliances are critical. Not only resources but political support are important for projecting legitimacy and holding sway over official decision making. Evans writes:

> Even the most well organized communities often lack the political clout to protect their own local interests, to say nothing of being able to advance more universalistic goals. For communities to be effective political actors, they must be able to find the allies, either in the form of other, similarly situation communities or in the form of organizations with extralocal scope. (2002, 19)

Fighting alone will likely not yield success. NGOs may be significant allies to community organizations, but global actors, concerned citizens across cities, and public officials are also critical resources. When community organizations develop alliances as part of any strategy, they should be more likely to achieve their objectives. The case studies illustrate examples of the potential reach of alliances and the effect of allying with various actors.

Government Capacity

Even when there is the political will to act in the interests of community organizations, capacity may limit government responsiveness. To respond to the demands of community organizations, governments must have the capacity to provide additional benefits or restrict development in a way that benefits low-income communities. According to Tilly (2006, 2008), government capacity involves the extent to which the government influences the distribution of populations, activities, and resources (Tilly 2006, 21). Public resources and the scope of authority limit what governments are able to do, and it may be that the demands of community organizations fall outside of the limits of what is possible.

Political Shifts

A number of factors influence political shifts and divert resources and attention, including a sudden event, such as a terrorist attack or a mass shooting; a planned mega-event, such as the Olympic Games; political upheaval at any level of government; and economic crisis. Organizations may adapt their strategies to reflect these shifts, but political will and government capacity are also be impacted, depending on the event. When there are significant atypical events, the impact of community organizations will be increasingly limited, regardless of organizational strategies.

Laws

Finally, existing laws clearly shape the outcomes that are achievable regarding low-income housing and issues of displacement. In the case of Brazil, Brodwyn Fischer (2008) argues that there is a "perpetual state of ambiguity" around property rights, in which de facto permanence is never legalized. Though Brazil enacted significant legal protections for those living in informal settlements, executing those rights when notices of eviction are issued still presents a challenge. Unlike the Brazilian Constitution, which specifies that housing is the right of all citizens, the U.S. Constitution does not provide any such guarantee. The provision of housing by government is never guaranteed, and, in fact, many would argue that housing assistance should be the responsibility of charitable organizations, if not individuals themselves. But the United States does have "squatters' rights" to provide ownership of property to residents of abandoned properties, and eminent domain to ensure that the government pays property owners fair market value when the expropriation of property is necessary for the public good. Compared to Brazil, the United States has a more developed legal system, if not greater authority to ensure everyone the right to a home. The outcomes of community organizations' efforts that rely on the force of law may therefore be different across these two contexts.

To summarize, the foregoing discussion yields the following arguments regarding intervening variables between strategies and outcomes. First, organizations with greater capacity, in terms of social capital, networks, leadership, and alliances, will be more likely to succeed in achieving their desired outcomes. Second, fewer financial resources or fractured priorities will limit the ability of government officials to respond positively to organizations' demands. Third, political shifts limit the will of officials to address housing needs, and, finally, legal ambiguity in Brazil, in particular, limits the law from working in the favor of community organizations or low-income residents.

Conclusions

This chapter provides the theoretical basis for assessing the three main questions in this book regarding the nature of strategies, the factors behind the decisions of community organizations to engage in certain strategies, and the outcomes these strategies produce. The activities of organizations concerned with displacement and affordable housing for low-income residents vary in cities across the United States and Brazil, but here I argue that their strategies may be differentiated into four main categories: inclusionary, indirect, overhaul, and exit. On the basis of the trend toward emphasizing the right to the city and the right to housing among grassroots organizations and academics, I have argued from the beginning that community organizations will pursue strategies that enhance their ability to directly work with public officials to shape policy and programs and seek legal protections for low-income residents. In reality, though, we also see that community organizations pursue various means to achieve their goals, and the question then becomes why they choose certain strategies at different points in time or maybe even concurrently.

The second half of the chapter lays out a framework for assessing why organizations choose the plan of action they do. I have argued that ideology and the relationship with the state interact to strongly determine the strategies that organizations pursue. In addition, political opportunities shift strategies on the basis of changing perceptions of relevance and effectiveness, and resources shape the capacity of organizations to engage in political and judicial institutions either on their own or as part of networks.

Maney et al. (2012) suggest that we can measure the impact of strategies on differences in outcomes by controlling structural factors and focusing on the decision process, by comparing each strategy to the others, or by looking at changes in outcomes over time in one case in which different strategies are at play. Looking across cities, particularly those across the North-South divide, controlling for all potential structural factors is impossible. Nonetheless, the cases to follow demonstrate similarities in the challenges to low-income housing and in the barriers to political will and government capacity to solve these issues. Simply comparing one strategy to another is also analytically implausible in that organizations often engage in a mix of strategies at once or over time. To the extent, possible, however, I do try to trace causal pathways to understand how different strategies lead to different outcomes. In the case study chapters, the objective is to identify points of convergence and divergence across cities while also focusing on the specific decision processes within each case over roughly half a decade.

The success of various strategies will never be perfect or complete, and the choice of strategies always reflects trade-offs. As Paul Dosh (2010, 26) wrote, "There are not automatic 'winners' in terms of strategy choice. Rather, the success of a chosen strategy rests on how well it reflects existing constraints." Often success is not ideal, but rather relative to the environment in which organizations operate. Stone et al. (2015) argue that success may be defined as "readily imagined" positive-sum scenarios, which in terms of housing may include mixed-use and mixed-income housing developments. But whether moving to a new community represents a positive gain or negative outcome will depend on the perspective of the community and individuals themselves. "Success" may be difficult to uniformly define across contexts, but the cases allow one to judge whether different strategies lead to variation in the outcomes that groups do achieve.

Though the theoretical framework for understanding the three questions I have posed is complex, complexity is the reality for community organizations on the ground navigating actual political contexts and seeking to refine their particular vision for the future of their cities. In the case studies to follow, these questions are put into perspective and analyzed to determine how well this framework reflects the reality of each city and each organization's experience.

3

Resisting Removal in Rio de Janeiro

Narratives of Rio de Janeiro often portray the city as either the "Cidade Maravilhosa" (Marvelous City), known for its beautiful vistas and iconic landmarks, or the "Cidade de Deus" (City of God), known for poverty, violence, and police corruption. Of course, neither scenario accurately represents the city, but the dueling images do much to explain the current issues fueling displacement and access to affordable housing. As Rio was host of the 2014 World Cup and the 2016 Olympic Games, the government and residents alike wished to portray the city in the best possible light, emphasizing the natural beauty and the rich cultural traditions that coexist in the city. Public officials hoped the positive images of the city generated through these events would spur lasting investment and tourism long after the games passed. Critics charged, however, that in their quest for international prestige, city officials sought to push the poor farther out to the periphery rather than directly addressing poverty, inequality, and the causes behind violence.

Between 2009 and 2015, the administration of Mayor Eduardo Paes initiated processes of removal against 77,000 people, most of whom lived within the city's favelas or informal settlements (Popular Committee 2015). The large number of removals was surprising, given

A version of this chapter was originally published as Maureen Donaghy, "Resisting Removal: The Impact of Community Mobilization in Rio de Janeiro," *Latin American Politics and Society* 57, no. 4 (2015): 74–96.

that the government's urbanization policies of investing in infrastruc-ture and services and issuing land titles to residents had largely re-placed the former authoritarian regime's policy of removal as a means of controlling the population of squatters in the city (Perlman 1976, 2010).[1] A removal, in which the government calls for residents to va-cate their homes with or without compensation, had been viewed as politically untenable, especially since politicians rely on votes from low-income citizens. The number of evictions under the Paes admin-istration, however, exceeded the combined number of evictions that occurred under the administrations of Pereira Passos (1900s) and Carlos Lacerda (1960s), the nondemocratic regimes historically most associated with evictions in the city (Azevedo and Faulhaber 2015).

While the World Cup and the Olympics hastened the implementa-tion of infrastructural projects and removals of residents from favelas throughout the city, the games were only part of an ongoing process of gentrification that occurred over the span of a decade. Discovery of oil off the coast in the 2000s drove the federal government, private corporations, and research centers to invest significant resources in the city and state at the same time the World Cup and Olympics gen-erated an infusion of money for construction from the federal govern-ment partnering with private firms. Rapid investment drove up prices in the city, leading some residents to seek more affordable accommo-dations elsewhere, but investment also meant that the city and state governments increasingly initiated processes of removal against those they claimed were in the path of development. Individual homes and livelihoods were at stake, but so was the future of entire communities (Angotti 2013). Because of this, community organizations formed the locus of resistance to the government's orders for removal.

There is a long-established literature on favela politics in Rio de Janeiro in which authors debate the evidence regarding strategies resi-dents use to secure services and the ability of residents to access demo-cratic institutions. For instance, Gay (1994) finds that the choice to engage in clientelistic politics versus protest and negotiation led to very different long-term consequences for two favelas in the city. While cli-entelism won benefits in one community, organization and protest in the other staved off removal by authorities. Gay concludes that chang-es in the relationship between civil and political society are key to en-during change for favela residents. Both Bryan McCann (2014) and

Fischer (2008) argue that lack of de facto political rights and legal ambiguity over property rights hamper the ability of Rio's favela residents
to achieve full benefits and a sense of permanence in the city. Both
authors note increasing urban activism in which residents demand
greater political rights. Each of these authors documents the importance of knowing one's rights and pushing political leaders and legal
institutions to ensure the practice of those rights.

What is missing from these accounts, however, is an analysis of the
specific ways in which community organizations carry out resistance
strategies and how their strategies lead to outcomes. Though Gay provides evidence of the benefits that accrue to those communities that
do not engage in clientelistic behavior, he does not assess how communities counter the power of private-sector interests in the city, increasingly important as Rio strives for global recognition. Further,
though McCann (2014) and Fischer (2008) document the increasing
use of the language of rights to make demands, they do not link this
framing to strategic decisions.

For this case study, I focus on the community of Vila Autódromo,
a neighborhood in which more than five hundred families lived adjacent to the site of the main Olympic Park on the edge of the Barra da
Tijuca neighborhood. To some, the case of Vila Autódromo represents
one of the most successful recent resistance efforts in Rio, and the
residents' association garnered significant international attention for
their persistent efforts to remain in place. The eventual outcomes,
however, were far from satisfactory for all residents. I would expect
payoffs to the community as a result of their indefatigable efforts, but
the incomplete nature of the community's success must be viewed as
one of the many cases of significant mobilization across the globe in
which outcomes rarely satisfy all of residents' desires. For this case, I
undertook fieldwork in Rio and the community of Vila Autódromo in
2012 and 2016, but because of the ongoing nature of the conflict, I also
collected evidence through online interviews, news reports, and social
media posts during the intervening years. Analyzing one community
over time allows one to understand the evolving nature of mobilization. The close geographic and symbolic association with the games
and the residents' strong resistance make this community ideal for
assessing the clash of interests among residents, local officials, and
business interests.

Through this case I document the strategies this community used and the ways in which a strong ideology based on the right to the city coincided with a weak relationship with the state. The mix of these factors led the community to seek mediation through the Defensoria Pública, but also autonomous solutions, or exit strategies in which they created a new social network to counteract the weight of their opposition. Shifts in political opportunities linked to protests in June 2013 provided an incentive for the mayor to respond positively to the community's demands, and the national political turmoil and global image of the games in 2015–2016 ultimately led to achieving the goal of permanency for the few Vila Autódromo residents who remained in place. To date, the response to this one community has not led to long-term institutional change, nor does it provide evidence that a new era in community influence is really afoot in Rio. However, it may point to the *possibility* of a series of decision points creating change. Vila Autódromo's response is a case of sustained organization by one community in a sea of communities facing numerous challenges and suggests the viability of exit strategies for those facing removal.

Background

Since democratization, the city of Rio de Janeiro has elected mayors primarily from center-right parties. Mayor Eduardo Paes of the Brazilian Democratic Movement Party (PMDB) was elected in 2008 and again in 2012. During his time in office, Mayor Paes maintained a strong relationship with the governor of the State of Rio de Janeiro, Sérgio Cabral, also of the PMDB. In 2015–2016, however, the corruption scandals plaguing the entire country came home, with Cabral indicted on bribery charges related to the renovation of the Maracana Stadium. Along with the swing to the right across the country, in 2016 Rio elected former evangelical bishop Marcelo Crivella to be its next mayor, defeating progressive Marcelo Freixo of the Socialist Party (PSOL).

The city of Rio de Janeiro has a long history of urban conflicts, particularly since industrialization drove growth in the favelas in the mid-twentieth century. In contrast with other cities in which informal settlements have developed in peripheral areas, in Rio the favelas are scattered throughout the downtown and interspersed with wealthy neighborhoods. As McCann writes, the result of this territorial pattern has meant that "the poor could never simply be pushed to the outskirts of the city, and conflict over urban space became central to urban life" (2014, 12). McCann documents the 1970s experience of the Vidigal favela, which successfully defended the right of residents to remain in place and spurred the mobilization of residents' associations in favelas across the city to fight for their rights despite the presence of an authoritarian regime. Since democratization in the mid-1980s, the number and size of favelas and irregular settlements have only increased, particularly in the de-industrializing north side of the city and the west side of the city, areas traditionally lacking in amenities and transportation options.

In the early 1980s, Leonel Brizola was elected governor of the state in large part as a result of his connection to the early favela movements. Under Brizola's leadership, the state largely withdrew policing from the favelas, in recognition of abuses perpetrated by the police in the past. But the administration failed to implement new policing efforts, leaving a void in the rule of law within the favelas for several decades. During this time, most favelas saw material upgrades, but the absence of the state perpetuated a view of the favelas as lawless, violent neighborhoods separate from the rest of the city.

In 2008 the state of Rio began implementing a form of community policing known as the Unidades de Polícia Pacificadora (UPPs, Police Pacification Units). The UPPs focused on approximately forty favelas with the goal of driving out drug traffickers, providing a constant police presence, and implementing social programs. While the UPPs did succeed in reducing violence in the favelas in which they operate, the communities first selected to receive the program were mainly in tourist areas, with the intent to improve security for the World Cup and Olympic Games. Now that the games are over and the city is bankrupt, the future of the program is unclear.

Spending for both the 2014 World Cup and 2016 Summer Olympic Games led to significant contention and mobilization in the city. In June 2013, protests in Brazil that began in response to a ten-cent increase in bus fare spurred protest in cities across the country. Demonstrators rallied against corruption in city, state, and national governments and decried the amount of public money spent to host the 2014 World Cup and 2016 Olympic Games. One year later, at the start of the

2014 World Cup, international news reports focused on not only the rivalries between national teams but also the clashes between protesters and police outside the stadiums. Following the protests in June 2013, city mayors retracted the increase in bus fares, and left-leaning President Dilma Rousseff reacted with proposals for reform and promises of solidarity with the protesters. Nonetheless, protests continued, signaling the frustration of urban residents over the slow pace of reform and the federal and city governments' quest for international recognition rather than attention to residents' needs. Though these protests took place in cities throughout Brazil, Rio de Janeiro saw some of the largest and most contentious actions. In 2015 and 2016, economic crisis and political turmoil leading to President Rousseff's impeachment brought out further divisions in the country and renewed criticism over the massive spending for the games. In June 2016, the state government of Rio de Janeiro declared a state of emergency in the face of fiscal collapse, and the state was unable to deliver salaries to police, firefighters, and other public-sector workers.

Displacement and Affordable Housing in Rio: Removals, Rising Prices, and Gentrification

Current challenges to housing for low-income residents in Rio are the result of a combination of market-induced price hikes, gentrification, and state-led removals. The city is home to about 6.5 million people, second in size to only São Paulo within Brazil (IBGE 2014a). Among cities across the world Rio saw the fastest rate of growth in the cost of living—86 percent—from 2008 to 2014, making Rio the eleventh-most expensive city in the world.[2] In addition, from 2008 to 2014, the median cost for rent in the city increased by 114 percent (Zap 2015). In large part because of rising prices, from 2011 to 2012 the number of families without "adequate" housing increased by 10.5 percent in the city (Fundação João Pinheiro 2015). Comparing median monthly incomes to average rental prices confirms the problem. According to the 2010 census, the median monthly income in Rio was approximately $755 (IBGE 2014b), while the average cost to rent a one-bedroom apartment in 2015 was $774 (Numbeo 2015a).

In Rio, low-income residents have traditionally crowded into centrally located favelas on steep hillsides, the wealthy preferring to live directly along the city's coastline. The city's favelas have constituted the largest source of affordable housing in the city, sheltering approximately 24 percent of city residents largely outside of the regulated housing market (Williamson 2015a). Now these favelas are undergoing drastic change as police interventions reduce the threat of violence and urbanization projects improve basic services in many of the favelas with the most desirable ocean views and central locations. The UPPs serve to combat drug trafficking and make favelas safer for residents, though their presence also drives up real estate and rental prices within these communities (Flor and Marinho 2013). To respond to the expanding need for affordable housing throughout Brazil, through the Minha Casa Minha Vida (MCMV) Program and the Program for Accelerated Growth (PAC), the federal government has committed significant resources to new low-income housing construction and the urbanization of a number of informal communities. In Rio these programs are now being used to urbanize centrally located favelas.

In a sign of the changing times, celebrities are rumored to have purchased homes in the city's central favelas (Williamson 2015b). Locally, people refer to these forces of gentrification as "white removal" or "market removal." As programs to regularize land titles reach a growing number of favelas, these properties are more often subject to market forces and are sought by those priced out of the existing rental and ownership market as well as wealthier people seeking to capture the stunning hillside views.

While rising prices and gentrification clearly impact the lives of residents across the city, state-led removals continue to be a significant source of displacement that affects whole communities—more than 77,000 residents. Under Brazilian law, removals, or evictions, may take place only under limited circumstances: when the legal owner of the property petitions to take back possession of the land, when the land is needed for projects to benefit the public, or when the homes are situated in an area of environmental risk (Ministry of Cities 2013). Contradictions in the justification to remove residents from their homes as well as the process in which the government undertakes the removals led the Popular Committee for the World Cup and Olympics in Rio, a group that comprises community members, activists, academics, and other groups, to charge the government with abuses of citizens' rights.

For example, several years after the government removed the community of Restinga/Recreio to make way for the construction of the Transoeste Bus Rapid Transit,[3] the land still stood empty. This led to claims that the city was principally interested in removing residents in order to present the image of a "clean" city to the world (Popular Committee 2013). In the same manner that South Africa relocated townships prior to the 2010 World Cup, and Beijing and Atlanta removed homeless from the streets for the Olympic Games in 2008 and 1996, respectively, Rio was a "staged city," as Solomon Greene (2003) describes the means by which cities use mega-events to create an image of development.

Brazilian citizens faced with removal for any purpose are to be given fair notice before they are forced to leave their homes and then either fair compensation for the value of their homes, relocation to public housing, or assistance to purchase a new home (Ministry of Cities 2013). Residents claim, however, that their rights to due process have often been violated in the face of eviction. Some residents report being given only an hour's notice before they were forced to vacate. Others came home to find the housing authority had marked their home with a big X, indicating the home would be torn down. In addition, activists charge that some residents received little or no compensation as legally required (Popular Committee 2013). Though public housing offers security of tenure, residents complained that the units were far from their original homes and did not provide the same quality of life as individual dwellings (Popular Committee 2012).

Narrative data from the Popular Committee have also demonstrated that many of the communities removed were unorganized. For example, in Restinga/Recreio, residents claim that the government forced them to move quickly without any compensation in place because they were unorganized. Several years after the city government destroyed their homes, residents were still fighting for indemnity payments (Justiça Global 2012). The Popular Committee's report suggests that organization was an important factor in removals in that the greater the resistance to removal, the greater chance the residents were able to delay or stave off eviction, or secure higher indemnity payments for those who were forced to move. The report, however, does not go into detail about the specific resistance strategies that led to different results. More systematic analysis is needed to determine what factors of community mobilization ultimately led to greater success in reversing the process of removal or securing greater benefits.

Vila Autódromo: Resistance in the Face of Removal

The case of Vila Autódromo provides evidence regarding the evolving strategies of communities affected by removals and the broader process of gentrification. It represents an exceptional case of community mobilization because of the high degree of organization among residents. While much has been written in the United States and international media about Vila Autódromo and the general problems of removals in Rio,[4] this chapter contributes a more careful analysis of the strategies carried out by the community and its relevance to our understanding of the impact of communities on development.

In comparison to other cases of removal in Rio, the case of Vila Autódromo is both representative and an outlier. On the one hand, in the universe of cases, removals tied to construction for the Olympic Games were more likely to have yielded partial or complete removal than those cited for environmental risk (Popular Committee 2013). On the other hand, Vila Autódromo numbered among the larger communities under threat and therefore had less likelihood of facing complete removal. What really set the community apart, however, was the persistence of the struggle and the strategies local residents undertook. The case both confirms expectations and adds to our understanding of the selection of strategies and reasons behind eventual outcomes.

Below I detail the ways in which the community built their strategy around legal intervention, a steadfast dedication to remain in place, and use of the international media. While the community adhered to a strong belief in their right to the city, a weak relationship with the state led them away from inclusionary strategies toward autonomous exit strategies. In addition to the government's capacity and will to respond to their efforts, volatile political and economic tensions over the period also influenced the community's strategies. In the end, the residents were able to wear down opposition within the government and expand the potential influence of civil society within the urban regime, which may well serve as a model for other communities worldwide to persist in their efforts even if complete success is unattainable. The broader institutional and political environment ultimately remained largely unchanged, but for this one community, long-term struggle demonstrated the possibilities for the people overcoming the opposition of the state.

Background

Fishermen first occupied the community of Vila Autódromo, situated between a lagoon and a racetrack, in the 1960s. Though the community still lacked paved roads and proper sanitation, in 2012 approximately five hundred families lived in homes incrementally built over several generations. Property values in the Barra da Tijuca neighborhood where Vila Autódromo is located skyrocketed during the 2010s as a result of the development of large luxury condominiums and gated communities and in anticipation of overall growth from the Olympic Games.[5] In 2009, the city government provided notice to residents in Vila Autódromo that they would be removed because of the construction of the main Olympic Park next door (L. Silva 2012).[6] The community had also been subject to two previous notices of removal, including one in 2007, when the government sought to remove residents before the Pan-American Games. In 2009, the city declared that the community had to be removed to make way for the construction of two main avenues. Later the government announced that the community must be removed because Brazil had made a commitment to the International Olympic Committee to construct the TransOlimpica BRT line through the property.

In 2011 the city government released a solicitation for the concession to the public land and the creation of a public-private partnership to manage the Olympic Park. The solicitation stated that after the games, 75 percent of the Olympic Park land, which included Vila Autódromo, could be used for a large residential project (Barros 2013). In response, the community petitioned a judge to suspend the solicitation on the basis of the fact that the removal was based on future real estate potential and not the public interest. The judge granted the request, but the city administration responded by changing the justification for removal to that of environmental risk.

About 60 percent of residents in Vila Autódromo had titles of possession (*titulo de posse*), which gave them the right to occupy the land for ninety-nine years and pass it on to their children.[7] Having this legal right to the land should have provided residents with extra security against removal, and, in fact, several judges upheld the rights of the residents to stay on the basis of their right of possession.

The residents' association's first demand was "no to all removals." They rejected the government's assertion that it was necessary to remove any of the five hundred families in the community. In the event that the government refused to allow the residents to remain in place, however, the secondary demand was for them to be relocated to a comparable house with infrastructure located close to their current location (L. Silva 2012). In 2012, the government proposed moving residents to a new condominium building, known as Parque Carioca, not far from their existing homes. The residents' association still argued that the condominiums were not comparable to their current homes, and throughout 2013 almost all residents refused to negotiate over relocation or indemnity payments.

In August 2013, Mayor Paes invited leaders from Vila Autódromo to a meeting. Following the meeting Vila Autódromo released a public statement announcing:

> After years of resistance and struggle, Vila Autódromo achieved a commitment from the Mayor: Vila Autódromo and its residents will not be removed. . . . The Mayor recognized there had been mistakes in the treatment of the community and affirmed he is willing to open a round of negotiations based on the permanence of Vila Autódromo and its urbanization. The eventual cases of resettlement can be made in the same area, if a resident so desires. The Mayor also presented options for resettlement in the Parque Carioca apartments or compensation at market rates. (Vila Autódromo 2013)

The mayor's announcement reflected a reversal of his previous statements in which he repeatedly said all residents would be removed. He left open the possibility that residents might choose to relocate to Parque Carioca or receive indemnity payments to leave, but he concluded that these would mostly be voluntary dislocations. In addition, the mayor established a committee of residents and technical advisors to direct the process of urbanization outlined in the community's plan for development, described below.

Following the announcement, community members were hopeful that the mayor's office would follow through with its promises. But by the end of 2014 residents complained that urbanization plans had stalled, and in the meantime about two-thirds of residents had either accepted units in Parque Carioca or indemnity payments to relocate elsewhere (Wrede 2014). The city government made leaving the community increasingly attractive, with offers of market-value payments for properties. Those who decided to stay were forced to live amid the rubble of their neighbors' former houses as the city government demolished most of the vacated homes. In March 2015 the mayor issued a decree for the demolition of about fifty homes, clearly a departure from his previous declaration that no one would be forced to move. Many of the remaining families continued to fight, but the community had been torn apart in what residents described as a "war zone" (Souza 2016).

In May 2016 the city administration finally agreed to an urbanization plan to benefit the remaining members of the community, which included about twenty families out of the original five hundred. The modest houses, which were delivered right in time for the start of the Olympic Games, were built along a single street and have the benefit of paved roads and sanitation services. Though very far from a decisive victory, the mayor's acceptance of the community's right to remain in 2013, the construction of public housing nearby instead of in the distant periphery, market-rate indemnity payments, and the eventual urbanization of the remaining community all represented a clear break with the city administration's original plans. Vila Autódromo residents' strategic vision and determination serve as a model for communities under threat of removal elsewhere.

Strategies

The goals, targets, and tactics of Vila Autódromo demonstrate a pattern of resistance in which residents realigned their efforts depending on ongoing responses to their initiatives and new opportunities. The components of the community's strategies changed to reflect new realities over time, though the primary strategy of resistance rather than negotiation remained central to their activities.

The primary goal of the association was always for the entire community to remain in place and for the government to invest in improving services and infrastructure. As time passed, however, and residents became more apprehensive that the city government would not agree to residents remaining in place, they also called for inclusion in public housing nearby or market-rate indemnity payments for those who preferred to move elsewhere. They did not seek to change the existing administration in the city, even though there was an election in 2012, nor did they take part in the city's participatory institutions or argue for institutional change.

The targets of the community's efforts included those they thought could bring about change. Through legal action they sought to impact the ruling of local judges, which meant building the case for why residents should remain in place. One proactive solution for the urbanization of the community was the creation of a Popular Plan in conjunction with the Universidade Federal de Rio de Janeiro (UFRJ) and the Universidade Federal Fluminense (UFF), which targeted the mayor and his administration. Over the course of a year, the community association held assemblies to prepare a detailed needs assessment and proposal for the urbanization of the community. The resulting Popular Plan included cost estimates for rehousing residents living along the lagoon, sanitation infrastructure projects, and educational programs for both youth and adults. Once the plan was completed, leaders from Vila Autódromo sought to present it to the mayor to persuade him of the benefits of urbanization over removal. Leaders in the community knew that they must frame adoption of the plan in practical terms that the mayor's administration could not refute (Guimarães 2012). As such, they calculated that the plan would cost about 35 percent of the amount it would take to relocate them to newly constructed apartments.

At the same time, the community realized they would need better leverage with the mayor to gain his approval. With the help of the Rio-based NGO Catalytic Communities (CatComm), university supporters, and others, the community targeted international media outlets to present their story to a global audience. As Theresa Williamson (2016), executive director of CatComm, noted, they saw an opportunity to present a new narrative of favelas, as many key international media outlets—the BBC, NPR, the *New York Times*, and *Global Mail*—brought correspondents to the city. Residents from Vila Autódromo

worked with CatComm to present their own timeline of events, ultimately to alter the global perception of the city so that Mayor Paes
would see the political and economic benefit of responding positively
to their demands. As noted by Sandra Maria de Souza, a resident leader from Vila Autódromo, they worked with many organizations, but
the international press gave them a voice that was fundamental to their
struggle. At the end of the day, former residents' association president
Altair Guimarães believed it was the power of money rather than the
judiciary or the government that would decide their fate, and, as such,
their resistance had to also target economic interests. By projecting a
negative image of the Brazilian government, the city of Rio, and corruption in the private sector to the world, they hoped to generate
enough fear of backlash in terms of investment and tourism dollars to
influence the city government in their favor.

The community's tactics—legal redress through the Defensoria
Pública, protest, developing the Popular Plan, and publicizing their
story in the international press—aimed to achieve empowerment in
the political process that would decide their fate. On several occasions
community members met face-to-face with Mayor Paes to present the
Popular Plan and discuss their desire for urbanization, but these
meetings came only after significant outside pressure from street agi-
tation and the international media. For example, in August 2012 residents staged a protest to secure a meeting with Mayor Paes in which
they presented the Popular Plan. Though the mayor received the plan
and said he would respond in forty-five days, it took many more protests and actions before he finally did respond a year later in his announcement that the community could remain in place.

By all accounts (i.e., personal interviews, observation, news reports), the community chose not to engage in corrupt or clientelistic
politics. In an interview from July 2013, Guimarães reported that he
had received "indecent proposals" to end the fight in the community,
but he concluded that because he was "always fighting out in the open
with the politicians" they didn't try to buy him off anymore (Barros
2013). Residents' association leaders in Vila Autódromo calculated
that they had more power through the use of judicial actions, protest,
and media attention than they would have through pledging loyalty
in exchange for potential benefits. Across Rio, other communities

have not made the same calculation. As one resident commented during a meeting of a group called Favela Não Se Cala (the favela does not stay quiet), "In many cases, the residents' association has been bought by the city government—residents get special treatment for not protesting municipal actions" (RioOnWatch 2013). Clientelism, then, appears to be alive and well, even as many other residents' associations and individuals participate in citywide groups to publicize and protest removals. Critically, though, clientelism appears to be more of a factor in securing special benefits than in actually preventing the removal of residents.

The strategies of this community may be defined as a mix of exit and indirect, according to the typology I have outlined in this book. They certainly did not attempt to change policies or programs from within, preferring to use the international press to generate pressure on public officials. Ultimately they did need to negotiate directly with the Paes administration to secure relocation, indemnity payments, and urbanization, but the source of their empowerment came from the outside rather than from working within the state.

What Factors Influenced the Strategies of Vila Autódromo?

The case of Vila Autódromo demonstrates the ways in which the variables of ideology, the community's relationship with the state, political opportunities, and resources interact to influence the choice of strategies. First, the community association believed that to be effective and to reframe the debate about removals, they needed to depersonalize the struggle and frame their story in terms of their rights as citizens. The choice of the residents' association to say no to all removals rather than negotiating over benefits rests on the framing of the issue in terms of rights as well as practical experience. Guimarães stated that the association would not negotiate because "we have the right to be there; it's not about removal or no removal, but about the value placed on our lives" (Guimarães 2012). The community's previous experience with threats of removal provided them with knowledge of the legal system and the rights they possessed within Brazilian law. For several decades the community had relied heavily on Brazil's system of civil public defenders (Defensoria Pública) to challenge the government's right to evict them. When the community faced removal prior to the Pan-American Games in 2007, the judicial system worked in their favor to allow them to remain in place.

At the same time, Guimarães stated that they recognized that judicial action alone would not suffice to counteract the weight of the government's desire to redevelop the area for "real estate speculation" (Guimarães 2012). They had been subject to removal in the past and won the right to stay, but when once more faced with the prospect of removal, community leaders understood the problem to be much broader than their own situation. They began to view their own struggle as part of the ongoing gentrification of the city, involving removals of residents by government order as well as a push to the periphery of the poor who were no longer able to afford the city. They concluded that the judicial system could be only part of the answer. In practice, this often meant combining judicial actions with protest and taking their case to international institutions and media. For example, when the government declared that the community needed to be removed because the area was at environmental risk, residents and supporters protested outside city hall and demanded documentation for the claim. When a judge ordered that houses located within twenty-five feet of the lagoon be removed according to federal regulations, the community filed an injunction to stop the eviction and also petitioned the International Olympic Committee, citing rights violations against forced removals.

The rights-anchored ideology of the community led them to seek redress through the judicial system, but just as importantly the system shaped their understanding that laws alone would not solve the problems of forced evictions and lack of affordable and secure housing options. The creation of the Popular Plan came out of this frustration with the legal system and the community's desire to generate their own vision for their neighborhood and for the city. But this course of action is also a symptom of the weak relationship between informal settlements in Rio and the state. As McCann (2014) detailed, the state had been largely absent from favelas in the city in terms of providing security, infrastructure, services, and social assistance. In Vila Autódromo, residents had a particularly contentious relationship with officials from the Secretariat for Housing, which they criticized for violating their rights to information, ignoring court orders, and intimidating residents into accepting offers to move without informing them of their options (Guimarães 2012, L. Silva 2016).

Distrust of the city government led the community away from inclusive strategies and toward community-led planning and international exposure, or what I characterize as exit strategies. Though Brazil has developed a number of innovative participatory institutions at all levels of government, communities in Rio typically do not rely on these institutions as mechanisms for policy change. According to Valério da Silva, "Many spaces for participation exist in Rio, but the real policy making lies outside these spaces. We are told here are your options, now choose what you want to do" (V. Silva 2012). In other words, participatory institutions in the city do not invite debate but rather serve as mechanisms to legitimize the options government officials have already devised. Professor Carlos Vainer from the UFRJ also noted that the community planning process in Vila Autódromo, which he led, did not involve government representatives because residents were suspicious of any process in which civil society is invited to the government's table. He argued that when the government controls these types of participatory processes, communities always start off from a point of weakness because the government has already brought their ideas. It is up to the community to change the government's mind. The process of community-led planning differs in that residents have the opportunity to present their own vision first, in advance of negotiation with the state. According to Vainer, people need to acquire the right tools for resistance to be effective (Vainer 2012). In this case, residents needed to learn the language of urban planning in order to know their options and translate their vision into a concrete plan the city administration could plausibly implement. The resulting plan reflected the residents' belief that the community belonged to them, and as such they had the right to plan for the community's future as they saw fit, much as David Harvey defines the right to the city ideology (2003). Importantly, though, the community still sought to persuade government officials to implement the plan and did not seek outside donor assistance.

In the community's pursuit of the goals of remaining in place and implementing urbanization measures, their weak relationship with the state led them to seek international attention instead of pursuing bilateral negotiations with the municipal Secretariat for Housing. Resident leaders did not feel they had a voice within the institutions of government and therefore exited the local political sphere to target the international press and citizens who might act in solidarity. Their resulting strategy involved appeals for public support rather than petitioning public officials directly. In March 2016, as the city government announced it would demolish all remaining homes, the community began the "Urbaniza Já" campaign through social media, in which they urged people from around the world to record and post videos appealing to the mayor to urbanize the community. In response, Vila Autódromo received hundreds of videos from journalists, actors, academics, and other citizens within and outside Brazil.

Because community leaders did not agree with the group's portrayal by the local media, they viewed the international press as a more effective means to draw attention to their cause. As Luiz da Silva related, they believed the main news outlet in Rio, O Globo, to be fundamentally dishonest, and he pointed to a number of falsehoods reported by the paper, including that the majority of residents wanted to leave the community and that residents were simply gaming the system for more money (2016). Silva argued that in order for the residents' association to have influence, they needed "to educate people who did not understand the history of the community to see them as citizens rather than as invaders," but he did not believe that could be achieved using traditional media in the city.

Further, the community's distrust of the political system was also reflected in their lack of ambition to change it. As noted above, though there was a municipal election in 2012, which occurred after the fight to save Vila Autódromo began, the neighborhood association did not invest time or resources into supporting or running candidates for election. At the time, Mayor Paes was enjoying considerable popularity, and his reelection was never really in question. According to staff from FASE, an advocacy and research organization based in Rio, only two City Council members demonstrated solidarity with any of the communities under threat of removal related to the games, and both of them were from the Workers' Party (PT) (FASE Coordinators 2012). Traditionally, however, the PT has not had a strong presence in Rio. Though the housing secretary at the beginning of the removal process was from the PT, the neighborhood association accused him of deceit and corruption and never considered him an ally (Guimarães 2012). Without significant political allies, changing the political regime was an unlikely strategy for this small neighborhood association.

In both summer 2013 and spring 2016, large-scale protests targeting Olympic cost overruns brought significant international attention to Rio and the negative consequences of mega-event development. In these two time periods, assisted by CatComm and other NGOs, Vila Autódromo capitalized on the attention focused on the city to promote the community's story as a symbol of the greed and inequality fostered by the games. A number of international news outlets, including *The Guardian,* the *New York Times,* and the BBC, reported on the experience of Vila Autódromo in relation to the protests.[8] In fact, the location of the community next to the Olympic Park was a considerable asset in their resistance efforts. According to community leader Luiz da Silva, "The athletes involved in the games should not want the mark of suffering on their medals" (L. Silva 2012). The community carefully connected the image of the games to the fate of their community. They used the language of rights in their demand to remain in place, and the Popular Committee for the World Cup and Olympics—mentioned above—promoted the community as the primary example of government greed and corruption associated with preparation for the games.

The community benefited from the resource of social capital accumulated during years of struggle, which allowed them to present a united front to the media and others. The residents' association cultivated social capital through biweekly cultural events and ongoing meetings to update residents on their activities and government responses. In addition, and unlike many other communities in Rio, they did not face incursions from drug traffickers or militias intent on overtaking the residents' association (McCann 2014). Ultimately, having faced previous threats of removal was a key factor in creating a strong group identity.

The community also enjoyed a high degree of civic capacity and strong leadership in the personality of their presidents, Altair Guimarães and, later, Maria da Penha. At every opportunity Guimarães shared his personal story of being evicted from two previous favelas before building his home and his life in Vila Autódromo. Residents identified with Guimarães's longing for security and his fatigue with a city government that he saw as more concerned with profits than people (Vila Autódromo Residents 2012). His leadership enabled connections to other groups around the city even if none of the community members had formal political experience before the struggle. In addition, by linking to universities to develop the Popular Plan, residents received valuable advice and recall that they learned a great deal about how to present their demands through these relationships. Though a lack of allies in the administration hindered the community's ability to reach government officials, they were thereby able to remain independent and unco-opted.

Nonetheless, like most communities, Vila Autódromo struggled with maintaining enthusiasm for participating in protests and other activities. At a protest meant to solicit public support for the community's cause held outside city government offices in July 2012, one resident of Vila Autódromo wearily expressed to me her disappointment that the same few people always participated in protests. No matter the time or the day, she said that it was difficult to get people to participate because they complained that nothing changed as a result (Vila Autódromo Residents 2012). The creation of the Popular Plan, in which residents saw the personal relevance of making sure the plan suited their individual needs, and securing supporters across the city for protests and around the world for advocacy campaigns helped to overcome the obstacles of eliciting participation.

In sum, the case demonstrates the influence of a rights-based ideology and a weak relationship with the state as well as the impact of changing political opportunities and resources. A rights-based ideology led Vila Autódromo to depersonalize the struggle and focus on making the legal case for the community's permanence on the site, but a distrust in the system and the current administration also led them away from participatory processes and negotiation toward community-led planning and the international media. Global attention to Rio during times of mass protest created the political opportunity for the community to attract increasing international media attention while also boosting the potential economic threat to the city of negative press surrounding the community's removal. Finally, the location of the community, and the high degree of unity among residents, allowed them to serve as a symbol of resistance to mega-event development everywhere and reject initial offers from the city government that did not meet their demands.

Does the case of Vila Autódromo represent a new era for community activism? While in the past neighborhood associations may have turned either to clientelistic tactics or revolutionary ideology, this case does suggest a shift toward public negotiation and moderation of rhetoric. Perhaps of concern, though, is that the community used the democratic institutions of the judicial system, yet they did not view elections and participatory institutions as positive means toward resolution of their campaign.

Outcomes

This case demonstrates the influence of a variety of actors that worked both for and against the perpetuation of Vila Autódromo as a community as well as the effect of the community's strategies in avoiding removal. On the one hand, leaders in the community recognized their antagonists as not only the government but also private real estate and construction companies that stand to profit from redevelopment in the city. On the other hand, academics, journalists, and NGOs partnered in legitimating and promoting the legal rights and interests of the community and acted as their advocates in the city and abroad. The long-term struggle in Vila Autódromo influenced leaders' understanding of their rights and how to use the judiciary to their advantage, while the failure of the judicial system to stave off the threat of eviction despite residents having previously secured land titles led them to believe that the judicial system alone would not guarantee their long-term security. The community both relied on the language of rights to forward their claims and recognized the practical need to argue on economic terms and hit the government in the wallet through negative publicity.

As I argue in Chapter 2, the outcomes of the efforts of community organizations depend on the extent to which they are able to overcome opposition to their claims in addition to the capacity of the government to respond favorably. In cases of land disputes, government actors and private developers alike tend to oppose the permanency of low-income communities situated in increasingly valuable real estate areas. The case of Vila Autódromo shows that resistance against such opposition is not futile. From all accounts, the mayor of Rio did not really change his heart regarding removal of the community. Nonetheless, Vila Autódromo won two significant victories in overcoming the city government's opposition to the community's permanency on site: the first in 2013, when the mayor reversed his previous statements that all of the community would be removed, and the second in 2016, when the remaining families negotiated for urbanization. Though the administration never operationalized the Popular Plan as promised, and many residents gave up the fight to stay in place and accepted other alternatives, the actions of the community still appear to have served them well compared to other communities in which residents were not provided nearby public housing or unprecedented market-rate indemnity payments (RioOnWatch 2015b). For those twenty remaining families who received newly constructed housing units in the community, leaders report that urbanization is a victory in that they will be able to serve as a model to other communities engaged in resistance, even if the victory is incomplete because the original community no longer exists (L. Silva 2016; Souza 2016).

Ability to Overcome Opposition

Vila Autódromo managed to overcome opposition through significant unity, building new social networks, and capitalizing on political opportunities. With most residents remaining united, they worked to negotiate with the government as a collective rather than as individuals. Though many would later accept relocation or indemnity payments, their early unity ensured they would be offered units nearby. There was also greater transparency in the negotiation of monetary settlements. In contrast, in communities without a strong leader or group unity, such as in the sprawling Morro da Providência, consensus has been more difficult to achieve, and the individual negotiations pursued by some residents weakened the community's bargaining power. The smaller size of the community and long-term cohesion in fighting eviction helped Vila Autódromo to unify under a coherent strategy. The continued resistance of families left the mayor with little choice but to negotiate for urbanization (Souza 2016; Williamson 2016). After years of legal action and increasing incentives to leave the site, the final option for removal of the few families that remained would have been by force. Given the international interest in the community, removal by force would have jeopardized the city's image within weeks of the opening ceremonies for the Olympic Games.

Vila Autódromo's strategic actions also led to a significant expansion of the breadth of actors with an interest in preserving the community. Stone argues that the composition of an urban regime changes over time as different groups have access to *institutional resources* and form *new social networks* (1989, 4). The urban regime for development in Rio, defined as those who have the power to make governing decisions, comprises city government officials who make decisions regarding land use and dole out land and contracts to private-sector companies to carry out construction work. Through campaign financing, the private sector in turn holds sway over the decisions of government officials. In the 2012 mayoral election, eight of the top ten donors to the mayor's party, the PMDB, were construction or real estate companies.[9] Leaders in Vila Autódromo claimed that their intended removal was a direct result of this relationship: companies that supported the mayor expected cheap access to the increasingly valuable land the community occupied (Guimarães 2012; L. Silva 2012).

In order to reshape the power to make decisions in this urban regime, then, Stone would argue the community needed greater access to institutional resources and social networks. Through their connections to domestic and international NGOs, including Amnesty International and the Urban Age program at the London School of Economics,[10] as well as international journalists, they achieved the formation of a new social network concerned with the plight of the community. Previous research in Rio (Arias 2004) and internationally (Keck and Sikkink 1998) identifies networks among local and global civil society actors as key to effecting political change. These networks are particularly important for disrupting the urban regime status quo. However, to change incentives for government officials, resistance efforts by this new network needed to influence institutional resources by disrupting the supply of money from the state and federal governments as well as revenues from tourism and investment.[11]

A shift in political opportunities generated by the mass protests of June 2013 and 2016 stoked fear of disruption. The motivation for the mayor's changing position regarding Vila Autódromo in 2013 stemmed from panic regarding losses of both political support and international prestige. Following the protests, approval ratings for President Dilma Rousseff fell from 57 percent to 30 percent, while ratings for Rio State Governor Sergio Cabral fell from 49 percent to 25 percent, the lowest of any governor in the country. By July, Mayor Paes's approval rating had also fallen from 50 percent to 30 percent.[12] From the federal level down, officials felt the pressure to respond to protesters' anger regarding public spending for the games. President Rousseff invited urban reform movement leaders to meet with her in Brasília, and Mayor Paes followed suit by inviting members of the Popular Committee for the World Cup and the Olympics to meet with him in Rio.[13] The mayor then visited a number of communities under threat of removal, publicly proclaiming that the government had made mistakes by not engaging residents in dialogue. In the case of Morro da Providência, the mayor announced he would suspend the construction of an infrastructure project that would require removals of residents.

Still, Vila Autódromo stood out as a particular symbol of violations associated with the games because of the international press the community had received.[14] Giselle Tanaka, a leader in the Popular Committee, described the mayor's decision to allow the community to remain in place as a "strategic retreat." As Tanaka explained, even then the mayor could not force a violent eviction because of the global focus on Brazil and the community's worldwide notoriety, but the community would also not let him pass through the gates for a photo opportunity without the promise to allow them to remain in place (Tanaka 2014). The community's strategy to say "no to all removals" and refuse to negotiate on any other grounds appeared to back the mayor into a corner from which he needed to offer residents the opportunity to stay if he wanted to be seen as responsive to the needs of those negatively impacted by the games.

Mayor Paes relied on close ties to President Rousseff and Governor Sergio Cabral to fund development programs such as MCMV and other infrastructural projects in the city. He had a political incentive as well as a monetary one to act in accordance with the president's desire to quickly respond to civil society demands. At the same time, international financial institutions, including U.S.-based Fidelity Investments (2013), warned that overspending by the government and mass public dissatisfaction would decrease the potential gains from investment in the country. Given their strident activism and global networks, Vila Autódromo was well situated to serve as a political symbol of conciliation. The mayor had an incentive to signal to investors that he was aware of the challenges facing the city but was fully capable of addressing any issues.

Concern for his political future and legacy as the mayor of Rio during the World Cup and Olympics clearly motivated Mayor Paes's behavior in July and August 2013. After the announcement in 2013 that no residents would be forced to leave Vila Autódromo, however, the political opening passed. Residents charged that the mayor's administration embarked on a campaign to divide the community by convincing some residents to leave for Parque Carioca while making life increasingly difficult for those who remained. For instance, residents reported that the city government removed public telephones from the community and built a temporary wall across the main access road that impeded entry to the children's park (RioOnWatch 2014). Toward the end of 2014, the administration began negotiating indemnity payments for residents that were closer to market value and reached over half a million dollars in some cases. These higher payments were not made out of the goodness of the mayor's heart. In an interview in May 2015, Mayor Paes stated:

> I find [paying high compensations] absurd and an unacceptable business. Yet, the fact remains that at some point someone came and legalized the situation of these people. At a certain moment in time, a band of NGOs, international organizations, political parties and public defenders defended these guys. . . . And this is the result: people who do not need it are receiving a fortune to vacate a public area. Demagoguery rules, hypocrisy comes, and this is what happens. And we were only able to empty the area after lots of negotiation. There've been six years of negotiating this. (Berta 2015, translation by RioOnWatch)

The mayor blamed not only civil society but also sympathetic politicians and public defenders for the fact that his administration agreed to market-rate payments. As a report by MIT scholars Lawrence Vale and Annemarie Gray (2015) found, the higher payments to residents still remained about 50 percent lower than market-rate compensation should have been, given the value per square meter in the Barra da Tijuca neighborhood. Still, despite the mayor's complaints, paying more to the residents permitted his desired outcome. As Guimarães lamented, once the amount of payments to residents increased, the fight largely ended (RioOnWatch 2015a). The association's quest to fight the city could no longer compete with the lure of large payouts. The residents' association continued protests, and international media pressure was sustained, but the backsliding on promises clearly showed that while the political moment of 2013 mattered for the decision to allow residents to stay in place, the long-term impact was ambiguous.

Nevertheless, for the small contingent of residents who remained in place, unity, the international press, and further mass protests in 2016 enabled their eventual victory. In April 2016 about fifty remaining residents took to the streets to block traffic in protest of continued construction around the community without plans to implement promised urbanization. As Williamson argued, Mayor Paes still did not really understand how big the movement around Vila Autódromo had become, but the strength of the "Urbaniza Já" campaign surprised him and he knew he didn't want more bad press (2016). A new round of stories from media outlets such as CNN, NPR, the BBC, *The Guardian,* and Bloomberg News focusing on Brazil's political and economic turmoil leading up to President Rousseff's impeachment questioned Rio's preparedness for the Olympic Games and included mention of Vila Autódromo's latest struggles (Charner 2016; Loeffler 2016; Griffin 2016; Garcia-Navarro 2016; BBC 2016).

Even within Rio, Mayor Paes needed to reconcile a declining economy and mounting municipal debt with his record as the mayor who hosted both the World Cup and the Olympic Games. As quoted in *The Guardian,* Larissa Lacerda, an activist with the Popular Committee on the World Cup and Olympics, stated that "It is not just the chaos of the schools and hospitals, but the cost of living and the huge traffic jams, and Eduardo Paes is watching all this. . . . The urbanisation of Vila Autódromo has appeared to Paes as a possibility to keep some political capital at a time [when] he is losing popularity" (Griffin 2016). By building a visual symbol of responsiveness to the needs of low-income residents, Paes hoped to stave off further criticism.

The Vila Autódromo case demonstrates that the exclusionary power of the urban regime in Rio remains strong, though political dynamics and well-designed strategies enabled a measure of success for community resistance. Traditional urban regime theory explains the coalitional politics involved in city governance and the need to reshape the interests of actors with the "power to" make policy decisions (Stone 1989). The events in Rio in 2013 and 2016 provide evidence that shifts in political opportunities were vital to changing those interests and incentives of policy makers. Though limited interaction with the state was initially problematic, mass protests and continuous press surrounding the games incentivized the city government to respond to the new network of concerned organizations and individuals around the world. Long-term change in approach by the city administration, however, appears unlikely, and skepticism among community members regarding meaningful political change remains high. As Sandra Maria de Souza explained when I asked how they seek power within the city, "It's not really possible to have power, to fight capitalism, but we hope our victory represents hope for the ability of communities around the world that resistance can work" (2016). Williamson (2016) also agreed that change in Vila Autódromo came about because of a critical moment in time that brought issues to the surface, but real change takes decades. Influence through participatory institutions, in particular, won't happen until people actually vote for change of the administration.

Conclusions

The findings in Rio de Janeiro point to a number of broad conclusions. First, the case of Vila Autódromo demonstrates that an ideology based on the right to the city and the need to protect individual and collective rights does not necessarily lead to strategies of inclusion. When combined with a weak relationship with the state, a rights-based ideology instead leads communities to seek autonomous or exit strategies rather than working within the confines of the city government. In this case "exit" meant appealing to an international audience for support once the community recognized the limits of the judicial system for redress. The community did rely to a large extent on a key democratic institution—the Defensoria Pública—to provide some measure of inclusion into government, as the office for housing within the Defensoria Pública negotiated on the community's behalf and brought both sides of the conflict together. But seeing the ineffectiveness of the legal system and of the Defensoria Pública to protect their right to stay in place led Vila Autódromo's leadership to seek empowerment outside of the state.

As Fischer (2008) argues, residents of Brazil's informal settlements have never achieved full inclusion into the city in part because of ambiguity in the procedural enforcement of the laws. On the basis of their past experiences with legal institutions and continued inability to gain true stability of tenure, communities such as Vila Autódromo now understand the importance of reinforcing judicial efforts with protest and global advocacy. The right to the city ideology provides a framework for community organizations to understand their struggle within a larger process of reformulating the city to reflect their needs. Rather than personalizing the struggle, broadening the debate added legitimacy and appeal to global audiences who identified with the challenges of inclusion.

Second, the resources of the community, including social capital, played a key role in the formulation and implementation of strategies. Civic capacity and political alliances also determined how strategies were put into action and whether they had the intended effect. Lacking allies within the municipal administration, the residents' association relied on ties to university faculty and NGOs to publicize their story.

Third, the community's exit strategy proved critical in eliciting immediate proposals, but long-term change may be elusive. A strategy to appeal to outsiders to elicit pressure for change within the regime assisted this community in achieving benefits, but it does not appear to have changed any fundamental power relationships within the city. To generalize, it could be that exit strategies are more effective for short-term remedies than broader institutional or political change.

Fourth, though the finding that shifts in political dynamics influence the outcomes of community mobilization may not be surprising, this case demonstrates that changes in the political structure are also associated with expanding networks in the urban regime. In this case the creation of new policy networks regarding removals became important as mass protests provided an opening for greater attention to the issues. Government officials and members of the private sector had greater incentives to incorporate the interests of those concerned with removals in order to preserve the image of the city for investment and tourism. In the long term, a development-driven urban regime is difficult to crack, and other events may need to converge in order to provide openings for inclusion. But when the political opportunity arose as a result of mass demonstration and demands for democratic accountability, Vila Autódromo's residents were poised to benefit from the government's desire to appear more responsive to citizen demands.

Finally, though previous literature on favelas in Rio has focused on the use of clientelism for eliciting benefits, this case shows that the strategies of some contemporary communities have moved beyond direct negotiation with the state. Elected officials may be concerned with garnering votes, but they also recognize the need to satisfy private-sector interests as campaign contributors and partners in development projects. Community organizations, therefore, have broadened the scope of their advocacy beyond negotiating with government officials. Future analyses of mobilization should start with the expectation that organizations incorporate assessments about future risk and reward on the basis of past experiences and their understanding of the plurality of actors involved.

4

Neighborhood Transition and Housing for Low-Income Residents in Atlanta

In 1989, Clarence Stone published his widely cited book *Regime Politics,* in which he described the coalition forged between public officials and the private sector to generate growth in Atlanta's downtown in the latter half of the twentieth century. The city represented the traditional closed development regime in which community organizations generally lacked the power to set the urban agenda and direct the distribution of resources. In viewing the case of Atlanta nearly thirty years later, the question is whether anything has changed. Is there a "new era" in Atlanta as Stone et al. (2015) now posit exists in other U.S. cities? What is the organizational environment in the city and to what extent do community organizations now influence the policy agenda and distribution of resources?

To assess these questions, I specifically review the experience of the Old Fourth Ward neighborhood and the work of the Historic District Development Corporation (HDDC). Atlanta's Old Fourth Ward has traditionally been the home of working-class black residents. The neighborhood sits right outside the city's downtown and features numerous historic homes and sites, most famously the childhood home of Martin Luther King Jr. and a museum dedicated to his legacy. In the fictional narrative *Them,* author Nathan McCall (2008) examines the history of the Old Fourth Ward and the conflicts that arose as whites entered the primarily black neighborhood in the 1990s and 2000s and were widely viewed as invaders with completely different tastes and lifestyles. McCall succinctly describes the historical trajectory of the Old Fourth Ward in his writing:

> When the neighborhood was first built, whites lived in most of the area, especially up on the northern end of Randolph Street. In the 1920s, blacks following factory jobs moved down on the opposite end, near Auburn Avenue. To keep the boundaries clear, whites changed the name of their end of Randolph to Glen Iris Drive. When blacks kept coming, white folks hauled tail out of town. Blacks moved into the fine Queen Anne cottages, bungalows and shotgun houses and claimed the place for themselves. The main drag on Auburn Avenue eventually came to be widely known as "the richest Negro street in the world." In time, though, the ward suffered as black tax dollars were steered to the white areas in Atlanta. City neglect and more integration gradually siphoned middle-class blacks from the neighborhood. As the single-family homes, duplexes, and apartment buildings fell into disrepair, the Old Fourth Ward declined. In the late 80's, a smattering of blacks began trickling back . . . a decade later, blacks had begun a steady push to revive the ward. (2008, 23–24)

McCall sets the scene for the clash between African Americans who were part of the revitalization of the neighborhood in the 1980s and 1990s and new white residents hoping to take advantage of the neighborhood's charm and central location in the 2000s. He vividly depicts the historic racial divisions in the neighborhood and the resentment that ensues when white residents return, thereby raising prices and bringing with them trendy restaurants and bars.

The HDDC existed throughout this transition, striving to preserve racial diversity and the original character of the neighborhood. As a community development corporation, the HDDC grew from the mission to revitalize the neighborhood through homeownership, but their mission also drives them to participate in advocacy and planning processes related to the preservation of affordable housing in the neighborhood and in the city at-large.

As the analysis below demonstrates, a weak relationship with the state and a conservative ideology have meant the HDDC came to rely on market strategies and persuasion of officials to forward their agenda of preventing displacement and promoting affordable housing in the neighborhood. The market-driven focus fits the purpose of their origin as a community development corporation. But leaders also recognize the need for broader change in city policy to complement their approach. For instance, leaders were involved in both the development of the BeltLine Trust, a fund to ensure continued provision of affordable housing along the BeltLine path transforming the city, and an inclusionary zoning law passed in 2016. The promise of city revenue from the BeltLine's creation generated goodwill toward developing the BeltLine Trust, while a political opening created by the election of a new City Council member served to move forward the push for inclusionary zoning. Still, lack of formal inclusion, mobilization of residents, and stable funding sources hamper the ability of the HDDC and others to significantly reform housing policies, programs, and institutions in the city.

Background

Atlanta, a midsized city with approximately 500,000 residents, has been led by a Democratic mayor for most of the past two centuries. Politics in the city are somewhat fragmented by the overlap of two county governments—Dekalb and Fulton—within the city boundaries. In addition, political tension often arises between the Democratic-led city administration and the Republican-led state legislature. The political orientation of the successive Democratic administrations, however, has remained relatively stable, particularly in recent decades. Mayor Kasim Reed, who was elected in 2010, has led his administration through a process of economic revival following the 2008 national financial crisis that severely impacted Atlanta. Since the 1970s, the city has been known for its predominantly African American leadership and focus on attracting the headquarters of multinational corporations, which now include the Coca-Cola Company, Delta Airlines, Home Depot, and CNN. The city strives for global prominence, and in the past few years Mayor Reed has advanced the city's global integration through a planning process to increase export capacity in addition to other efforts to attract investment to the city (Katz and Daley 2013).

The 1996 Summer Olympic Games proved to be a pivotal moment for redevelopment in the city. The beginning of the federally funded

HOPE VI program, which sought to replace public housing with mixed-income communities, coincided with the awarding of the games. In the most publicized instance of displacement, the city demolished the Tech-wood and Clark Howell Homes public-housing communities in order to make room for the Olympic Village, with the original intent that residents would be offered units in newly constructed mixed-income housing once the Olympics were over. In the meantime, most residents received rental vouchers. By 2000, only seventy-eight families, or 7 percent of the original tenant population, were rehoused in the new mixed-income community (Vale and Gray 2013). By 2007, the Atlanta Housing Authority had dismantled almost all public housing in favor of mixed-income developments and rental vouchers. Citywide, about thirty thousand residents were displaced as a result of the destruction of public housing, and only 17 percent were relocated to new subsidized units (Oakley, Ruel, and Reid 2013). Despite the scale of the changes to housing policy in the city, there was little opposition from residents or outside groups to the demolition of public housing in favor of mixed-income communities. The policy trend in Atlanta followed the paradigm shift in U.S. housing policy, with scholars arguing that deconcentration of the poor was necessary for poverty alleviation and reducing the violence and crime associated with public-housing complexes. Follow-up surveys, however, have found mixed results as to whether residents are better off in terms of income and quality of life than they were before living in concentrated public housing (Hankins et al. 2014).[1]

Current issues of affordable housing in Atlanta are exacerbated by a high degree of inequality. The city has the distinction of being the most unequal city in the United States: the top income earners in the city (those at the ninety-fifth percentile) earn twenty times the amount of low-income earners (or those in the twentieth percentile) (Berube and Holmes 2015). In addition, over 25 percent of the population lives below the U.S. poverty line (U.S. Census Bureau 2015). In the past few decades, demographic shifts have also significantly changed the face of the city. Between 1990 and 2010, the percentage of the population that identified as black fell from 67 percent to 54 percent, while the white population increased from 31 percent to 38 percent (U.S. Census Bureau 2015). The presence of large corporations and the city's reputation for having a relatively low cost of living have attracted significant numbers of young, often white, professionals.

In fact, the cost of living in the city has been on the rise. As the demographic of residents has changed and the population has risen over the last decade, rental and home prices have increased dramatically. According to the American Community Survey, 54 percent of renters pay more than 30 percent of their income to housing, which means they are "cost-burdened," as defined by the U.S. Department for Housing and Urban Development (ACS 2014). From 2006 to 2013 the vacancy rate dropped from 16 percent to 9.9 percent, indicating increases in demand were outpacing increases in supply. During the same time period the median monthly cost for rent increased about 8 percent per annum, though in the past few years, *monthly* increases of 5 percent have been commonplace (Zumper 2016). From 2010 to 2014, the city lost one-third of apartment rentals costing below $750 per month (Immergluck, Carpenter, and Lueders 2016). In 2016, the median monthly cost for a one-bedroom apartment in Atlanta was $1,300, and $1,650 for a two-bedroom (Zumper 2016), while data from 2014 show the median annual income hovered around $46,000 (ACS 2014). Assuming an annual rental cost of $15,600 for a one-bedroom apartment, a household earning the median income would be paying 33 percent of its before-tax income in rental costs. For those able to purchase a home, median home prices are relatively low for a major city at $234,000, but prices are on the rise, with an increase of 15 percent in just one year, from 2014 to 2015 (Zillow 2015).

Though Atlanta has been perceived as an affordable city, increasing rental and home prices demonstrate that the city is not affordable for all, and rapid increases in prices jeopardize the future of inclusion in the city. In addition, as housing advocate Mtamanika Youngblood points out, the affordable housing that continues to exist is often "not safe and decent, particularly in neighborhoods of color" (2015). New construction is overwhelmingly luxury rentals in gentrifying areas of the city rather than moderately priced units spread throughout the city (Immergluck 2015).

In 2005, the Atlanta City Council approved the construction of the BeltLine, a twenty-two-mile walking and biking trail built alongside old railroad tracks that is meant to unite neighborhoods across socioeconomic status and revitalize the city. Popular perception of the project is largely positive, as it provides leafy trails, parks, arts programs, and fitness classes. The project is a major attraction for the city, but the BeltLine also has its critics, who argue that planners have not adequately accounted for the need to protect affordable housing as gentrification occurs along the circular path (see Mehrotra 2014). On the east side of the trail, which was constructed first, market-priced rents now soar far above average: a three-bedroom apartment in a newly built luxury complex along the BeltLine starts at $3,400 per month (Editorial Board 2014).[2] According to the director of housing for the BeltLine, James Alexander, the project did not result in significant displacement of existing residents in the construction zone because much of the area around the path was abandoned industrial property without residential units. But planners did expect that gentrification around the BeltLine would result in the erosion of affordable housing in the surrounding neighborhoods over time, especially because new building would likely not target the low-income market. The BeltLine Trust was therefore established by the city in conjunction with the nonprofit BeltLine, Inc., with the goal of providing funding for 5,600 units of workforce housing to maintain diversity in the neighborhoods along the BeltLine. In addition, a homeownership program led by this BeltLine partnership assists low-income buyers to purchase homes along the path, particularly in areas of the city where vacancy rates are still low. While Alexander admits that the organization is behind in meeting its goals of providing affordable housing, it continues its efforts to secure funding and meet housing needs in the city.

Gentrification around the BeltLine in the Old Fourth Ward and adjacent areas along the east side of the path has certainly changed local demographics, even if not all of the effects are directly attributable to the BeltLine's construction. As James Fason, executive director of the HDDC, explained, over time there has been a significant problem in the neighborhood as homes turn over and there are fewer and fewer affordable homes for sale. Unlike in Washington, D.C., and other cities, in Atlanta displacement caused by condo conversions and rising rents as property owners sell off buildings has not yet occurred (Alexander 2015). As in D.C., however, landlords may be holding on to properties waiting for appreciation and not making improvements (Fason 2015). Displacement has occurred more as a result of rising rental and home prices than from evictions from previously affordable housing. Because Atlanta does not have rent control, and state statutes prohibit it, the city cannot act alone to quell the tide of rental increases.

Housing policies and programs in Atlanta are directed by three main agencies, the Atlanta Housing Authority, the Atlanta Office of Housing and Community Development within the Department of City Planning, and Invest Atlanta. The Atlanta Housing Authority (AHA) owns and manages affordable housing units both in traditional "public housing" buildings and in mixed-income communities. As in other U.S. cities, the Housing Authority also supports tenant-based voucher programs, project-based rental assistance, supportive housing arrangements, and homeownership programs. As mentioned above, the AHA led the effort to dismantle the city's stock of public housing projects and replace them with mixed-income communities. According to Deirdre Oakley, professor of sociology at Georgia State University, in the process, the AHA gained a reputation for heavy-handedness that is only now changing under new leadership (Oakley 2015). With few properties left to manage, the AHA focuses mainly on redevelopment of former public housing sites and planning for next steps (Youngblood 2015). The Office of Housing and Community Development within the Department of City Planning then provides fiscal oversight and management of state and federal contracts, conducts research on fair housing, and provides funds to community housing development organizations and for-profit developers for affordable housing. The Department of City Planning also houses the Neighborhood Planning Units (NPUs), which are advisory councils that comprise neighborhood residents who review zoning requests and report their recommendations to the Zoning Board.

Invest Atlanta, formerly known as the Atlanta Development Authority, is tasked with promoting economic development broadly in the city, and this mandate includes the planning and financing of affordable housing. In particular, Invest Atlanta has been involved in moves to regulate construction and redevelopment to promote affordable housing through bond financing. In a city long-focused on promoting itself as a global center for business, Invest Atlanta's role in the direction of urban policy and planning is pivotal. Nonprofit housing developers have not always viewed Invest Atlanta as a critical actor in the production of affordable housing, since they mostly rely on the Low-Income Housing Tax Credit (LIHTC) program, which is run by the state of Georgia rather than the city government. But, according to Kate Little (formerly of the Georgia State Trade Association for Nonprofit Housing Developers and now president/CEO of Georgia ACT), as leaders move the agency into promoting affordable housing regulations for development, nonprofit developers do view them as a source to direct advocacy efforts (Little 2015). In the recent Housing Strategy Report (2015), Invest Atlanta proposed the initiation of inclusionary zoning rules.

In sum, the city of Atlanta is changing as a result of new money, new business, and new residents. Though in the past residents did not face significant challenges in securing relatively affordable housing, as formerly affordable neighborhoods gentrify, questions about displacement and maintaining economic and social diversity multiply. Issues of where resources are spent and who benefits may be at a critical junction in the city, and the impact on future policies, programs, and institutions related to development remains to be seen.

Organizational Environment and Strategies

Among the housing advocates, government officials, and academic researchers with whom I spoke in Atlanta, there was a consensus that the organizational environment for housing in the city is quite weak. Longtime activist William McFarland, relationship manager for the organization Georgia Advancing Communities Together (Georgia ACT), lamented the lack of mobilization in a city that has a strong history of civil disobedience, particularly during the civil rights movement (McFarland 2015). At the root of demobilization, he argues, is not contentment with the status quo, but rather lack of funding for advocacy efforts. According to HDDC current board chair and former director Mtamanika Youngblood (2015), organizing efforts in Atlanta are hampered by a lack of resources from private foundations and a lack of corporate support for housing and redevelopment that one finds in other cities, such as Cleveland or Chicago. McFarland also mentioned a lack of trust in elected officials and the absence of universities working in communities to help identify and articulate concerns. Finally, there is the perception that Atlanta has not had an affordable housing problem because there are still affordable units spread throughout the city even if the median cost of housing is on the rise.

The demolition of public housing and the dispersal of low-income residents to far-flung neighborhoods also discouraged the organization of residents around housing issues. But in Youngblood's view, the demolition of public housing was partially the *result* of weak organizational capacity rather than the *cause*. Most of the process of tearing down public housing—providing rental vouchers to some and units in newly built mixed-income communities to others—faced little opposition. According to Georgia State University professor Deirdre Oakley (2015), there was not a strong resident coalition through this process and there is not one today. In the 1960s, Atlanta's tenant organizations were a powerful force, but in the 1970s when President Nixon announced that there would be no more construction of public housing, the tenant councils began to crumble (Hankins et al. 2014). During construction for the 1996 Olympic Games, residents from several neighborhoods around the principal Olympic Stadium did mobilize for protests, concerned with how they would benefit from new construction in their midst. As a result, residents secured a percentage of the profits from parking sales to benefit the surrounding community. Since then, according to McFarland (2015), there have been few instances of people taking to the streets.

Community Development Corporations (CDCs), with money largely from the federal government, have become the main organizations in Atlanta interested in displacement, revitalization, and new affordable housing. Though as nonprofits they generally run their projects with a social mission to assist low-income residents, they are not necessarily interested in organizing tenants or other residents who might fight against new developments (Little 2015). In addition, most of the development by CDCs is for single-family units rather than multi-unit rental buildings. Without the purpose of organizing tenants, CDCs in general may be less likely and able to mobilize low-income residents.

In addition to CDCs, the Atlanta BeltLine Partnership is an active nonprofit focused on displacement and the provision of affordable housing, seeking to ensure that affordable housing remains a part of the in-town neighborhoods. Through the tax-funded BeltLine Trust, the organization's goal is to construct new properties and renovate existing properties to provide "workforce housing." Even though they are actively working on issues of housing, they have not engaged in significant advocacy campaigns through which they might mobilize residents. Leaders from Georgia ACT, an association of nonprofit developers in Atlanta, which played a critical role in the development of the BeltLine Trust, now monitor state and local legislation and partner with larger state organizations for lobbying efforts (Little 2015). But they too remain relatively insular and do not widely promote the cause of affordable housing beyond the state capitol or the halls of city government.

According to the few active advocates in the city, many organizations, including CDCs, took a hit from the financial crisis and the cut to federal budgets in the late 2000s. With less federal funding, an increasing share of housing projects has been led by for-profit developers rather than nonprofits. The financial crisis also had an effect on the locus of lobbying. Georgia ACT worked at the state legislature on issues related to foreclosures and predatory lending. A newcomer to the city, Occupy Atlanta briefly took on issues of foreclosures through occupations and protests, though they have not been able to sustain long-term activism.

The HDDC's strong social mission stands out as one that has fostered significant progress revitalizing the Old Fourth Ward neighborhood. Critics argue that CDCs in Atlanta have historically lacked significant capacity for housing production compared to CDCs in other cities (Walker and Weinheimer 1998), but the HDDC may be the exception to the rule. Founded by Coretta Scott King, the HDDC grew from the mission "to facilitate the preservation, revitalization, and non-displacement of residents in the Martin Luther King Jr. National Historic District" (HDDC 2016). According to Youngblood (2015), the HDDC's first executive director, the guiding principles of the organization were to revitalize in a way that would be viable for people of mixed incomes. They were particularly concerned that low-income, elderly African Americans would be displaced against their will as a result of rising costs associated with gentrification. In the 1980s the Old Fourth Ward had become riddled with gambling, prostitution, and drugs, but the HDDC started with renovating dilapidated properties along the corridor of Martin Luther King's birthplace and, supported by Coretta Scott King, they largely succeeded in transforming the area.

Thirty years into the organization's work, HDDC leaders are struggling with how to keep low-income residents in the neighborhood amid renewal. Though they initially bought blighted properties, held them in a land bank, and then sold them to low-income buyers, at present many of those original residents are aging and want to move on or cash out to make a profit. According to Fason, many residents struggle with increasing property taxes and the cost of home repairs on aging homes. The HDDC's current investigation examines how land trusts might be used to allow for some turnover but keep low-income people from being priced out of the neighborhood. By managing a number of rental properties, the HDDC can also continue offering low-cost housing in the neighborhood even as home prices rise.

According to Fason, the HDDC's work has been a success in that the area is beautiful and much safer that it was a few decades ago, but in reality, regular workers like teachers and police officers can no longer afford to live there (Fason 2015). The rents on the HDDC's properties are still the most affordable in the Old Fourth Ward, Fason stated, but the dream of homeownership that is now beyond reach for many is really what they would like to promote. Youngblood reported that by around 2000 they could see that though displacement was not yet a problem, the rapid increase in values would make it difficult for people of modest means to continue to buy houses in the neighborhood. The HDDC started taking losses on the sale of properties to sell to low-income buyers in order to maintain the neighborhood's diversity. A few times, however, the HDDC felt burned when buyers turned around and sold the property for a profit. Still, as City Council Member Kwanza Hall, who represents the Old Fourth Ward, commented, the Old Fourth Ward needs the HDDC in the neighborhood as a socially conscious actor in the market, in part because the CDC can take on riskier and more innovative projects than private developers out for a profit (Hall 2016).

When the financial crisis hit Atlanta around 2008, the HDDC also fell on hard times, though they did still have a number of publicly funded projects. Even before the financial crisis, the HDDC found it difficult to generate interest among the banking community to create some kind of fund for generating affordable housing. The impetus for the BeltLine Trust, then, was to have a stable, tax-funded source for housing preservation and construction.

Strategies

The primary goals of the HDDC have always been to maintain diversity through nondisplacement and the creation of affordable housing through the process of revitalization, and Youngblood described the goal of influencing public policy for affordability as vital to the HDDC's current strategy. Youngblood believes that the credibility of the HDDC—the oldest CDC in Atlanta—from preserving affordable housing in the Old Fourth Ward should provide substantial legitimacy in the policy realm. In 2016, she described the goals of the HDDC as threefold: (1) using reputation and clout to influence the Old Fourth Ward and the rest of the city, (2) sharing with other neighborhoods the development savvy achieved, and (3) transferring the housing currently owned into a community land trust. For the last goal, Youngblood anticipated seeking money through federal programs or potentially from private foundations.

Elected and appointed officials, specifically the commissioner of planning and urban development, council members for their district and at-large, and Fulton County commissioners, are the HDDC's main targets. The HDDC's work also falls within the housing advocacy community in the city, which, as Youngblood notes, basically includes Georgia ACT and the BeltLine Affordable Housing Advisory Board. In addition to the affordable housing projects implemented within the neighborhood, the HDDC's tactics include meetings with officials, speaking at forums, and providing consultative services. Using knowledge gained through the years, the HDDC would now like to work with other neighborhoods to educate residents and nonprofits about the technical issues involved in building affordable housing and preventing displacement. When I asked whether the HDDC would like to see formal mechanisms for inclusion within the City Council or Invest Atlanta, Youngblood responded that they would like an oversight committee within the council to monitor whether policies are carried out in practice, but the creation of such an institution did not appear to be a current priority.

In 2016 the City Council of Atlanta passed an inclusionary zoning ordinance in the city mandating that developers building with public funds reserve 15 percent of units for residents earning less than 80 percent of area median income or 10 percent of units for those earning less than 60 percent of area median income (Invest Atlanta 2016). The HDDC did not participate in the initial crafting of the ordinance, but Youngblood intervened in hot debates between housing advocates and for-profit developers over the negotiation of the details. She worked to convince each side that the deal might not be what they would like, either because it didn't go far enough or went too far, but that it was a necessary compromise.

Finally, the HDDC also participated heavily in the establishment of the BeltLine Land Trust. Youngblood reported that it took a long time to convince all of the stakeholders that the trust would be in their best interest. The HDDC argued that the trust was a means to create a permanent subsidy for affordable housing, rather than the usual fifteen-year subsidy created through federal programs, and that mixed-income communities would always be vital to a hot-market city like Atlanta.

Community participation has been difficult to garner in Atlanta, but several organizations are working to preserve and generate options for affordable housing in the city. The HDDC can be considered both a nonprofit housing developer and an advocate for citywide policies and programs to prevent displacement and promote affordable housing. The strategies of the HDDC can be characterized as indirect in their attempt to persuade government officials, though perhaps efforts toward neighborhood development could be defined as an exit strategy because of the use of the market and federal funds to prevent displacement. As Youngblood has gained more experience in the field, she has been offered more opportunities for consulting and taken on a mediating role, which could be construed as insider influence, though the organization has not pressed for formal incorporation in terms of participatory institutions or formal employment as a community liaison. Overhaul strategies do not appear to have ever been part of the HDDC's or other housing organizations' efforts in Atlanta.

Motivations for Strategies

Atlanta's organizational environment is weak, and a strong urban development regime serves to explain why those organizations that do exist, like the HDDC, have acted cautiously to advance their demands. The ideology of the HDDC and other groups in Atlanta is quite conservative, without any mention of the right to housing or the right to the city. Despite the Democratic orientation of the city, the relationship between housing organizations, such as the HDDC, and the city administration has often been strained, though at times housing activists have maintained strong connections to City Council members and other officials who assist in moving the housing agenda forward. In 2016, the election of a new council member, Andre Dickens, combined with the surge in housing prices provided a political opportunity to press for new inclusionary zoning legislation. Limited resources, however, continue to restrict the activities and the goals of the HDDC and others in the city.

Ideology

In a conversation with James Alexander (2015), director for Housing at the Atlanta BeltLine, we discussed the often-heard view in Brazil that housing is a right of all citizens and that the right to the city forms the basis for inclusionary goals among many urban organizations. Alexander was intrigued by this ideology, commenting that no one in Atlanta ever talks about housing as a right. According to Youngblood (2015), the strategies of advocacy organizations in Atlanta follow the southern tradition of "politeness." As she remarked, "Rather than raising hell, we talk and negotiate." They are not inclined to make a lot of noise and cause disruption because it would be perceived as radical or inappropriate for the local context. Fason (2015) of the HDDC also stated that they are being strategic by not engaging in disruptive politics because they don't want to be labeled as "activists," a term that he says has a negative connotation in Atlanta. Many of the HDDC's board members have been influential members of the community, and the rank and file do not want to put them in a difficult position or burn any bridges that might serve their interests. While Youngblood as HDDC board chair is quite outspoken, she is also strategic. She does not damage relationships that could potentially help the HDDC's cause.

This conservative ideology has manifested itself in the HDDC's strategies, which pursue incremental rather than rapid change. In 2016, when Council Member Dickens brought a bill before the City Council to require inclusionary zoning in publicly funded projects, Youngblood counseled him that it was important to tell stakeholders that this was the beginning and not the end of opportunities for affordable housing. In her words, "This was one tool in a box of tools, and they have to do things incrementally to get anything done" (Youngblood 2016). You need to start where you can control the resource—in this case public dollars going toward new development—and then work toward influencing other actors. There is a southern tendency toward patience and a slower pace of activity than is reflected in the continuous demands of organizations in Washington, D.C., and other cities.

It is also the case that the tendency toward cooperative activities is the result of a long history of cooptation, or what might be labeled clientelistic behavior. In the past, mayoral candidates would campaign in public housing complexes, making promises to residents in exchange for votes at election time and then returning the next time an election was at hand (Oakley 2015). The destruction of public housing not only dispersed residents who may have organized for affordable housing but also removed the potential for politicians to cater to residents as a geographically rooted voting bloc. Past cooptation generated an environment of cooperation and acceptance rather than expectations that contentious politics lead to positive results. The strategies of the HDDC and other organizations in the city reflect past cooptation as well as present reticence to mobilize residents for radical, structural change.

In sum, the ideology of organizations in Atlanta, including the HDDC, is mainly conservative in terms of the tactics in which they are willing to engage and demands for which they are willing to fight. Housing is not seen as a right but rather the result of personal achievement or possibly the benevolence of government. Race, however, plays a large role in the HDDC's call for preserving affordable housing in order to maintain neighborhood diversity. To achieve this goal, the conservative ideology will need to shift to accommodate strategies that produce greater structural change.

Relationship with the State

Historically the HDDC's relationship with the mayor's office and City Council members has not been strong (Hall 2016). There was a degree of distrust of elected officials among leadership in the HDDC and residents in the neighborhood because the Old Fourth Ward was viewed as the depressed, poor black stepchild of the city. Recently, however, the relationship has begun to improve. The current district council member for the Old Fourth Ward, Kwanza Hall, purchased a home through the HDDC some years ago and believes strongly in the mission of the HDDC, especially as it relates to preserving the legacy of Dr. King (Hall 2016). He has worked to update the Historic District guidelines to enable redevelopment of properties for new purposes, a move that he believes encourages greater investment in local business development.

Tax abatement is one issue in which the current relationship between the HDDC and the city government has shaped the HDDC's strategies. Because members of the HDDC board are in leadership positions within the city government, they have been able to use their offices to push forward reform of the property tax system to protect long-term residents from rapid tax increases (Fason 2015). Fason also reports they have regular contact with Council Member Hall and a county commissioner who lives in the community. HDDC leaders know, however, that to be reelected, these officials have to balance the interests of the HDDC with the interests of other constituents in the community, many of whom are considered "newcomers" who do not necessarily share the same goals. Leaders of the HDDC know they can set up meetings with officials and their interests will be considered, but they are also realistic in not expecting too much from elected and other public officials with whom they might have personal relationships. Their approach is thus conservative in terms of the extent to which they rely on insider access to forward their agenda.

In terms of the city government at-large, Youngblood characterizes their relationship as mutually beneficial in that the government has money to allocate to housing and the money is needed for the HDDC to spend on housing projects (2016). If the relationship is defined by financial resources, however, she says it could always be stronger with more money. As a rule, in the HDDC's view, the organization's voice has not been heard within the mayor's office, which has been more concerned with private development than neighborhood revitalization. In 2016 Youngblood provided consultative services to the commissioner of the Department of City Planning, which would appear to give her and the HDDC a level of inside influence within the agency and may indicate greater willingness to work with housing advocates on official development policy. The stature that comes with Youngblood's experience with housing in the city and her ability to speak her mind while maintaining cordial relationships provide her with the capacity to engage government officials to seek more funding or new policies for the city. For example, because of her experience working with both for-profit developers and nonprofit advocates, Council Member Dickens regarded her as a valuable mediator in the discussions preceding the enactment of the inclusionary zoning law.

To definitively characterize the relationship between the HDDC and the state as either strong or weak oversimplifies matters. At various moments and with certain government officials, the relationship has been close, based on mutual trust and insider access, but even then the expectations for influence appear limited.

Political Opportunities

Political opportunities in the form of new leadership reshape the strategies of organizations that see these new officials as allies or at least fresh ears. According to Council Member Dickens (2016), he recognized that his election created a political opportunity for housing advocates, and in a sense the advocates felt they could teach him how to do his job because he was so inexperienced. Nonprofit leaders would come to him and tell him "let us help you" as they connected his own narrative coming from humble roots to the imperative of addressing affordable housing. Dickens reports that advocates constantly provided him with advice about how to be more effective in meetings, and they would send him readings to understand pertinent issues. He knew they sought him out because everyone else had already heard their message, and he says they had his ear from day one. At the same time, they provided him with valuable fact-based information that made his job easier. With a seat on the Invest Atlanta Board, he was also influenced by reports showing how few newly built in-town residential units were affordable and was further motivated to reduce concentrated poverty in the city.

The presence of Council Member Dickens, a young African American man who had come from a low-income background, provided housing advocates with a serious ally within the City Council.

They used this alliance to further the goal of inclusionary zoning by assisting the council member in designing and negotiating a new law. The HDDC and others were pushed toward this strategy by the opening Dickens's election presented, though the relationship remains indirect via their influence on the council. They have neither achieved nor even sought an institutionalized voice.

Resources

Two variables—the lack of community involvement and the dearth of philanthropic support—limit the strategies of the HDDC. As Nathan McCall recounts in his 2008 book, *Them,* there have often been conflicts among and within neighborhood associations in the Old Fourth Ward, particularly as long-term African American residents clash with newly arrived whites. According to Fason, one concern among the new owners has been that affordable housing will bring down property values (2015). Many of the new residents want trendy restaurants and dog parks, which are not the priority of the HDDC and many long-term residents. While there are several very active neighborhood associations based on geographic divisions in the Old Fourth Ward, the HDDC leaders have not formed strong relationships with these groups, and most community residents are not involved in the HDDC's work. The neighborhood associations actually have significant power in that they make decisions on zoning requests that then go to the official Neighborhood Planning Unit (NPU) and eventually filter up through the appropriate agency. The HDDC, then, cannot completely ignore the neighborhood associations but to date have found no way to genuinely connect with the members of these associations.

The HDDC's strategies are both the result and the cause of the limited engagement with the community, particularly newer white residents. Their strategy to preserve affordable housing by attracting more funding from current federal and city programs does not involve mobilization of community resources. If the community were engaged and supportive of the HDDC's efforts, their strategies might also rely to a greater extent on large-scale advocacy campaigns, which might in turn result in increased funding or changes in policy.

Activists also consistently mentioned the lack of philanthropic partners in the city as a hindrance to their work. As Youngblood said,

"Any advocacy effort needs some support, and we don't have a foundation like Cleveland or Chicago. There's nothing in Atlanta that even comes close to that. There's little public support and very little corporate support" (2015). Most of the funding that goes to the HDDC now comes from developer fees or the revenues generated from the properties maintained. During the financial crisis in 2008, the HDDC and other CDCs lost most funding from private banks. The drop in bank funding has persisted and makes it difficult for CDCs to maintain their role in property development. The one major philanthropic organization that has worked in Atlanta, the Casey Foundation, also pulled back resources during the financial crisis.

The goals of the HDDC are circumscribed by both lack of participation and financial resources, which limits the ability to reach policy makers and engage in broad-based tactics. As such, efforts mainly rely on the reputation of leaders and the strength of the historic connection to Martin Luther King.

The HDDC's strategies to influence government officials to expand existing programs have mainly been indirect, but use of the market to generate affordable housing could be considered an exit strategy as well. More recently, political opportunities have strengthened their relationship with the state and shifted their advocacy efforts within the City Council, though a conservative ideology and lack of resources continue to limit broad structural changes that might provide greater inclusion in decision making and in the long-term housing solutions.

Outcomes

In the past, the activities of housing advocates in Atlanta have largely followed the dictates of federal housing policies and resources. Recent advances in policies at the city level, however, include the creation of the BeltLine Trust and the inclusionary zoning ordinance. The BeltLine Trust is funded by tax allocation district (TAD) funding and was expected to generate $1.5 billion in bonding capacity over twenty-five years. The trust also anticipated an additional $25 million from the federal government and $60 million from a capital campaign (Atlanta BeltLine 2017).

The trust, however, ran out of money around 2013, and three years later officials were still debating how to create a new funding source (Dickens 2016). In 2005 those involved in the creation of the trust imagined that there would be a series of bond issues to provide continuous funding, but a reduced volume of investment and legal issues have stalled the intended accumulation of funds (Alexander 2015). Because the trust is supposed to be funded by bonds, Alexander did not think they would be able to go to the Housing Authority, Invest Atlanta, or anyone else to ask for more money. The trust was established without significant opposition from the private sector or other stakeholders in the city, in part because it would not take revenues away from other programs or create disincentives for competition, but it has also not been a major source of affordable housing creation. Building a new funding source outside of the TAD, however, could incite greater contention if it were to upset funding or development opportunities for the private sector.

Even if the trust were fully funded, Youngblood argues that it's really too late to prevent the disappearance of affordable housing in the Old Fourth Ward and around the BeltLine more broadly. To some extent she blames the success of the HDDC in revitalizing the neighborhood because, as she put it, "now that there are attractive and nice places to live, who can afford them?" (Youngblood 2015). In reality, the organization has yet to really figure out how to address this problem, nor have they had support from city officials to generate projects or policies to preserve affordable housing, such as rent control. If the trust continues to receive funding, the strategy to engage with public officials to create the trust should have some effect in providing new workforce housing in the area, but there is currently no end in sight to the erosion of affordable units. The strategy of promoting homeownership in the Old Fourth Ward has not had the intended long-term effect of inclusion.

The Ordinance for Affordable Housing put forward by Council Member Dickens and supported by the HDDC represents a step forward by the city government to recognize the increasing problem of affordability in the city. In this instance, the strategy of the HDDC was to influence all stakeholders to see the value in passing some reform. The ordinance, however, is not without its critics. Council Member

Kwanza Hall, representing the Old Fourth Ward, believed that the percentages in the ordinance are really too small to have great effect and that the city really needs a coherent nondisplacement plan that would include the input of residents, landlords, banks, and government officials, along the lines of what might be considered an inclusionary strategy. Hall recognized the need for greater inclusion of stakeholders in policies and planning, but to date there has not been any real movement in that direction.

In fact, in the last decade Clarence Stone's original findings regarding regime politics in Atlanta appear to be alive and well. As Youngblood stated, "Businesses run cities, and the business that runs Atlanta is development" (2015). She says they are constantly pushing against a "very lucrative and very uninterested industry." For instance, the HDDC tried to work with the Urban Land Institute on inclusionary zoning long before the recent ordinance, but its efforts did not go anywhere. According to Youngblood:

At the end of the day we're talking about land and real estate. The fact that development is the business of Atlanta has an impact on politics and public policy. We go to the mayor and say one thing and the developers come in and want something else. Real estate has really impeded our ability to get the kinds of things that would ensure low-income families have a place in the city. (2015)

Youngblood was pessimistic that a change in strategies would significantly alter the power of the real estate sector in the city. In the mid-2000s she was involved in a proposal for inclusionary zoning that she thought would appeal to everyone, but private developers told her they could not do affordable housing and still compete in the market. Further, developers did not see any benefit in catering to the low-income market when they were successful selling units at the higher end. Though government officials said they supported the idea of inclusionary zoning to satisfy demand for affordable housing, they never moved on it.

What changed in the intervening years that led to the adoption of the inclusionary zoning ordinance in 2016? Two variables: a worsening crisis of affordability and city leadership. These factors encouraged the success of negotiation among stakeholders, though continued resistance from business weakened the strength of the enacted policy. The inclusionary zoning ordinance does not go far enough for critics like Council Member Hall, but it should move the city forward in preventing future exclusion of low-income residents and at the very least signifies that community organizations do have *some* influence on housing in the city. At a board meeting for Invest Atlanta in June 2016, Dawn Luke, senior vice president for community development, made the case for the importance of the inclusionary zoning ordinance, highlighted by the release of the Brookings Institution report finding Atlanta to be #1 in income inequality among U.S. cities (Berube and Holmes 2015). She cited other research indicating substantially rising housing costs as evidence that quick action was imperative. Mayor Kasim Reed, chair of the Invest Atlanta Board, then acknowledged the hard work of Council Member Dickens in ensuring the passage of the ordinance. The mayor had included the law in his State of the City speech several months earlier in a new effort to prioritize housing in the city's agenda.

As the mayor recognized, the ordinance likely would not have passed without the efforts of Council Member Dickens. I asked Dickens what influence community organizations had on his decision to introduce and negotiate the ordinance. His response was that as a new member he was not really worried about votes and elections; rather, he personally believed in the need to address housing issues and had the facts to support his own convictions. Clearly, the personal leadership of Dickens mattered for a change in policy as much as solid evidence on the need for proactive reforms. Dickens admitted that he faced opposition from for-profit developers and that he had to respect their opinions because they add value and revenues to the city, but as he noted, "We have to make sure that developers don't just flip dirt for profit, but for equity as well" (2016). He had to convince developers that they couldn't abandon the low end of the market. After holding a series of one-on-one meetings with nonprofit and for-profit stakeholders, Dickens arranged a joint forum, facilitated by Youngblood. In a nearly unanimous vote, the ordinance passed the City Council, a victory that Youngblood attributed to Dickens's leadership in addition to mounting evidence forcing council members to recognize the extent of the affordability crisis in the city (2016).

In our interview, I asked Council Member Dickens whether the success of the joint forum might bring about a more formal arrangement to allow for inclusion of community organizations in the policy-making process. He responded that he would like to see greater inclusion, but that a formal institution would be difficult to manage. He was also concerned that community organizations are not democratically elected and may not actually represent the people. Instead, he seeks to be accessible and available to all who want to meet with him directly.

In this case, external events, especially the election of Council Member Dickens and research documenting increasing problems of affordability in the city, rather than primarily internal organizational characteristics, such as social capital or alliances, led to partial victories for the HDDC and the housing community in Atlanta more broadly. Seeing a political opening, Youngblood worked with Dickens and others to promote passage of the ordinance. The ordinance itself may have some effect on generating greater inclusion of low-income residents in the city, but its effect may be limited, given the bill's narrow scope, particularly as the zoning rules apply to only new publicly funded projects. The momentum for further reform, however, has begun, and it will be up to HDDC leaders and others to figure out how to bring about more radical changes, such as rent control, land trusts, or direct housing subsidies to preserve affordable housing in the city.

Conclusions

The case of Atlanta and the HDDC demonstrates the constraints community organizations face because of limited mobilization, weak funding, and the absence of commitment to structural change. The conservative ideology that has led the HDDC to step gingerly in order to maintain cordial relationships does not disrupt the chain of power in Atlanta, which Youngblood has described as dominated by the real estate sector. As a nonprofit dependent on federal and local funding, the HDDC must to some extent defer to public officials, but without disruption of the power structure in the city, changes to policies and programs have been weak. The election of a new council member provided a political opportunity, which, when combined with evidence of the growing inequality and issues of affordability in the city, spurred the City Council to action to pass the inclusionary zoning ordinance. The question is now how far these two factors—new leadership from within the City Council and greater awareness of the problem—will motivate continued action. For instance, rent control could be one progressive policy reform that would prevent increasing costs from pricing out existing renters in the city, but this type of policy that disrupts the real estate market in the city will likely not come about without significant pressure from constituents. Perhaps more likely in this southern city would be a higher percentage of low-income housing set-asides for projects with public support or the creation of a developer-funded low-income housing trust fund, but again, these types of programs will require interruption in the power of the real estate sector currently dominating Atlanta. Though the HDDC indicated some desire for inclusive institutions to work from within on implementation and oversight of government programs, inclusion does not appear to be a main priority for the near future.

Traditionally, housing needs in Atlanta have seemed less urgent than in other cities because of the relatively low cost of living, but as a result of millennials' and seniors' preference to live in cities, the current crisis of affordability will likely only worsen in the coming years. The long tradition of the development regime in Atlanta depressed mobilization of low-income residents and generated cynicism for change among the few seasoned housing activists. This cynicism is reflected in the limited efforts to further mobilize residents to the cause, but it also affects the depth of the goals they seek to achieve. Apathy and reluctance to rock the boat are part of the story that explains the difficulties facing those advocates who are working to preserve and provide low-income housing. But it may be that the current level of mobilization leads to long-term strategies to elicit incremental change in which better outcomes are negotiated bit by bit. Small changes alone constitute progress in this traditionally conservative city.

5

City Center Development in São Paulo

In January 2013 I first visited the long-abandoned but newly occupied Maúa Building in the city center of São Paulo. Within the building I found a well-organized, clean community with individual families struggling to construct and maintain households within small spaces and with limited amenities. The building sits adjacent to the Luz subway stop and several museums, but many of the other neighboring buildings are also abandoned or highly degraded structures with limited commerce on the ground floors. The Movimento de Moradia da Região Central (MMRC) occupied the building to provide temporary, affordable, centrally located housing to its members, but also to motivate the city government to invest in renovating buildings in the city center for the low-income population. At the time, the new administration of Mayor Fernando Haddad was assessing whether to proceed with a public-sector–private-sector partnership to revitalize the city center, known as the Nova Luz Project. As I admired the organizational capacity of the MMRC and its members to maintain this occupation for as long as necessary to secure permanent housing, I also wondered about the overall plan of the MMRC and the broader movements for housing within the city. What were the strategies to ensure the provision of affordable housing and prevent displacement of residents, particularly in occupations or informal settlements, that would enable the low-income population to be a part of the city's overall economic growth and development?

São Paulo is a case in which urban development has crowded out low-income residents while also failing to create a livable downtown for residents of all income levels. The city has in place a number of participatory institutions and legal protections, but it is unclear how these institutions and laws function in practice to provide a voice and concrete solutions for residents. Leaders of the housing movements in São Paulo have been fighting for years for participatory institutions and legal instruments, so I would expect these movements to now be engaged in strategies that promote their implementation. But in reality, the question is whether movements view these institutions as spaces in which to invest their time and resources or whether they see the need to engage in other types of strategies to advance their goals.

From 2012 to 2016, I made a number of trips to São Paulo in order to meet with housing movement leaders, researchers, academics, and government officials to understand the ways in which movements working in the city center carry out strategies and achieve results. Though state-led removals of residents to make way for infrastructure projects were still commonplace in São Paulo, lack of affordable housing throughout the city presented the greatest threat to displacement and inclusion. During this period, the local housing movements were engaged in an intense process of occupation of abandoned buildings in the city, both to serve the immediate needs of citizens and to force negotiation with the government to increase the number of projects for low-income housing. In the city center, housing movements were mainly fighting for enforcement of zoning laws, increased investment in renovating city buildings, and constructing new low-income housing, though they were also fighting against displacement of residents in informal settlements. I found that while the movements used new democratic institutions to advance their claims, they also recognized the need to act contentiously to motivate implementation.

The strategies of the movements profiled in this chapter were inclusionary, but with significant reliance on indirect strategies as well. An ideology based on the right to the city mixed with a close relationship with the state motivated inclusionary strategies, but not without a reliance on influencing key administration actors as necessary to ensure promises were implemented. To a large extent this case confirms the hypothesis that a rights-based ideology and strong relationship with the state leads to inclusionary strategies, but the case also demonstrates the ways in which indirect strategies still play a significant role in movement strategies. Further, this case illustrates the development of strategies under a left-leaning regime as well as the limitations posed by resources in a slowing economy. Under a relatively friendly administration, the housing movements were able to generate promises for reform, but economic recession in the country, municipal fiscal shortfalls, and political turmoil jeopardized the implementation of those promises.

Background on São Paulo

Since democratization in the late 1980s, the city of São Paulo has cycled between mayoral administrations from the Worker's Party (PT) and more conservative parties. From 2006 to 2012, Gilberto Kassab of the center-right Democratas Party (DEM) presided as mayor over a rapidly growing city, both in terms of population and wealth. In 2013, Fernando Haddad of the PT entered office with the economy booming, though by 2014 the economy and the PT's national popularity were both in decline. In general, housing advocates in the city have viewed the PT as an ally and mayors from other parties as probusiness. The movements' strategies and the outcomes of their demands likely responded to this cycle of leadership.

The scale of local housing challenges in São Paulo befit a global megacity. With a population of approximately twelve million people in 2014 (IBGE 2014a), São Paulo experienced a 33 percent increase in population between 1990 and 2012 (Brookings 2012). While it is viewed as the financial capital of the country, awash in luxury condos and helicopters ferrying the superrich above the local skyline, it is also well known for striking levels of inequality and crime. Approximately one-third of city residents live in inadequate housing as defined by a Brazilian statistics agency (Fundação João Pinheiro 2013). According to the Secretariat for Housing's calculations, in 2008 the city had 1,567 registered favelas, 1,060 irregular settlements,[1] 523 public housing buildings, and 1,698 *cortiços* (tenement houses), providing shelter to millions of families (Secretaria Municipal de Habitação, Cidade de São Paulo 2008). Lack of formal market housing for low-income residents perpetuates the challenges of informality. While the *median* monthly income in the city stood at approximately $240 in 2010, the *average* income was approximately $1,500, distorted by very high incomes at the top. Rising prices exacerbate inequalities. According to *Numbeo*, a website that compiles data on housing, metropolitan area home prices increased by 208 percent and rent increased by 97.5 percent between 2008 and 2014. Average monthly rental costs of about $600 for a one bedroom and $1,200 for a three bedroom made living in the city center out of reach for most residents (*Numbeo* 2015b). Between 2011 and 2012, the official housing deficit—the gap between those residing in existing housing stock and those needing housing—grew by 18 percent, indicating that the market was not supplying housing to suit the needs of a large portion of the population (Fundação João Pinheiro 2013).

In the early 2010s a real estate boom that grew out of economic prosperity in the city and the country as a whole exacerbated existing patterns of inequality. According to Coslovsky (2015), real estate developers raised considerable amounts of money by becoming publicly traded companies and quickly bought up land in São Paulo with lucrative plans for development. At the same time, owners of long-degraded buildings sought to cash in by repossessing their properties and selling them to the highest bidder. The municipal and state governments compounded the building boom with plans for large transportation projects and redevelopment plans.

As a consequence of rising prices in the center, the city experienced a boom in population living in the periphery, with a population the size of Uruguay commuting from the eastern zone to the city center every day (Parkin 2014). The size of the housing deficit and the population living in informal settlements demonstrate the breadth of housing challenges, but the spatial segregation of residents illustrates the magnitude of the particular challenge in building a more inclusive city. Census data show a strong negative correlation between income and distance from the city center, with the majority of the poor living on the peripheries, with vastly different experiences of violence, schooling, and social conditions compared to more central areas of the city where residents experience fewer incidents of violent crime, higher-performing schools, and higher standards of living (Torres et al. 2003). These disparities make the ability to live in the city center all the more important for creating access to opportunities for low-income residents.

Brazilian scholar Mariana Fix (2001) argues that the patterns of segregation in São Paulo are the direct result of state interventions by which the poor have been dislocated to make room for amenities for the rich. For example, large numbers of poor residents were removed along the waterways in the city to enable the construction of roads that ultimately benefit automobile commuters. Though the city purports to address the problem of affordability through the expansion of programs for new construction and regularization of land titles in informal settlements, urban planners from URBEM, the São Paulo–based Institute of Urbanism and Studies for the Metropolis, argue that by 2024, 700,000 affordable housing units for those earning zero to three minimum wages will be needed, fewer than half of which are planned by the city government.[2] The result of this lack of affordability has been an explosion in not only the population of the periphery but also informal settlements (i.e., occupations) throughout the city, led both by social movements and unorganized individuals (Barbosa 2015).

At the same time that there have been more occupations, there has also been an increase in state-led removals of residents from informal settlements, some of which have existed for decades. In the early 2010s, the real estate boom, in addition to infrastructure building, led to this increase in removals.[3] As in Rio de Janeiro, municipal and state government agencies informed residents that they must leave their homes either because they were in "areas of risk," the property belonged to someone else, or the government needed the land for public works projects. Tenure has always been precarious for residents living in informal settlements, but since governments at the federal, state, and municipal levels in the past two decades turned toward urbanization and regularization as housing solutions, the mass evictions typical of the dictatorship were no longer as common. As residents in informal settlements make up a considerable voting bloc, and voting is obligatory, mass evictions have been viewed by advocates as politically untenable. Nonetheless, the increasing price of land and large projects in the city have meant increasing notices of eviction for low-income residents.

The city of São Paulo, then, has experienced the twin problems of displacement and lack of affordable housing common across growing cities. Social movements, government officials, and private-sector developers all seem to agree on the importance of developing the city center to resolve many problems in the city, including infrastructure and transportation, but progress in this direction has been limited.

Housing advocates charge that there has never been a consistent plan regarding affordable housing in the center, though there have been a number of state-led development efforts. Under the administration of PT mayor Luiza Erundina in the late 1980s, provision of social housing in well-located areas rather than the city's periphery became an important political issue, and policy makers began to debate the idea of inclusionary zoning and a master plan for the city (Sigolo 2015). During the 1990s, these ideas lost traction under more conservative leadership in the city, but in the early 2000s the administration of PT mayor Marta Suplicy generated the Morar no Centro (Living Downtown) program, which included plans to reclaim abandoned buildings for social housing. Lack of interest from the private sector, issues of financing, and uncertain ownership rights to these spaces, however, still made intervention in the center difficult (Sigolo 2015).

Eduardo Marques (2013) argues that São Paulo maintains a traditionally closed policy process in which bureaucrats and officials interact with private companies in networks that ultimately shape land-use regulations, infrastructure policies, and the construction of large urban projects in the city. Whereas in the United States scholars argue that growth motivates the formation of elite coalitions (Molotch 1976), in Brazil urban coalitions are based on land production, urban renewal, and large-scale public construction projects from which private contractors derive large profits. In turn, much of this profit is reinvested in political campaigns (Marques 2013). SECOVI, the most important association representing developers in the city, uses both participatory institutions and personal contacts to promote their interests in the city's master plan, land regulations, and housing programs (Donaghy 2013; Marques 2013).

The largely neglected city center has been a major target of state-led development efforts. In the 1990s, the state government, led by the center-right Partido da Social Democracia Brasileira (PSDB), first tried to revitalize the city center through the preservation of cultural institutions. In 2005, the municipal election victory of the PSDB refocused development planning around the central train station, which has been known for prostitution and a concentration of crack addicts and the homeless. Mayor Gilberto Kassab promoted the redevelopment project known as "Nova Luz" as a public-private partnership to transform the crumbling city center. Many social movements opposed this redevelopment project because of its explicit focus on gentrification without detailed plans for affordable housing (Barbosa 2013; Souza 2013). Even though the project was put on hold with the election of PT mayor Haddad in 2012, numerous poor residents had already been removed from the area as initiated by the state and municipal governments or by landowners repossessing their property. The official reason for cancellation was that the program was no longer financially viable (Scruggs 2013). Even though Nova Luz was never implemented, movements charge that real estate speculation led to rising prices in the center.

For its part, the Haddad administration supported a public-private partnership for redevelopment, led by the state government, called Casa Paulista, which is a smaller-scale program that aims to provide affordable housing through mixed-use developments. The plan is for the state- and city-level governments to contribute approximately R$10,000 (Brazilian Reais) for each unit of social housing, while the federal government's Minha Casa Minha Vida (MCMV) Program pays for the remainder of construction, and private developers pay for the land.[4] Housing activists, including Benedito Barbosa—attorney and activist for the União Nacional por Moradia Popular (National Union for Affordable Housing [UNMP]), Central de Movimentos Populares (Central Organization of Popular Movements [CMP]), and Centro Gaspar Garcia—objected to the plan in favor of directing greater resources to expropriating existing buildings for renovation into social housing units.

Any redevelopment plan is mandated to respond to the city's laws regarding inclusionary zoning and the city's current master plan (Plano Diretor). In 2002, São Paulo was the first municipality in the country to approve a city master plan, which includes regulations to put into practice the constitutional provision that requires all land be used for a social purpose. These regulations included such provisions as time limits for property owners to repay back taxes before the property may be seized by the municipal government. The plan also established the "Special Zones for Social Interest" or ZEIS (Zonas Especiais de Interesse Social), in which 80 percent of new development is to be for those earning less than six minimum salaries (Sigolo 2015).[5]

Though density bonuses and cost-sharing through the MCMV Program are meant to incentivize developers to build affordable housing in these zones, the problem is that rising costs in the city have meant many developers still do not consider it profitable to build affordable units (Samora and Hirata 2012). According to an executive from SECOVI, they agree that reurbanization and renovation are key to future sustainability (SECOVI 2012). The problem, however, is that initial federal guidelines set the maximum price per unit at R$65,000 (about U.S.$20,000). According to the top executive of Cury Construction, a major builder of low-income properties, it is impossible to build at this price because of the cost of land in the center of São Paulo (2012). Even with incentives from the MCMV Program, he and other developers preferred to build on the periphery where land is cheaper. In fact, none of the units built in the first round of the MCMV Program were built in São Paulo. In the meantime, the city does offer other programs for regularization of land titles, urbanization of informal settlements, subsidized housing, and temporary rental vouchers, but most of these efforts target the periphery rather than the center of the city (Barbosa 2015).

In 2015, financial and political crises at the federal level threatened to disrupt MCMV and other social programs. As Barbosa explained, the city government relied so strongly on the MCMV Program (rather than investing in other types of programs to supply low-income housing) that any reduction in funding would have meant the absolute loss of housing programs in the center. The appointment of a conservative housing secretary in the early years of Mayor Haddad's administration also left the housing movements insecure over the future of housing policy, though a more leftist housing secretary named in 2015 allayed some of their discontent. The four-year plan for housing generated by the City Council in 2015 called for creating 55,000 social housing units through MCMV, assisting 200,000 families through regularization of tenure, and improving communities through urbanization, impacting roughly 70,000 families (Barbosa 2015). Barbosa, however, expressed skepticism about the ability of the municipal government to reach these goals, given financial constraints at both the municipal and federal levels.

The problems of displacement and affordability confronting São Paulo make living in the central urban districts impossible for the very residents that are the backbone of expanding development. The problem of affordability has not been caused by excess unemployment, but rather by prices outstripping paychecks (Barbosa 2015). Though the city has some programs in place to address the needs of low-income residents, community organizations have sought increasing resources, enforcement of zoning laws, and implementation of programs to ensure future inclusion. Attorney Benedito Barbosa of the União dos Movimentos de Moradia (Union of Housing Movements—UMM) summed up the situation:

> Everything is difficult and everything is slow. This generates a certain frustration, a certain indignation of the movements because everything is so difficult to put into practice and get mobilized. The government always has beautiful words. . . . [E]verything is moving, everything will be coming out, . . . but in practice everything is dramatic, very difficult. We're living in a war-torn city. It's cruel what is happening in the periphery of São Paulo, the extreme East, the South, and the center. So we have a city with many occupations, land tenure conflicts, many evictions. We have large investments in big projects like the highways, the works of the Metro, the works of the Rodoanel [beltway encircling the city], all of these have a great impact on low-income families. There's a conversation about how we will indemnify or provide for the families, but there is never a conversation about the future.

To Barbosa and other critics, the primary problem in the city was that the government lacked the will and capacity to fully address housing needs. In the meantime, low-income residents incurred the negative effects of development. Given the presence of innovative democratic institutions in the city, we might expect more in terms of inclusive governance. Brazil as a whole is well known for its use of participatory institutions at the municipal level to bring together citizens, civil society organizations, and government officials for budgeting, planning, and policy-making purposes, and the city of São Paulo has several key participatory councils targeting issues of urban development. The city has a participatory council for housing, which is responsible for managing a portion of the city's housing budget and formulating regulations for housing programs (Donaghy 2013) and a participatory council for urban policy that is responsible for overseeing the implementation of the city's master plan. Additionally, the city houses the statewide Defensoria Pública, a branch of the judicial system mandated by the constitution, which is tasked with representing low-income citizens in legal disputes, including those against the state. Important questions, then, involve how movements in the city are using these institutions to address the myriad housing challenges discussed above, and further, what have been the results from these inclusionary strategies?

Organizational Environment and Strategies

The contemporary urban reform and housing movements in the city of São Paulo emerged from the struggle for democratization in the 1980s. Since then, housing movements have strongly influenced the adoption of self-construction housing programs, created new policy alternatives, and inserted themselves into the large policy community focused on housing in the city (Lopes 2012). Luciana Tatagiba (2010) argues that housing is the primary issue area for which direct political action remains commonplace. Given the stakes for job opportunities and other public services the center could provide, in the past decade redevelopment in the city center has been a major driver of this activism. Movements have seen themselves as fighting against the neoliberal, market-driven model of development and toward the reinsertion of the municipal government in financing and construction of viable solutions to the shortage of dignified housing (Barbosa 2015).[6]

Holston (2008) argues that activism in São Paulo around housing issues was created by the circumstances in which informal settlements, or favelas, began. In the 1980s, political parties, churches, and social movements increasingly organized land invasions, and the mobilization involved in the process of occupation often led to successfully avoiding eviction and securing property rights. Holston finds that the process of building their own homes and communities created "new kinds of public participation, conception of rights, and uses of law to redress the inequities of their residential conditions, primarily as they struggled to develop and legalize their housing stakes"

(2008, 23). Even earlier, in the 1970s, neighborhood associations had begun to make connections across the city once they recognized they had similar issues around which to rally.

This tradition of collective mobilization to achieve rights and benefits continues. During the time of this study, the main movements for housing, particularly in the center of São Paulo, included the União dos Movimentos de Moradia (Union of Housing Movements—UMM-SP), the Frente da Luta por Moradia (Front for the Housing Struggle—FLM), and the Movimento dos Trabalhadores sem Teto (Roofless Worker's Movement—MTST). The goal of the UMM-SP, founded in 1987, is to unite smaller community movements that work with the homeless and residents of favelas, *cortiços* (tenements), occupations, and other informal settlements to fight for the right to dignified housing, urban reform, and cooperatively built projects (Barbosa 2015). Though they engage in contentious activities when they feel it is necessary, they are also heavily engaged in the development of participatory institutions, regulatory mechanisms, and legal institutions to promote the right to housing. The primary objective of the FLM is to occupy abandoned buildings in the city to publicize that these buildings have been sitting empty for years and to bring the government to the table to negotiate over housing programs in the city center (Borges 2015). The MTST grew from the model of the Movimento dos Trabalhadores Rurais sem Terra (Landless Rural Workers' Movement—MST). Often cited as the largest social movement in Latin America, members of the MST carry out occupations of rural land that, they argue, do not fulfill a social function as required by the constitution. Members of the MTST, then, carry out occupations in the city, arguably adopting a more radical, Marxist-oriented political position than the FLM or UMM. This chapter focuses on the UMM and the FLM rather than the MTST. The former have been the most active over time in the fight for low-income housing in the city center, though the MTST's role is now important in collective mobilization in the city.

A number of nonprofit organizations also work on issues of housing in São Paulo and coordinate with the housing movements for conferences and advocacy. For instance, the Polís Institute is a research-centered organization that works with the movements in the city on capacity building. The Gaspar Garcia Center for Human Rights provides legal assistance to communities struggling with tenure security and works to improve the legal system for the poor in the city. In addition, the university sector, particularly through the Faculty of Architecture and Urbanism at the University of São Paulo, serves to articulate the concept of housing as a legal right and provides practical assistance in developing new projects and regulatory institutions.

The following analysis details the goals, targets, and tactics that made up the strategies of the UMM and the FLM from roughly 2012 to 2016. Though the two movements appeared to diverge in their focus on occupations and participatory institutions, in practice they often engaged in joint activities. The variation in their approaches, however, provides a means to understanding the motivations behind strategies within the same environment. Looking at both movements provides insight into why the movements diverged on certain goals, targets, and tactics while unifying on others.

Over the past five years the primary goals of the movements in São Paulo included (1) preventing removals of residents in informal settlements or occupations, (2) generating more housing for low-income residents in the city center through expropriation and renovation of existing buildings and construction of new units, and (3) directing the creation and implementation of a new master plan for city planning. Each of these goals involved targeting specific actors and developing both contentious and cooperative tactics. Overall, movement efforts in the city were characterized by a mix of inclusionary and indirect strategies.

Removals

The goal of preventing removals of residents relied first on using legal institutions to enforce existing laws regarding tenure. Relying on the court system, individuals, communities, and the movements that represented them generally sought the assistance of the Defensoria Pública (Public Defender) to mediate their claims against removal. But as Anaí Rodrigues (2012) from the Housing Sector of the Defensoria Pública explained, pressure outside of the judicial system was also a large part of the process to confront eviction notices. The targets of actions to prevent removals included both responsible judges and public officials. As such, tactics often involved protest and direct negotiation as well as legal actions.

The movements were also involved in efforts to pass new laws regarding land conflicts by lobbying legislatures at the federal, state, and municipal levels and participating in housing and urban policy councils across levels of government. For example, the UMM members were involved in a campaign for a new provision stipulating that those being evicted should have access to a public defender before the order for eviction is carried out. In the Municipal Council for Housing, the UMM generated a resolution regarding the mediation of land conflicts. Opposition to proposed laws regarding land conflicts at the federal and state levels came from rural landowners, while at the municipal level private developers and property owners sought stronger protections against squatters. Part of the goal of these housing movements was to generate compliance with the constitutional provision that land should be used for a social purpose and hold property owners accountable for failing to pay taxes on vacant properties.

In addition, the movements sought to collectivize the struggle through protest and regular *jornadas*, or "conferences," in which government officials, activists, and concerned citizens met to discuss current challenges and solutions. For instance, themes of the *jornadas* included megaprojects, violations of the right to the city, and the role of the judicial system in mediating land conflicts. Further, the movements worked with faculty and students from the University of São Paulo to create an Observatory on Removals in which they cataloged and monitored the experiences of communities throughout the city.

Provision of New Units

In addition to preventing displacement, a goal of the UMM and FLM was to create as many housing units as possible for low-income residents through a mix of renovation of existing buildings and new construction within the city center. This involved identifying abandoned buildings that could be renovated and increasing resources dedicated to construction. As Osmar Borges, leader of the FLM, stated, "The primary goal of the FLM is to bring workers closer to consolidated areas close to jobs, transport, and services" (2015). The targets of their efforts were officials from the Secretariat for Housing, which controlled the implementation of construction programs, including the MCMV Program. At the federal level, the movements also initiated an effort to earmark a portion of the MCMV Program to fund projects led by housing associations, now known as "MCMV-Entidades." Their activities included a mix of protest, occupations, and bilateral negotiations as well as participation in municipal councils. Several leaders also worked in both the municipal Secretariat for Housing and the federal Ministry of Cities.

In 2015, as Brazil dealt with fiscal crises at all levels of government, the movements in São Paulo began a campaign to ensure that funding would not be cut for housing programs, especially the third phase of the MCMV Program. Members from the movements staged a large protest on Avenida Paulista, and UMM members camped out overnight in front of the Caixa Econômica Federal—the agency responsible for program funding—to bring attention to budgetary issues. A smaller group traveled to Brasília for protest and to meet with President Dilma Rousseff.

Both movements also relied on the tactic of occupations as a means of providing central, affordable housing and as a means of coaxing the government into renovating city center buildings. For example, during a week of protests in April 2015, the FLM carried out occupations of sixteen abandoned buildings around the city. According to Borges, the purpose of the occupations was to get the city government to make good on promises to expropriate city center buildings and move forward with building renovations. The strategy was to influence the decisions of policy makers rather than exiting the chain of governance through autonomous housing solutions. They called for more investment at the federal level but also greater contributions of money from the state and municipal governments. As Borges stated, the FLM began out of a frustration that other movements for housing in the city had moved away from "the direct struggle for dignified housing." Once members of the FLM undertook an occupation, the focus was on negotiating with the city government either to allow the new residents to stay in place, for the government to renovate the abandoned building, or for rehousing the residents elsewhere. Occupation, then, was not in itself a strategy, but rather a tactic to achieve empowerment through bilateral negotiations and action on previous promises. Again, movement activists based their right to occupy abandoned properties on the provision that all land should have a social function. They called on the municipal government to expropriate buildings for which owners had not fulfilled their tax obligations and enable low-income residents to reside in the buildings.

The UMM invested a great deal of time and energy in the participatory councils as a means of influencing policies in the city center, though in the mid-2010s they returned to the strategy of occupations with more coordination and intensity than in the past (Barbosa 2013, 2015). In 2013 the UMM staged sixteen occupations in the city center, and Barbosa said this type of resistance would continue as long as the municipal government refused to provide long-term solutions for housing (Barbosa 2013). Even with a change in 2013 to the PT administration of Mayor Haddad, the UMM and allies continued with occupations as a means of bringing attention to housing. Nonetheless, the UMM still sought to strengthen participatory councils through the mandate of greater responsibilities and dedicated resources to achieve their goals. Barbosa explained that as a movement they need to have the capacity to perceive when it is the right time to negotiate, when it is time to have a vote or deliberate in a council, and when social pressure is key to shaking up the institutional agenda. While he recognized that deliberative spaces would not solve all problems, he believed the struggle would be even slower without them, and the housing movements needed to have equilibrium between more cooperative and contentious activities (Barbosa 2015).

Urban Planning

Last, the movements in São Paulo sought to influence future development to promote inclusion in the center through the city's master plan. In 2014, the movements participated in public forums, carried out mobilizations, and staged an encampment in front of the municipal legislature to push forward their agenda for the city's new master plan. In particular, the new master plan expands the Special Interest Zones (ZEIS) and states that the majority (60 percent) of the 80 percent of units reserved for those earning less than six minimum salaries must be for those at the bottom rung, earning less than three minimum salaries (Secretaria Municipal de Urbanismo e Licenciamento 2014). That is to say, if there were one hundred units constructed in the ZEIS, eighty would go to low-income residents, but sixty of these would be reserved for the lowest-income citizens. This model

prevents developers from catering to only those at the top of the low-
to middle-income grouping and mandates greater targeting of the
poorest of the poor. As Barbosa acknowledged, however, even as they
celebrated the approval of the legislation, the city needed policies, programs, and resources in place to really implement the law. Moving
forward, then, their goal was to push the Secretariat for Urban Development and the city administration to uphold the new zoning law.

One means by which the movements sought to influence implementation of the master plan was through the participatory Council
for Urban Policies. Though the council was not new, it had renewed
importance after the passage of the new master plan. According to
Borges of the FLM, "the Council for Urban Policies has the power to
distribute nearly R$300 million for the expropriation of buildings in
the center for low-income people and we feel that we can influence
the budget through these direct participation channels" (2015). Even
though participation in the councils was not their primary strategy,
the FLM recognized their practical importance. The council was also
responsible for establishing the perimeters of the ZEIS. Barbosa of
the UMM explained that there were a lot of questions about how the
ZEIS law would be carried out in practice, and it was vital for them
to have a voice through the council to formulate regulations and allocate resources (2015).

These two movements—the FLM and the UMM—existed within
the same political, economic, and institutional arena and yet differed
in their emphasis on the primacy of participatory institutions in their
mission to prevent removals and secure affordable housing for low-
income residents. At the same time, they were both pragmatic and
willing to engage in varying strategies to forward their agendas. The
strategies of these movements could be classified as inclusionary, in
that they focused on achieving a greater voice in decision making and
increasing protection of rights, but indirect strategies involving bilateral negotiation also strongly complemented their work.

Their goals aimed to change the structure of the physical city by
providing more units of formal housing for low-income residents in
the currently degraded but increasingly valuable center. These goals
included having a greater voice in the long-term planning for the city,
directly allocating resources, and enforcing the legal rights of citizens.
But the goals of physical and political inclusion were not accomplished

without significant public pressure and disruption through protest and occupations in an effort to influence government officials to follow through on their promises.

Motivations for Strategies

Strategies in São Paulo built on the long-term struggle for more participatory institutions as well as the long tradition of collective mobilization to achieve rights and benefits. The right to housing as enshrined in the Brazilian Constitution of 1988 was the explicit goal of the housing movements in São Paulo, particularly the UMM, which formed through the fight for democracy. For the past several decades movements in the city have stated their goal broadly as the right to "dignified housing," with the right to the city increasingly framing their rhetoric in the past ten years. The reliance on rights was a response to both ideology and now the institutional mechanisms in place that provide for inclusion in decision making, protections for residents in informal settlements, and also inclusionary zoning laws. The struggle over the past thirty years to put into place participatory councils, laws to enforce Brazil's right to housing, and ZEIS meant that strategies shifted toward making sure the ideals of these instruments were put into practice (Hirata 2012). This meant engaging with the legal system, though they also still needed to motivate policy makers to comply with the provisions as written. Strategies to elicit interest and action by policy makers relied, then, on the movements' relationship with the state, political opportunities, and resources.

Ideology

Ideology shapes ideas about the appropriateness of certain strategies over others. Given the long history of organizing based on the claim to rights among informal settlements in São Paulo, as documented by Holston (2008), I would expect the citywide housing movements today to frame their goals in terms of their rights as guaranteed by law and the right to the city as a vision for inclusive development. Both the UMM and the FLM claim the right to housing and the right to the city, but for the UMM more than for the FLM long-term structural change has been prioritized as a means to achieving these rights. The latter movement's focus has been more the immediate fulfillment of housing needs. The question, then, is whether ideology motivated a divergence in strategies.

The UMM and the FLM differed on the value of participating in and pushing for the participatory councils, though neither viewed the councils as the answer to all problems. Within the Municipal Council for Housing, members deliberated on rules for the implementation of programs and the allocation of resources, though they constantly challenged the interests of the private sector and government officials on the council (Donaghy 2013). Borges of the FLM argued that it was often a waste of time to argue with the government via the council when the group could be out protesting (Borges 2013). In reality, he said, the council controls very little money, and final decisions are actually made by the Secretariat for Housing even when there is a vote in the council. In addition, Borges argued that as a movement they needed to remain autonomous in order to confront whatever government happened to be in office. He explained:

> The movement has to have its own role. We cannot be imprisoned by our relationship with the government and the political parties, and we have to take to the street to ensure we get what we demand. They [government officials] have their role in the government, and they have to complete their role to sit at the table, to dialogue, to say what is and is not possible, to say what they can and cannot promise, but make it clear what will be done. . . . When the movement mixes in the relations of the government, they begin to think with the mind of the government, the mind of the party, and the legislature, and so then you are at the mercy of the decisions of the government.

Borges feared cooptation of the movement and a loss of autonomy by working within government institutions. Nonetheless, there has been FLM representation in the Housing Council, and decisions made in the council regarding which buildings would be expropriated for funding under the MCMV Program were important to them. Participation in the Housing Council as well as the Urban Development Council was therefore a practical necessity for Borges, but not necessarily an ideological one.

Conversely, Barbosa of the UMM explained that what the policy and management councils, including the Housing Council, provide are spaces to be constructive in proposing alternatives and not always to react to the government's proposals. He believed that raising the political consciousness of the movement's members was a vital part of the movement's struggle, and integrating members into participatory spaces enabled them to have a more direct voice in the political process than they ever had before. His views represented a worldview in which reform came from changing the structure of political representation rather than influencing the interests of policy makers who ultimately control decisions.

Given the experiences of both movements, ideology did lead to participation in these deliberative spaces, though practicality also played a role in explaining strategies of inclusion. Given that the institutions existed, they presented an option for engagement even to reluctant participants, but the reason the institutions existed and continued to function was the persistence of the UMM and others that believed deeply in the need for structural change through inclusion in formal institutions.

Relationship with the State

Alliances with the administration in power, insider access, and trust all defined the movements' relationship with the state. From 2013 to 2016 there was an allied government in power in São Paulo, which meant that strategies did not involve changing the political regime. This has not been the case over time, however. In 2013, the administration of Mayor Haddad (PT) took over from that of Mayor Gilberto Kassab, with whom the movements had a contentious relationship. The movements questioned the legitimacy of the Municipal Council for Housing under the conservative Kassab government. Eventually the relationship broke down, and the council stopped operating for more than a year over a disagreement regarding the rules to elect social movement members to the council. Traditionally, movements in São Paulo have allied with the PT; in fact, many leaders receive salaries from the party. As such, at election time the housing movements, especially the UMM, work vigorously to ensure the election of PT candidates. Under the administration of Haddad, movement leaders reported a friendlier relationship, though they were dismayed when Haddad initially appointed a housing secretary from a more conservative party (Barbosa 2015; Borges 2015).

Even under a relatively friendly administration, the process of occupations increased, according to Borges, because the movements needed to ensure that the government moved forward with its promises. Though theory would predict that the movements would be more likely to engage in cooperative tactics when the government is an ally, the case of São Paulo demonstrates that movements will protest when they feel it will work, and when the administration is an ally, movement leaders feel they have the chance for positive response.[7] When I asked directly whether movement leaders felt they needed to stage occupations or protests to get meetings with the current mayor or the Secretariat for Housing, the answer was a definite "no." Borges reported there was an open door for dialogue, but the problem as they saw it was that the government's channels for implementing projects were inefficient. When FLM staged an occupation, the administration took the initiative to call for a meeting and negotiate to see what they could quickly put into practice. The challenge for the movement was not access but political will and the capacity to turn promises into action. An official within the Secretariat for Housing likewise told me it is natural for the movements to engage in this type of pressure because the process of implementation is very slow, and officials expect that protest is a part of advocacy in the city (COHAB 2015).

Leaders from the UMM also capitalized on insider access and long-standing ties to the PT at the federal and municipal levels. For example, a leader of the UMM went to work with the MCMV Program in Brasília in order to create the portion of the MCMV Program supporting self-construction projects by housing associations. Another member of the UMM I met was a City Council member whom other members often sought out for advice and assistance. Barbosa and others have at times held liaison positions within the Secretariat for Housing, and they had a direct, long-standing relationship with Secretary for Housing João Sette Whitaker, a professor from the University of São Paulo appointed in 2015. For the UMM, insider access and an alliance with the administration facilitated their policy agenda and the functioning of participatory institutions, but leaders argued they needed to continue to engage in protests and occupations to keep the focus of the administration on their demands.

The movements' lack of trust in the judiciary to act fairly also shaped their strategies. According to Borges, a lack of trust in judges to uphold the constitution, the Statute of the City, and the master plan when applied to "squatters' rights" and penalties for absent property owners led directly to occupations as a means of protest. The FLM viewed the judges as being in the pockets of elite property owners and real estate speculators rather than being concerned with the social function of property. Borges argued that judicial bias was evidenced by the low percentage of eviction cases decided in favor of those who occupied the buildings.[8] The FLM's aim in engaging in occupations was to bring attention to judicial bias in order to motivate intervention by other government actors and put pressure on judges to uphold existing laws. In Borges's words, "Occupations give us the opportunity to invite the press and to ask public officials why they have not responded to the needs of the people" (2015). While the UMM did not disagree with this strategy, Barbosa also explained the importance of strengthening their relationship with the Defensoria Pública to influence judicial decisions. Through *jornadas*, leaders from the UMM hoped to educate the public defenders on the need for housing and for all sides to better understand and trust the process.

At the end of the day, the movements' relationship with the state was also ultimately influenced by the state's relationship to the private sector. The movements knew they must confront the power of the real estate and construction companies in the city in order to sway public officials. According to the website of the investigative news service Pública, in the 2014 municipal elections real estate and construction companies accounted for 57 percent of campaign contributions in the city (Belisário 2014). These companies had their own interests in promoting high-end housing in the city center and minimizing the proportion of less-profitable, low-income units in any new development. The power of the private sector motivated the movements to engage in electoral politics to elect candidates who were less engaged with business, but in reality they also knew that there was only so much they could do to compete with the city's profit motive. The presence of the private sector on the Council for Housing at times also reduced the incentive for the movements to rely on it as a means of policy change when government and private-sector votes aligned (Souza 2013). When governments are more aligned with the private sector, as under the Kassab administration, the movements tend to have less trust in the administration and less faith in the participatory process.

In sum, the relationship of the movements and the city administration between 2013 and 2016 was relatively strong in terms of communication and access. This relationship led them to engage in both inclusionary and indirect tactics to maximize their influence. A lack of trust in the judicial institutions motivated the movements to seek redress within the executive branch, and the power of the private sector challenged the movements to constantly press the government to keep their interests at the forefront of policy making.

Political Opportunities

Political opportunities that shift the strategies of movements present both openings and challenges to reform. An "opportunity" in this sense is not always the chance to positively influence the government's agenda but also the time in which to hold on to past gains. In São Paulo the election of Mayor Haddad represented a political opportunity to refocus housing policy in the city, while the economic and political crises from 2014 to 2016 at the national level presented a challenge to maintaining current programs.

The presence of the Haddad administration led to a greater push for partnership among civil society organizations. As Borges stated, through the process of occupations and negotiation they were "seeking the opportunity for more civil society involvement" and "what we should at least be able to initiate with this administration is a new chapter in the history of returning to partnerships with organized entities" (2015). The FLM's strategy shifted toward intensifying the process of occupations as a tactic in part because they saw an opportunity for engagement with the new administration. Under previous PT administrations, including Mayor Luiza Erundina in the late 1980s and Marta Suplicy in the early 2000s, more building projects were conducted through *mutirão* or *auto-gestão,* in which housing associations themselves manage the construction process and residents contribute sweat-equity to building the community. The strategy of the

FLM was in part to force negotiation as a means of promoting greater investment in such cooperative projects. During the previous administration, the UMM looked to the federal government to create the MCMV-Entidades Program to support projects built in *auto-gestão*, but they also hoped for greater cooperation under Haddad and increasing resources directed to the movements and housing associations themselves. Their strategy focused more on influencing the Secretariat for Housing and other agencies from the inside through appointments of allies and by participating with greater force in the councils. The UMM also had a strong investment in promoting the process of self-built projects and working with the city government to implement the MCMV-Entidades Program.

At the same time, the financial crisis throughout Brazil and the impeachment of President Dilma Rousseff in 2015–2016 brought a realization for the movements that the limited advances they had made in securing new projects through MCMV could be lost. Occupations were a means of keeping their demands in the public eye throughout the political and financial chaos. As Barbosa explained, "We carry out the occupations to say you cannot mess with the investments in social programs. The government says they have to pay debts and reduce inflation. This is the policy of fiscal adjustment, but we're saying this type of adjustment cannot mean cuts for social programs" (2015). The national-level political shift, then, did play a role in the increase in occupations and street protests, and the urgency of the need to protect social programs also necessitated face-to-face meetings with administration officials to secure promises of program continuation.

Resources

The movements in São Paulo benefited from the institutional resources of the Defensoria Pública (DP) and the participatory councils, but they were also strengthened by the capacity of members and connections to nongovernmental actors. The sum of these resources pushed the movements toward inclusionary strategies, though the practical need for indirect strategies remained.

Two resources encouraged the movements to use the force of law to forward their goals. First, the DP enabled the movements to engage in legal challenges, as the DP serves as mediator between judges and residents facing eviction. The Housing Nucleus of the DP also negotiates housing assistance, such as rental support, or inclusion in a housing program when an eviction is imminent. The movements sought to strengthen their relationship with the DP and viewed it as an ally against the state. In order to access the DP, most communities needed to link to one of the movements for support in navigating the process. In this way the movements collectivized the struggle against displacement. Though housing is often viewed as a private good, the fact that communities recognized the need to fight back collectively shifted the debate toward issues of community and the state of the city rather than individual need. Linking to other movements shaped individual communities' ideas about the right to the city through participation in forums and workshops in which citizens were taught their basic rights. In the sense that the movements were sitting directly at the table and able to challenge the government's power, mediation through the DP could be considered a strategy of inclusion.

Second, faculty and students at the University of São Paulo (USP) also served as a resource to the movements as they lent legitimacy and often evidence from careful research. For instance, USP faculty in urbanism and architecture mapped conflicts involving threats of removal in the city, which assisted the movements in publicizing the extent of the problem and directly providing legal assistance to those communities that needed it. Dr. Raquel Rolnik, a professor at USP and a former United Nations Special Rapporteur for Housing, advocated for São Paulo at the global level and provided analysis of property rights in the city. The institution of the DP and the support of academics both enabled the movements to broaden their struggle beyond individuals or single communities to promote citywide solutions to housing problems. The DP as an innovative democratic institution promoted inclusion through direct mediation among parties, and the support of academics provided greater capacity to the movements to engage the legal system.

The professional capacities of members, and, more specifically, the movement leaders, were also key for directing strategies. As an attorney, Barbosa represented communities within the DP, and other lawyers from the Centro Gaspar Garcia, a human rights organization, also represented movement members engaged in property conflicts.

Moreover, the leaders of both the UMM and FLM had decades of experience fighting for "dignified housing," and they knew the institutional rules and norms governing housing rights. Barbosa and others from the UMM had long-standing ties to religious organizations and the PT and were able to call on these ties for high-level meetings. The ethos of the PT and participatory democracy, as described above, also came out of the housing movements' origins. While the FLM did not choose to prioritize participatory democracy, it understood the system and how to use these institutions.

Finally, though participation can be difficult to motivate, especially among low-income residents, in the informal settlements of São Paulo a common identity did appear to generate significant participation and constituted a considerable resource for the movements.[9] As stated above, Holston (2008) argues that the process of auto-construction in informal settlements led residents to band together to make demands of the government for inclusion in the services of the city. The ability to motivate residents to protest and form organized occupations also enabled the movements to carry out these tactics.

Outcomes

Housing is a very visible form of social investment, but it can also be very expensive to please just a small number of people. According to University of São Paulo professor Marta Arretche, the municipality of São Paulo tended to take a lot of credit for small investments (2012). For example, when the administration signed the first agreement for MCMV, the municipal government contributed only R$5,000 for every unit, while the federal government provided R$80,000. At the signing with President Rousseff the municipality took substantial credit for the program. In fact, because of the cost of new construction, regularization programs had become more common across the country in the past two decades (Donaghy 2013). The availability of funding through MCMV, however, led the municipal government to focus almost exclusively on the federal government program for construction as a solution to housing, which Barbosa claimed was a serious barrier to implementing a variety of programs to address multifaceted needs (2015). In reality, though, according to staff from COHAB, the municipal government entity responsible for financing the construction of housing projects, the municipal government just did not have the capacity or resources to carry out additional programs (COHAB 2015).

The movements, then, faced the dual challenge of generating political will for housing while overcoming the problems of capacity at the local level. In the period under study, the greatest results of the movements' efforts came from indirect strategies, though the greatest promise for change came from inclusionary strategies involving implementation of the city's master plan and working within the participatory councils and the DP. Indirect strategies shifted the will of the city administration to act on implementing promised programs, but the councils enabled long-term planning and structural change in decision making. In the midst of political and economic crises, the capacity of the government to implement promises only decreased, but needs remained, and the movements worked to keep housing issues in the spotlight. The achievements of the movements as far as housing in the center of the city included the promise by the Haddad administration to build thousands of new units, the expropriation of occupied buildings for renovation, the cancellation of some eviction notices, and initiating penalties for abandoned properties under the master plan. These victories came through a mix of indirect and inclusionary strategies in which the movements sought power inside institutions and through negotiation with government officials using a variety of tactics.

As mentioned above, Mayor Haddad had promised to build 55,000 units of low-income housing in the city with funding from MCMV, the state, and the municipality. When Haddad entered office in 2013 his administration issued an "order of social interest" to expropriate at least nine movement-occupied buildings for renovation to be used for social housing. As a result of mobilization and pressure from the movements, 11,000 of the promised 55,000 units were to be built in *auto-gestão* with funding from the MCMV-Entidades Program. In 2015, housing associations (*entidades*) submitted proposals for the first 7,000 of these units. As Barbosa explained, the process of submitting proposals was quite difficult, but activists had great hope for the promise of the program. Each association first underwent a process of capacity building to enable it to participate in the selection process. Barbosa added, "The bureaucracy involved in the selection process is quite large and it will take a long time for these projects to mean housing for the people" (2015). Still, implementation of the program was considered a victory for the movements.

Among the projects in this program were three buildings occupied in partnership with the FLM that were slated to be expropriated by the city government and renovated with MCMV-Entidades funding: Maúa, Prestes Maia, and the former Hotel Lorde. To keep the city government moving forward with these projects, the FLM and the UMM staged a series of protests and occupations. For example, in April 2015 occupations led to an immediate meeting with the Secretariat for Housing in which the government agreed to deposit additional funds into an account toward the expropriation of the Prestes Maia building. During the meeting they discussed the motivation for the occupations—real estate speculation, the role of the judiciary, and the issue of expropriation of the buildings. Borges explained that these building renovations were "concrete projects in the central region that have come about through this process of struggle, and we have had important negotiations to bring about projects for the housing entities" (2015). Borges explained that they presented their demands and the government played its role by saying what was and was not possible to provide in the moment. He believed this separation of the roles was very important for autonomy in negotiations and allowed them to keep pressing for demands.

According to a staff member at COHAB, the movements also exercised influence in the Municipal Council for Housing in deciding which buildings would be studied and expropriated for MCMV funding. Though the staff member argued that available programs were really at the will of the administration in power and had very little to do with the activities of the movements (COHAB 2015), she recognized the influence of the movements in the details of program implementation: which buildings would be expropriated, who would be included in the projects, how much the municipal government would contribute in funding, and so forth, and these decisions were often decided within the Municipal Council for Housing.

The problem with the council remains the lack of resources dedicated to the fund for which the council makes decisions, but in the long-term the promise of these projects fulfills the goals of the movement as described by Nelson de Cruz Souza, coordinator of the Maúa occupation:

Occupations shouldn't last a long time because they are a form of pressure. . . . The objective of the movement is not simply to occupy. The occupation is a "foot in the door" [*porta de saida*] for families that need housing. If we simply keep doing occupations, filling them with people, we don't achieve anything because the provision of housing is not our responsibility but it is the government's. (2013)

The mix of indirect and inclusionary strategies appears to have motivated promises of action, but the implementation of these promises takes time and constant pressure and oversight by the movements. The beginning of the Haddad administration provided an opening for the movements to cement their demands, particularly as they had supported his election campaign. Government officials and movement leaders with whom I spoke admitted, however, that the goal of 55,000 units was mostly fiction because the money just wasn't there to carry out the projects. The indirect strategy of occupations followed by bilateral negotiation, however, did keep the promises of the administration moving forward. The promises may never be fully realized, but the movements will continue their activities to hold the government accountable through informal mechanisms.

Second, the movements prevented displacement of residents in several occupations through negotiation and use of the legal system. In 2013, Borges provided me with a list of occupations organized by the FLM in the city center. Three years later I asked about the status of the most prominent occupations, and all of them had survived threats of eviction. Two of the buildings on Avenida Rio Branco had received a notice of removal in which the owner claimed rights to the properties that had long been abandoned, but the judge ruled against the owner, citing the need for the property to fulfill a social function. The movements saw this as a major victory for upholding the rights of those living in informal settlements. The actions of another community, Jardim Edith, now serve as a model for avoiding displacement in the face of development. After the Centro Gaspar Garcia and the UMM filed and won a legal action to prevent removals in Jardim Edith on the basis of the claim that the government had offered below-market indemnity payments to residents, the groups worked with the DP and the municipal government on a plan to construct new social housing in the area instead of paying residents to leave. The movements learned from this model, in which mobilization and negotiation made a significant difference, and they now seek similar remedies in response to notices of removal.

Even with mobilization, however, not all occupations were ultimately successful in providing immediate shelter or a stepping-stone to other sources of social housing. Borges stated that sometimes after a judge ordered return of the property to its owner, the state mounted great pressure on the movements to vacate, for instance, by deploying police with tear gas and weapons, and the occupants had no choice but to leave. In these cases the organizational capacity of the movement was still important, but the legal decision backed by state power trumped their ability to remain in place. The lesson is that change within the legal system or laws to provide benefits to those evicted better serves the needs of low-income residents than protest or negotiation with executive branch officials.

Third, the movements fought for the creation of the city master plan to shape future development in the city. The municipal legislature's passing the master plan was in itself a victory in that it created the possibility for increasing low-income housing in the city center. Initial implementation of the law indicated that the plan would forward the goals of both the Statute of the City and the constitution. According to Leticia Sigolo, a staff member at the municipal Secretariat for Urban Development (SDU) responsible for implementing the master plan, one year after the plan passed, SDU had identified buildings that were not fulfilling their social function. In other words, these properties were found to have been abandoned by their owners. The SDU then notified the owners that they had one year to show the property was in fact being used for a social purpose or a tax would be imposed. After five years of failing to pay this tax, the property would then be transferred to the municipal government. The movements were very involved in identifying the properties that would receive the first notices. Buildings that were currently occupied by the movements, however, were not selected in the first round to receive notices because the movements feared owners would immediately file for *reintegração de posse* (return to owner), which could leave families without a place to live.

The inclusionary zoning provision of the master plan, which states that the majority of the total affordable units in the city center's Special Interest Zones (ZEIS) are to be reserved for the lowest-income citizens, will be much more difficult to implement. Setting the parameters for the ZEIS is the job of the Secretariat for Urban Development, but the resources for constructing housing must come from the Secretariat for Housing or the private sector. When the master plan was before the legislature, the movements fought hard to include this provision to allocate units specifically to the poorest residents, but the same problems of resources and reluctance from real estate and construction companies to build for the low-income market remained. SECOVI, the association representing construction and real estate companies in the city, also had representation on the Municipal Council for Urban Planning, and they were very involved in the creation of the new master plan. One concession to SECOVI was to increase the density allowed for building along the main thoroughfares of the city. Still, to build for the low-income market, private-sector companies are likely to rely on funding from the MCMV Program. As Barbosa explained, "In Brazil capitalism is capitalism without risk. Private developers don't want to take on the risk of low-income housing. They only want to enter into partnerships with the government where there is no risk" (2015). With potential cuts to MCMV, the possibility for new construction in the city center looks increasingly unlikely. The master plan expressed the best of intentions for creating low-income housing in the center, particularly for the poorest, but the economic reality may deter the fulfillment of the promise.

The strategy to influence the new master plan through protest and negotiation worked to secure its passage, but the long-term implementation of the plan will require vigilance on the part of the movements. The Council for Urban Planning will be key for locating any future projects and negotiating with private-sector interests to induce their building for the low-income market.

Speaking at the Habitat III Meeting in Quito, João Sette Whitaker Ferreira, secretary of housing for São Paulo under Mayor Haddad, lauded the accomplishments of the municipal administration in generating solutions for housing while citing the challenges that remain: the invisibility of housing as an issue in the eyes of the wealthiest people in the city; the long time frame to implement projects, often interrupted by elections; the difficulty of coordination among local, state, and federal officials; and the complexity of the juridical and political landscape. The strategies of the housing movements in São Paulo have led to achievements in reducing displacement, promoting access to low-income housing, and shaping the future of urban planning. These efforts clearly matter for the engagement of government agencies and the direction of policies and programs. But as Whitaker suggested, significant barriers to implementing these plans remain. Even with the political will to reform the city center with inclusion of low-income residents, the lack of capacity to move projects forward and engage the private sector impedes rapid progress.

Conclusions

The case of São Paulo largely confirms the hypotheses regarding strategies and outcomes: a strong ideology combined with a close relationship with the state leads to increasing reliance on participatory institutions and the judicial system, and these strategies serve to generate new policies and programs rather than simply increases in investment for existing programs. The movements' achievements included securing programs to renovate city center buildings, preventing displacement of residents in some occupations, and a new city master plan incorporating inclusionary zoning. What the case also shows is the importance of mixed strategies—inclusionary and indirect—to secure not only promises but also implementation. Restraints on government capacity across the federal, state, and municipal levels limit the ability of the city to follow through on the agreements they make with the housing movements, reducing the realistic impact of these community organizations. Still, the movements in São Paulo continue the fight across administrations and economic circumstances to push for the prioritization of housing in the city.

6

Citywide Growth and Gentrification in Washington, D.C.

Because Washington, D.C., is the national capital of the United States, its governance and financial health are closely connected to the federal government. Displacement of residents and the provision of affordable housing, however, are inherently local issues and are therefore dictated largely by local politics. In the 2000s the city began to experience rapid population expansion, predominantly fueled by upper-middle-class single adults and childless couples. Rapidly rising rents and home prices prevented low-income residents from moving within or into the District, and the cost increases also made the sale of previously affordable multi-unit properties and homes increasingly attractive to owners. Residents have fought back with a number of strategies to counteract the processes of displacement and have called for programs to increase the number of affordable units. This case demonstrates the effect of a close relationship with the state in developing strategies and the positive influence of long-term organizing on redistribution of resources.

This chapter focuses on the case of the Housing for All Campaign, led by the Coalition for Nonprofit Housing and Economic Development (CNHED). The goal of CNHED, a membership association made up of nonprofit community development organizations, is to ensure access to housing and economic opportunities for low-income residents (CNHED 2014). Living in the D.C. metropolitan area, I was able to observe the campaign's work over the course of two years (2015–2016) by attending meetings, advocacy trainings, rallies, and other events, in addition to carrying out interviews with key organizational members, journalists, and government officials. The campaign's website identifies its members as "people who work at affordable housing nonprofits, people living in affordable housing, and concerned D.C. residents like you!" As the case study demonstrates, leaders of the campaign were extraordinarily organized and proactive in designing their strategy to influence city officials to allocate more funding to housing programs. They developed a broad advocacy campaign that relied on inside connections to government to promote their agenda and outside efforts to mobilize and train supporters. In part because of the campaign, over a five-year period the issue of affordability reached the government agenda through the mobilization of constituents and persistent activities of organizers. As a result of the campaign's largely indirect strategies, the D.C. government increased the budget for key programs to prevent the loss of affordable housing. The increasing use of public testimony and direct meetings with residents and officials, however, speaks to the desire for greater participation in decision making, which may eventually lead to more formally inclusive governance institutions. For now, though, the campaign successfully used the institutional tools at their disposal to achieve demands, which signals that formal participatory institutions are not necessary to secure benefits for low-income residents in the city. But the case also suggests that while indirect strategies alone win benefits, politics as usual prevail, restricting the transformation of urban development.

Background on Washington, D.C.

The city of Washington, D.C., is exceptional in at least two regards: (1) it responds to federal rather than state control, and (2) since home rule began, the city has always had an administration and a city council led by the Democratic Party. The D.C. City Council is popularly elected by residents of the District, though the municipal budget must also be approved by the U.S. Congress. A substantial portion of the real estate in the city is also owned by the federal government, with 21 percent of the city's land controlled by a variety of federal agencies (Vincent, Hanson, and Bjelopera 2014). Despite the influence of the federal government, city politics are vibrant if not multiparty. In 2014, Mayor Muriel Bowser defeated incumbent Vincent Gray in the Democratic primary after he was implicated in a corruption scandal, and she went on to defeat independent challengers in the general election. As mayor, Bowser is seen as largely responsive to housing advocates, though she also has critics who charge that she is too closely aligned with private-sector elites. For instance, in 2012, Max Skolnik, a challenger for the seat on the City Council she held before becoming mayor, claimed that 37.5 percent of Bowser's campaign funding since 2006 came from "big-time developers, corporate bundlers and high-powered lobbyists" (Suderman 2012). The insinuation was that she was beholden to private-sector entities, which would have biased the decisions she made as a government official in favor of her privileged base of support.

Even though the vast majority of residents in the District are registered Democrats, important factions do exist based on race and class, particularly regarding the potential benefits of redevelopment. In a 2015 poll conducted by the *Washington Post,* 55 percent of African Americans stated they felt redevelopment was "mainly bad for them," up from 17 percent in 2000. Among white residents, only 15 percent of respondents viewed redevelopment as having a negative impact (Schwartzman, Hauslohner, and Clement 2015). Often, according to Aaron Wiener, former author of the Housing Complex column for the *Washington City Paper,* divides form between those residents who are prodevelopment and those who are antidevelopment. In his experience, "prodevelopment" residents tend to be younger and are less likely to be homeowners, while "antidevelopment" coalitions tend to form between upper-class white residents in the northwestern quadrant of the city who see no reason for change and poorer African American residents in the southeastern quadrant who believe change never means anything good for them (Wiener 2015). Politics, then, can be complicated by local geography, race, class, and the perception of the benefits versus costs associated with redevelopment.

Demographic data demonstrate the changing character of the city, which likely fuels current divides over the benefits of redevelopment. Washington, D.C., has long been a midsized city, with a current population of approximately 700,000 residents. But a reversal in mid-twentieth-century population decline since approximately 2000 has significantly altered the makeup of the city (Tatian and Lei 2015). Though former mayor Marion Barry famously nicknamed D.C. "the Chocolate City" for its majority black population, between 1970 and 2010 the black population declined from 538,000 to 309,000 (Tatian and Lei 2015). During this time, the black population fell below 50 percent, while the percentage of whites increased to 35.8 percent and the Hispanic population reached 10 percent. During the first decade of the new millennium, the city added 50,000 whites, 9,700 Latinos, and 7,900 Asians, contributing to the city's growing population total even as the number of black households continued to decline. According to research from the Urban Institute, the neighborhoods from which blacks have moved are largely the same areas into which whites arrived (Tatian and Lei 2015). The number of eighteen- to thirty-four-year-olds also grew by 35,000, and these millennials now make up about 35 percent of Washington's population.

In the 1990s D.C. struggled with how to reinvigorate the city center, which had fallen into severe decline. Though federal government buildings anchored many downtown areas, the city center was largely deserted after working hours.[1] In the late 1990s and early 2000s D.C. embarked on a deliberate development strategy in the downtown area to increase cultural attractions and restaurants that would appeal to high-income singles and childless couples (Sturtevant 2014). The influx of residents transformed the entire city, as people with higher incomes increasingly moved into previously low-income neighborhoods. Lisa Sturtevant (2014) finds direct evidence that lower-income, less-educated residents were more likely to move out of the District between 2006 and 2010, while higher-income, college-educated people were more likely to move into the city.

Like other cities across the world, Washington, D.C., has witnessed the problems of decreasing affordability, lack of protections for current residents, and lack of funding for programs to generate more affordable housing options as the city experienced significant economic growth and redevelopment. In Washington, D.C., the median cost of rent climbed 21 percent from 2006 to 2013.[2] Part of the "crisis of affordability," as housing organizations refer to the current state of the market in D.C., stems from the fact that the demand for housing is outpacing supply as the city's population rises (Tatian and Lei 2015). From about 2010 to 2015, the District added one thousand people every month, while the number of new units averaged only around three thousand per year.

The problem, however, is not simply supply but also the availability of housing units that fit the budgets of the low-income population. According to the DC Fiscal Policy Institute, from 2002 to 2013 the share of affordable rental units, defined as costing less than $800 per month, declined from 40 percent to 20 percent of the total, while the share of high-income units, defined as those costing above $1,600 per month, increased from 15 percent to 35 percent (DC Fiscal Policy Institute 2015). Though rents went up, the same report finds that wages during that time period were stagnant among earners below the fiftieth income percentile. For two-thirds of residents earning less than 30 percent of median income, housing now accounts for over 50 percent of monthly expenses (Reed 2012). According to the D.C. Office of Revenue Analysis, average home prices have also tripled in the city, leading to declining homeownership rates, particularly among low-income residents (District, Measured 2015). D.C. also has the distinction of having the highest average cost for household expenditures of any U.S. city, though the share for shelter alone is still greater in San Francisco (Scopelliti 2014).

Over the past few years, the threat of displacement has yielded landlord-tenant disputes in several of the remaining low-income apart-ment rental buildings in the downtown area.[3] As gentrification moves to new areas of the city that were once affordable, landlords are tempted to sell long-held properties. Residents who had lived in relatively affordable units are then forced to relocate in an increasingly competitive market. With the median rental price of a one-bedroom apartment at $2,000 in the city and the median household income at about $66,000, the numbers just don't add up for most seeking shelter that they can comfortably afford within the city (Zumper 2015).

In addition, like most cities in the United States, D.C. has moved to dismantle much of its public housing stock in favor of issuing rental vouchers or resettling residents in newly developed mixed-income communities, though not to the same extent as Atlanta. Over the past decade, with the promise of replacing every demolished unit with a new unit in a mixed-income community, the D.C. government's New Communities Initiative tore down approximately 250 public housing units, though the goal is to tear down and replace 1,500 units (New

Communities Initiative 2015). Long wait times for new units and bureaucratic hurdles have meant that most of the displaced public housing residents are actually receiving rental vouchers instead of newly constructed units (Wiener 2015). This type of displacement is not so much a direct result of gentrification but underscores the desire of government officials to improve neighborhoods through the deconcentration of poverty. The case of Temple Courts apartments illustrates the challenges of this program. Despite the initial promise of new units, in 2007 the residents of Temple Courts were forced to leave the soon-to-be-demolished community and received rental vouchers for what was supposed to be temporary rehousing. Six years later, a *Washington Post* report found that many of the residents had moved to suburban Maryland, though most "moved from one concentrated pocket of poverty to another, east of the Anacostia River" (Samuels 2013). Only half of the original residents eventually received new units in a mixed-income building not far from the Temple Courts site.

Beyond the New Communities Initiative, D.C. does have a number of policies and programs in place to deal with the issues of displacement and affordability. In the late 1970s, a grassroots coalition of residents proposed the Tenant Opportunity to Purchase Act (TOPA), which the City Council adopted into law in 1980 (Gallaher 2016). When properties go up for sale, TOPA guarantees that tenants will have the first opportunity to buy the property at market-rate prices, and in practice this means that tenants can either buy the property as a cooperative or assign their rights to a third party, usually a for-profit or nonprofit that agrees to maintain at least some subsidized units. According to Farah Fosse, director of the Housing Department of the Latino Economic Development Center, the D.C. government provides funding to nonprofit organizers to inform tenants of their rights and assist them in forming cooperatives, and the Housing Production Trust Fund, started in 2003, is meant to provide funding to developers and tenants for the purchase. In 2014, the Latino Economic Development Center, one of the two main tenant organizers in the city, assisted thirty-five tenant associations in the purchase of their buildings (Fosse 2015). According to a representative from another nonprofit in the city, Mi Casa, 117 buildings were eligible for TOPA during 2014 (Crouch 2015). Carolyn Gallaher (2016) found that, in practice, the TOPA process tends to operate more effectively in middle-income versus low-income buildings, but the law does provide unique protection to renters that is not available in any other city and does work more smoothly with the assistance of tenant organizers.

Rent-control laws, which limit the allowable percentage increase in rents per year, actually provide the largest stock of affordable housing in the city and therefore constitute a critical policy intervention in the District (Tatian 2015). Advocates are constantly working to close loopholes to ensure that more landlords abide by rent-control provisions, to revise the regulations to include even more units, and to create a database to track the rent-controlled housing stock (DC Preservation Network 2015). D.C.'s current rent-control regime, however, serves only those residents already in place who do not wish to move. Once current residents move out of rent-controlled units, the rent goes up, and this source of affordable housing is lost for future tenants.

D.C. also supports local programs that assist first-time homebuyers, provide vouchers for rental subsidies, and promote inclusionary zoning. Critics charge that these programs face critical funding shortages and delays in implementation that limit their effectiveness (DC Preservation Network 2014; Committee on Housing and Community Development 2015; Falcon 2015; Fosse 2015). Although the Local Rent Supplement Program (LRSP) has generated more recent rental vouchers in the city than the federal rental voucher program, as of 2016 the waiting lists for both programs were closed.

Despite its special status as the nation's capital, D.C. has fairly traditional institutions related to housing. The D.C. Housing Authority, like housing authorities around the country, receives funding from the federal government to administer housing vouchers and public housing programs. Using a mix of federal and local funds, the D.C. Department of Housing and Community Development (DHCD) administers programs "to produce and preserve opportunities for affordable housing and economic development and to revitalize underserved communities" (DHCD 2016). The director of DHCD wields significant power over citywide planning and distribution of resources, though the budget is set by the D.C. City Council. Between 2014 and 2015 the budget of DHCD increased over 100 percent, with a similarly large increase in 2016 (District of Columbia 2015, 2016).

Among housing advocates there is now a sense that D.C. is on the verge of losing significant numbers of affordable residential units as upward trends of rents and home prices permanently reshape the city away from the inclusion of low-income residents. As such, strategies in the past five years have vigorously promoted the preservation of existing affordable units. Creating new existing units must also be a goal to meet rising demand, but in the current environment preventing further loss has been the main priority of advocates and government responses.

The Organizational Environment and Strategies for Collective Action

D.C. has an active organizational environment in which a number of groups undertake coordinated efforts to promote affordable housing and mobilize affected residents. Organizations are able to successfully mobilize residents to engage in both institutional opportunities and outsider tactics, such as rallies. As Aaron Wiener, formerly of the *Washington City Paper*, explained, "There is definitely not a problem of apathy currently in D.C. People are very engaged and particularly willing to show up to testify to the City Council" (Wiener 2015). Residents not only are aware of the issues; they are also motivated to participate and tell their stories within formal institutions. Housing advocacy, however, is not new to the nation's capital. While in the late 1970s grassroots organizers fought for legislation to strengthen tenant protections, including TOPA, since the early 2000s paid advocates have worked to organize tenants, and nonprofits have sought to strengthen new and existing programs, including the Housing Production Trust Fund (Falcon 2015).

The four main organizations dealing with displacement and affordable housing in the period under study were: the Coalition for Nonprofit Housing and Economic Development (CNHED), Organizing Neighborhood Equity DC (ONE DC), Empower DC, and the Latino Economic Development Center (LEDC). These organizations each bring a distinctive strategy and worldview to the fight to preserve and create affordable housing in the city. All of the organizations focus on advocacy directed at city government institutions, including testimony at city council hearings, and to varying degrees each carries out demonstrations and rallies to mobilize residents to make demands. In brief,

CNHED's function is to lead the long-term Housing for All Campaign, whose goal is to increase the budget of city housing programs; the goal of ONE DC, according to resource organizer Dominic Moulden, is to mobilize long-term residents to organize for change in the context of human rights (Moulden 2015); the goal of Empower DC is to engage in general confrontational tactics in support of public housing; and the goal of LEDC is to organize tenants faced with eviction, among other advocacy activities. These organizations each have their own purpose and strategies, which at times limits the extent to which they work together. Community Development Corporations (CDCs) are also quite active in Washington, D.C. (Walker and Weinheimer 1998).

The focus here is on the Housing for All Campaign, led by CNHED, as an example of a successful long-term effort to influence policies and programs in the city. The campaign began in 2010, and their membership includes nonprofit housing developers, direct service providers, tenant organizers, and concerned citizens. According to Elizabeth Falcon, director of Housing Advocacy for CNHED and coordinator of the campaign, following the recession in the late 2000s the main demand of their organizational members across the city was more money to make existing programs effective in meeting the growing needs of residents (Falcon 2015). As such, the main demand of the campaign was for the D.C. government to invest in programs that fall across the full continuum of housing, including the Housing Production Trust Fund, the Home Purchase Assistance Program, the Local Rent Supplement Program, and the Permanent Supportive Housing Program (CNHED 2016). The campaign sought to preserve affordable rental housing, help the homeless into apartments and to get needed services, and assist first-time homebuyers.

A key goal for CNHED and other organizations in D.C. is preservation of existing affordable housing, especially subsidized dwellings. Preservation allows people to stay within their existing communities, which experts say is one-half to one-third cheaper than building new units (DC Preservation Network 2014). Therefore, a specific goal of the Housing for All Campaign was gaining the City Council's commitment to allocate $100 million for the Housing Production Trust Fund.[4] Coordinator Elizabeth Falcon believed a strength of the campaign was the focus on the four programs they targeted for budget increases rather than spreading their message among many demands. The $100 million for the Trust Fund provided a concrete goal by which to measure their success.

In order to increase the budget for housing programs, the campaign sought to influence the decisions of policy makers, particularly the mayor and members of the D.C. City Council. As Falcon noted, campaign members tried to "be the squeaky wheel wherever relevant" (Falcon 2015). They created their own moments for publicity by mobilizing members, such as during their annual rally and tenant town hall meetings, but they also made sure to have a presence at other political events, such as public meetings on budget proposals for the city. As Falcon explained it, their activities were never aggressive; rather, they pursued an "inside/outside" game in which they held meetings with government officials and pursued inside connections while also putting pressure on officials by mobilizing advocates and residents from around the city to make their voices heard at public events. Good relationships with the media also ensured their message reached residents and encouraged officials to respond.

A key institutional member of the Housing for All Campaign, the LEDC, also called on the District government to make regulatory changes to rent-control laws in order to strengthen enforcement and close loopholes in coverage (Kennedy 2015). Under the current system, a landlord can increase the rent 30 percent upon vacancy, which Phil Kennedy, the tenant organizing manager of the LEDC, argued encouraged landlords to get people to move out. The formula the LEDC proposed would base the allowable increase on how long the former tenant had lived in the unit. The primary focus of the campaign, at least until 2016, however, was on increasing funding rather than amending rent-control laws.

Mobilizing low-income residents to take part in the campaign was a key tactic of organizers. The campaign held a number of "advocacy trainings" in which leaders presented groups of residents—many of whom were leaders in tenant associations or simply residents in buildings threatened with eviction—with information about City Council members and how to craft personal testimony for council meetings. A handout at one training, titled "Tips for Council Testimony or Letter Writing Campaign," written in both English and Spanish, presented a simple script with talking points as well as pictures of the council members and their names, addresses, and committee assignments. The group talked about allies within the administration as targets of appeals and the way in which to present their stories to connect individual concerns to broader policies and programs. Following these trainings many of the attendees signed up to testify at council committee meetings. For instance, after one training in 2015, almost seventy people signed up to provide testimony in support of the campaign at one hearing of the D.C. Council Committee on Housing and Community Development. Council members were thoughtful and responsive during the daylong hearing. Behind the speakers sat members of the Housing for All Campaign, wearing bright yellow T-shirts bearing the campaign's logo.

The campaign also held an annual rally to bring together supporters and government officials. In February 2015, the rally attracted about seven hundred people, including Mayor Bowser and several council members. In 2016, the turnout was somewhat larger, and the mayor spoke of the achievements of the campaign in securing $100 million for the Housing Production Trust Fund and increases for other programs. In order to keep its demands center stage, the campaign timed the rally annually to immediately precede the release of the mayor's budget (Falcon 2015).

Because D.C. is a city that has always had a Democratic administration, the strategy of overhauling the political regime has always taken a back seat to other strategies for creating change. Across mayoral administrations there have been no significant changes in housing policy, and leaders I spoke with didn't expect candidates to differ substantially in their approaches to housing. In the most recent campaign in 2014, issues regarding housing figured prominently following a scandal at a D.C. homeless shelter, a cold winter in which the media scrutinized the rise in homelessness among families, and more than a decade of rising housing costs. Still, while seeking allies among political officials figured prominently in advocacy strategies, changing the political regime did not.

In sum, I would characterize the strategy of the Housing for All Campaign as primarily indirect, with an emphasis on grassroots organizing and voice through the use of testimony to the City Council. The campaign did not call for greater access to decision making but capitalized on the opportunity to present directly to City Council members in order to influence the budget and programmatic priorities. Without bilateral meetings and personal relationships with government officials as well as mobilization of affected citizens, however, the strategy for achieving a voice through City Council decisions was not as effective in achieving its demands. Its tactics worked together to promote the goals of preventing displacement and improving access to affordable housing.

Motivations for Strategies

The activities of the Housing for All Campaign were very logical and purposeful given the context in which the organization operated. I find that a relatively conservative ideology, a close relationship with the state, lack of political opportunities, and significant resources pushed the Housing for All Campaign toward indirect strategies. Increasing use of public testimony indicates a push toward inclusion in decision making, but also an acceptance of current institutional arrangements.

Ideology

In D.C. there is a definite divide between organizations based on ideology, with the Housing for All Campaign purposefully choosing to maintain a relatively conservative identity. The campaign's goal is specifically to bring tenants together in order to collectivize the issues of affordable housing, but this does not include using the language of rights to mobilize residents. According to Falcon, the campaign's design focused on practicality. The language of rights and also the term "gentrification" never seemed practical to her as the organizer (2015). She acknowledged that other organizations in the city, including ONE DC and Empower DC, took more radical approaches toward influencing the decisions of policy makers, but the campaign viewed their role in the city as less confrontational and more cooperative in order to achieve gains within the existing power structure. Campaign leaders recognized that the practical focus of the campaign sometimes limited members from taking on bigger-picture questions of how to restructure the system and that as a consequence of the focus, strategies generally hewed toward working within existing institutions and persuading government officials to improve existing programs and policies.

The makeup of the campaign's membership also shaped the goals and limited the desire for radical change. Many members are nonprofit developers who directly benefit from more money in the Housing Production Trust Fund to redevelop properties. Several organizational members also received money for tenant organizing, and they were to some extent reliant on the city administration for their own livelihoods as well as organizational survival. The reliance of advocates on city-derived funding would seem to have generated an atmosphere of compliance.

But a distrust of "the system" among low-income residents also perpetuated a conservative approach. When I asked a group of campaign members why people didn't seem to get angry about the lack of available rental vouchers and subsidies, one resident leader explained to me that people in her community didn't complain because they were afraid to lose what little they had. They didn't want to rock the boat for fear of losing everything. Another problem was fear of "speaking out" among the undocumented community. As the resident leader stated, instead of anger and protest, "advocacy is the cool and calm way to actually get responses" (Resident Leadership Team 2015). Members saw the most effective route to change as working within the existing political institutions rather than calling for systemic change.

The absence of housing as a right in Housing for All Campaign rhetoric, coupled with conservative strategies, actually ran counter to the idea that everyone deserves housing encapsulated by the campaign's title. Tenant organizers from LEDC, who make up part of the leadership team of the campaign, did report that they make sure to discuss with residents that "this is your city and you have the right to be here," but rights still did not shape the framing of the campaign (Fosse 2015). According to these organizers, people seemed to understand the language of rights as a claim to make demands rather than necessarily a legal question. But at the same time, the strategy of the campaign itself was basically to promote greater investment in existing programs to increase the availability of affordable housing rather than addressing issues of structural inequality or generating new programs, policies, and institutions that might provide greater voice or legal claims.

Then again, the law that the campaign sought to further implement—TOPA—was revolutionary in that it was designed to put the power in renters' hands to decide the fate of their own displacement. The TOPA process does promote "the right to the city" in that residents are given the power to put the brakes on the market sale of their buildings, and the campaign's insistence that the TOPA process must be facilitated by increasing money in the Housing Production Trust Fund does represent the campaign's desire to fulfill the promise of the law. The campaign talked a lot about the need for the city to invest in low-income people, without talking about housing as a right. The strategies of the campaign provided the opportunity for funneling individuals and communities with grievances into a broader struggle for affordable housing throughout the city.

Relationship with the State

The close relationship of the Housing for All Campaign to the city government was also critical to developing their strategies. Part of the closeness of the relationship stemmed from the nature of existing institutions. Campaign leaders did not call for greater inclusion in government because, as Falcon explained (2015), the D.C. government is already designed for inclusion—meetings are public, Area Neighborhood Councils encourage very local participation, and there are numerous opportunities to testify before the City Council—which meant that there were already strong formal mechanisms for people to be heard even if they did not have direct decision-making power. According to Falcon, because of its small size and the fact that it is always in session, the D.C. government has an ethos of being accessible to residents. D.C. may be different from other cities, such as New York, because it does operate much like a small town. In D.C., campaign members were able to do "walk-arounds" in which they dropped into the council members' offices to present their requests for action. In other larger or more adversarial cities this tactic would not have been possible. At a meeting to review the success of the campaign in 2016, one leader also described decision making as "coming from the bottom up" (Masliansky 2016).

Moreover, the relationship of the campaign to the city government was shaped by not only institutional opportunities but also the personal relationships of members with public officials and the presence of allies within the administration. Both the founder of the campaign and the executive director of CNHED previously served within the city government and were able to request private meetings with the mayor to present their budgetary goals. Former CNHED executive director Robert Pullman, who previously served as Mayor Marion Barry's chief financial officer and head of the Department of Housing and Community Development, decided on the $100 million goal for the Housing Production Trust Fund. The current director of the Department for Housing and Community Development, Polly Donaldson, was previously the director of the Transitional Housing Corporation, and an active member of the Housing for All Campaign. As Falcon explained (2015), the strength of the campaign came in large part from long-term relationships between leaders of CNHED, council members, and housing agency officials. CNHED also managed to mobilize other organizations to participate in the campaign because they knew CNHED to have direct channels into government. Several council members attended advocacy trainings, and many officials, including the mayor, attended the annual rallies held by the campaign.

Leaders in the campaign reported that institutions in the city promoted direct engagement, and mayors and City Council members generally expressed support for housing advocates as allies. They didn't see the need for greater institutionalized inclusion because they already had direct access to officials. Strategies for addressing displacement and affordable housing followed this attitude of relative satisfaction in that the campaign called for increasing investment in current programs rather than necessarily engaging in new policies and programs or creating new institutions. As Falcon commented (2015), even if D.C. did have more formalized avenues for participation, she did not believe these types of institutions would have enough resources to really make a difference for bigger-picture problems. She believed that only advocacy to the City Council and mayor's office would achieve significant gains in resources.

Political Opportunities

Elections in D.C. present opportunities to shift strategies toward supporting certain candidates, but the dominance of the Democratic Party in the District limits the contentiousness of elections. The organizational leaders with whom I spoke seemed to agree that there had not been much difference in the positions of mayoral candidates regarding housing in the 2014 election. In her campaign, Mayor Muriel Bowser pledged to support the $100 million goal for the Housing Production Trust Fund, the campaign's budgetary demand, but so did other Democratic candidates. The de facto one-party system in D.C., then, pushes organizations to work with the current regime rather than attempting to build support for outside candidates. Further, since federal law prohibits registered nonprofits from directly endorsing candidates, organizations can indicate to their members and other voters only that certain candidates are in support of their demands.

After the election, however, the new administration of Mayor Bowser did present opportunities for the campaign in terms of closer alliances. On the basis of her track record as a council member who did not really engage with the campaign, leaders did not expect the mayor to embrace housing as a top priority. But to their surprise, the mayor had, in Falcon's words, "designed her administration to be good on housing" (2015). As mentioned above, the new director for DHCD, Polly Donaldson, was a longtime supporter of the campaign, with a background in housing and homeless advocacy. The appointed deputy budget director also came from the nonprofit sector and had extensive research experience in housing policy. According to Falcon, these appointments actually meant that the campaign needed to schedule fewer meetings since these newly minted government officials already knew their issues and demands. Nonetheless, these appointments and the mayor's support allowed the campaign to further invest in an insider strategy.

The campaign also succeeded in taking advantage of political moments to garner media attention. For example, when the Housing Authority announced they were closing the rental voucher waiting list, the campaign held a rally on the same day because they knew the press would be covering the voucher story (Falcon 2016). Moreover, the campaign capitalized on outside events that captured the attention of D.C. residents. In 2014, the abduction and presumed murder of a young girl from a D.C. shelter brought renewed concern for the ability of the D.C. government to provide secure options for homeless children and families. The case directed the spotlight on the significant increase in homelessness among families as a result of rising rents and home prices, creating momentum for housing issues in the 2014 mayoral race. At that point the Housing for All Campaign was already one of the most visible campaigns in the city, and they had built a narrative that there were practical solutions to the sometimes seemingly intractable problems in the District. The $100 million figure for the Trust Fund provided a simple message for voters to assimilate, which encouraged candidates to pledge their support.

Resources

The Housing for All Campaign benefited from significant resources and capacity to achieve advocacy goals, increasing its ability to lobby officials and limiting its desire to seek radical political change. These resources include funding, a sizeable base of support, and an existing framework to support tenants' rights.

First, funding for CNHED shaped the interests of the campaign as well as providing them with the capacity to carry out their operations. CNHED receives funding from a number of philanthropic foundations and private-sector donors, as well as commercial banks that use CNHED's support to meet requirements under the Community Reinvestment Act of 1977. With the money received, CNHED can hire professional staff, maintain an office, hold events, and promote the campaign. The capacity of the campaign to network and reach government officials reduced the incentive for protest and instead led the team toward more cooperative tactics.

The campaign also viewed their residential leadership group as one of their strongest assets. The group's leaders were residents who had already secured victories for themselves, including homeownership and using TOPA to form a cooperative or a permanently affordable property. The group formed a strong contingent at City Council meetings, and the campaign relied on their stories to mobilize support for increasing the budget for housing programs.

Finally, the existing laws and institutions to assist tenants in the city served as motivation to increase the capacity of this policy infrastructure rather than creating something new. As mentioned, the TOPA process that was already in place spurred calls for its expansion. Resident leaders, in particular, who had witnessed firsthand the success of the TOPA process believed in it as a valuable tool for others across the city. Bob Pullman, the former director of CNHED, was involved in the original push for the Trust Fund, which was not funded in the 1990s. His experience led to the original goal for the allocation of $100 million in the Trust Fund. A number of lawyers who worked on housing issues, including those from Legal Service Providers, Bread for the City, Legal Aid, the Washington Legal Clinic, and Neighborhood Legal Services, also were involved in developing strategies for the Housing for All Campaign. In fact, it was attorneys affiliated with the campaign who were the impetus for seeking funding to enforce the existing provisions under TOPA. In addition, with pressure from LEDC and others, in 2009 the city established the "Fix It" court, as the Housing Conditions Calendar is popularly known, to enable tenants to sue landlords for needed repairs (Fosse 2015).

Outcomes

Even though access to officials was not a challenge for the Housing for All Campaign, Falcon noted that getting them to do what the campaign asked was sometimes another story. Was the campaign's strategy using insider-outsider tactics effective for achieving their goals? Have these strategies led to programs, policies, and institutions that will effectively reduce displacement and increase access to affordable housing? While the campaign was largely successful in achieving its goals, questions remain about the potential for long-term inclusion of low-income residents in the city.

Falcon explained, "The biggest thing we achieved was translating the old sentiment that it's so sad that the cost of housing is so high to *we are doing something* because the cost of housing is so high" (2016). In other words, their legacy will be the shift in thinking that there are concrete steps that can be taken to prevent displacement and provide affordable housing rather than simply lamenting the fact that living in the District is increasingly beyond the reach of too many people. The most prominent goal of the campaign was to secure $100 million for the Trust Fund, a goal that was accomplished in the 2016 budget following five years of advocacy. Falcon stated that "the campaign basically won everything we wanted. The foreclosure crisis and federal budget cuts set us back, but now there is more local money going to housing" (2015). Resident leaders felt the sense of momentum in the city. As one resident leader stated, "There was a gold rush for property under [previous] administrations, but now the pendulum is swinging back to affordable housing" (Resident Leadership Team 2015). Moving forward, the campaign's intention is to broaden the strategic plan toward expanding economic opportunities for low-income residents. The gains in funding for housing set the stage for further achievements.

In the CNHED's internal review of the Housing for All Campaign, CNHED director Steven Glaude remarked that "it was really important for everyone to wear yellow campaign shirts during testimony and council members really said that whoever made the most noise got the most money" (2016). Showing that the campaign had significant numbers of residents behind their cause and had vocalized their demands contributed to much of their success. At an "Advocacy Day" at the D.C. City Council sponsored by the campaign prior to the final budget approval for 2016–2017, Council Member Brianne Nadeau spoke to the crowd and emphasized the need for advocacy to push forward the housing agenda. She concluded by saying, "I'm with you and I'm glad you're with me" (2016). As a tactic, testimony to the council also had great impact because of the very local nature of D.C. politics (Fosse 2015). Without the need to respond to state legislators, the City Council is the locus of decision making, and having council members as allies is key to any advocacy strategy.

Support for the campaign from the City Council was evident in one meeting of the Committee on Housing and Community Development in February 2015. The chair of the committee, Anita Bonds, repeatedly assured those testifying that issues of access and affordability were on committee members' minds, and that the city needed to do more to address housing problems. Council Member Elissa Silverman appreciated campaign members' assertions that preserving existing low-income housing is much less expensive than building again, and she expressed enthusiasm for working with CNHED on preservation. The campaign also participated in the creation of the Preservation Strategy Group, which included D.C. housing agencies, the U.S. Department of Housing and Urban Development (HUD), and nonprofit developers. The Strategy Group issued a report detailing steps to be taken to preserve existing affordable housing, which was put in the hands of D.C. City Council members (Preservation Strategy Network 2014).

According to the theoretical expectations described in Chapter 2, I would expect that the indirect strategies of the campaign would lead to expansion of existing programs and policies, which coincided with the goals of the campaign. It is important to understand, however, how the campaign managed to influence public officials in order to persuade them that increasing resources for housing was in the best interests of the city. The strong civic capacity of the campaign, the alliances they formed across stakeholders, and their conservative demands all served them well in achieving their goals.

Internal Characteristics

The Housing for All Campaign benefited from a high degree of civic capacity, the ability to mobilize individuals around a common issue for a common purpose. According to a member of the campaign's Residential Leadership Team, the advocacy trainings taught individuals to pursue the issues they felt were most important, showed them to whom they could target their grievances, and provided them with the ability to craft a message emphasizing positive solutions. Residents learned practical lessons about the local budgeting timeline and how the process of testimony to council meetings works. The campaign connected constituents with the tools and information so they could act on their own behalf.

In the public arena, including rallies, town halls, advocacy days, and council meetings, members of the campaign then maintained unity in their messages. During testimony, each member would have a sheet with the "asks" from the campaign and would repeat the monetary requests as they recounted their individual stories or experiences working with city residents. Resident leaders did acknowledge the challenges they faced in converting participants in the advocacy trainings to long-term leadership positions in the campaign and generally sustaining commitment of supporters over time, even though the core group of resident leaders did exhibit great commitment to participation (Resident Leadership Team 2015). But the fact that the campaign filled a number of advocacy trainings with residents, the majority of whom had little previous experience with any form of political action, illustrated significant capacity for mobilization. The group also articulated a vision that wasn't particular to one population, such as residents who were homeless, renters, or residents of public housing, which meant that a variety of people could participate and not be divided by conflicting goals (Masliansky 2016). The goals for funding "across the continuum" mobilized residents and drove their outside strategy, which in turn sustained their ability to influence officials from the inside.

Alliances

Engaging a broad base of supporters made it difficult for politicians to ignore the Housing for All Campaign (Bilonick 2016). In addition to tenants' associations and nonprofits, the campaign specifically reached out to white millennials and for-profits involved in housing development in order to broaden the appeal of its message. By attracting more people to the cause, the campaign sought to influence policy makers who seek to cull voters at election time. Millennials proved useful to the campaign as volunteers. To the for-profits the campaign made a different case, in asking them to spread the word about the campaign's demands to their networks. Support through networking, then, served to reduce opposition from young voters and private-sector developers to the campaign's funding target.

In terms of securing increasing money for housing, forming good relationships with other nonprofits outside of the housing sector also proved to be a good strategy. Glaude reported that housing was the only municipal budget item that received an increase for 2016, and he attributed that to the fact that no other advocacy organizations in the city counter-messaged them (2016). Because no one directly challenged their budgetary requests, council members did not have to defend their "yes" votes.

Long-term governmental alliances were also critical. According to Jim Dickerson, founder and president of Manna, Inc., a nonprofit housing developer in the city, the Department of Housing and Community Development recognized them as allies years before. The agency needed constituents to show up at hearings to be able to push for increased budget allocations. In essence, officials rely on advocates to make noise and bring issues to the attention of the public in order to justify expenditures. Support from the Housing and Community Development committee chair, Anita Bonds, also contributed to the success of the campaign's strategy. To the crowd at "Advocacy Day" in May

2016, Bonds labeled the people in yellow shirts "her people," even as she described the lengthy process of conferring with tenants' associations and industry associations prior to introducing bills to the City Council. The biggest challenge to expanding rent control or increasing subsidies for affordable housing has been the Apartments and Office Building Association (AOBA). Leading a powerful industry that generates enormous revenue for the city, AOBA can count on the fact their opinions do matter to council members concerned about development. Bonds meets regularly with AOBA representatives in order to get them on board with her proposals, but as one of her staff stated, it is vital for the campaign to keep up the pressure so that the council member can say she is supporting the will of city residents (Weise 2016).

The power of AOBA in the city, however, was actually reflected in the strategy of the campaign to focus on budget increases for existing programs rather than expanding tenant rights, a move that directly reduced conflict with private-sector developers and property owners. Under TOPA, tenants have the right of first refusal to purchase properties, but the purchase price should be at market value. Landlords, then, cannot really argue against strengthening the ability of tenants to purchase through the allocation of resources in the Housing Production Trust Fund. The campaign's uncontroversial requests reduced opposition and increased the odds of success. To prevent further erosion of low-income and affordable housing, however, the campaign made plans to move forward in calling for stricter rent control legislation now that they have won these first victories.

Conservative Demands

The goal of $100 million for the Trust Fund was set in 2010, even as D.C. and the rest of the country were still reeling from the 2007–2008 economic collapse. Campaign leaders knew that their goal was not achievable in the short term, but they believed once the recession ended the government would be able to and need to dedicate significant resources to housing (Falcon 2015). Council members didn't really disagree with their requests, but the issue at the time was that the city did not have the money. As Falcon explained, "No one on the council said, 'no, the rent is not too high or we don't need more resources attached to housing'" (2015). The push back on the campaign's requests tended to be trade-offs for other valuable goals, and the strategy then was to capitalize on opportunities for citizens to vote for their number one priority for the city. For instance, in the transition to Mayor Gray's administration in 2010, on the mayor's website and in a town hall meetings residents rated housing as their number one priority (Masliansky 2016). The trend also continued in the town-hall-style meetings held by Mayor Bowser in 2015, after her election.

Conclusions

The Housing for All Campaign responded to the Washington, D.C., affordability crisis primarily by seeking to preserve existing housing for low-income residents by increasing the budget to enforce laws "on the books" and expand ongoing programs. The ideology of campaign members tended to reinforce satisfaction with existing ordinances and institutions and to press for practical goals they knew would be achievable. A close relationship with the state, a favorable political environment, and significant resources also reinforced the campaign's ability to seek solutions within the current system. In 2015–2016, the previous five years of mobilizing residents, training them for testimony to the City Council, and negotiating with officials paid off as the City Council adopted the campaign's budget requests.

The campaign's success was ensured in large part through the civic capacity the organization built among supporters and the alliances they sought to deflect those opposed to their demands. In the end, the conservative nature of the campaign's requests, in part reflecting the perceived capacity of the D.C. government to address housing challenges and in part reflecting the interests of their members, also allowed the campaign to succeed. Campaign leaders now say that with the groundwork complete, they will move on to strengthening rent control and creating economic opportunities for low-income residents, goals that are much more controversial and complicated than increasing budgetary line items. Issues of displacement and the availability of affordable housing will not be solved by the campaign's efforts alone, but their strategies added to the growing sentiment that D.C. needs to act and that there are solutions that can garner broad-based support.

7

Toward Democratization of Urban Development?

What do these disparate cases tell us about the future of democratizing urban development to produce more inclusive cities? In sum, more democratic cities will require both a shift in thinking among community organizations about the value of inclusive governance and, further, a shift in the mentality of public officials and private-sector interests to view housing that is affordable to low-income residents as a solution to poverty rather than as a problem for development. These cases demonstrate that to reflect the goals of inclusion, the strategies of organizations need to move toward demanding greater voice from within the state, even as political opportunities, public advocacy, and strong laws remain key to bringing about victories for low-income housing. To a large extent, I find that community organizations are not relying on inclusionary strategies but rather find greater security and presumed effectiveness in indirect strategies of influence from the outside. The outcomes of these efforts do often successfully promote urban inclusion through prevention of displacement and investment in affordable housing, but, without further institutional reforms that reflect the norm of inclusive governance, community organizations still lack significant control over public decision making. To generate innovative solutions to housing and respond to the needs of low-income residents, community organizations will need to forcefully push for a voice from the inside.

The implication of the research is that ideology among community organizations and the relationship of these organizations with the state are both key to deepening democratic urban development. On the one hand, a rights-based ideology is not enough without a close relationship with the state as it leads to disengagement from reforming local politics. In the case of Rio, a rights-based ideology but a weak relationship with the state led the community to exit from local politics in order to expand the community organization's power to prevent displacement. But, as the moment of the Olympics passed, local politics remain largely unchanged. On the other hand, a close relationship with the state leads to complacency regarding broader structural challenges without a more radical ideology. In the case of Washington, D.C., the Housing for All Campaign met their goals by influencing local politicians, but without greater institutional inclusion they will always be at the mercy of decisions by others. The case of São Paulo demonstrates that a rights-based ideology combined with a close relationship with the state is also not a magic bullet toward greater inclusion in the decisions shaping urban development. Significant barriers, including financial capacity and uncontrollable political shifts, still limit the ability of community organizations to influence the implementation of policies and programs for housing. Finally, with neither a rights-based ideology nor a consistently strong relationship with the state, Atlanta housing activists are left to pursue incremental change without a transformation in local politics.

Strategies in Practice

In Chapter 2 I proposed four types of strategies pursued by community organizations: inclusionary, indirect, overhaul, and exit. Does this typology match the efforts of community organizations on the ground? Yes, though it is clear that organizations rely on a mix of strategies to push forward their agendas and that replacing the administration through an "overhaul" strategy was not overtly relevant in any of these cases. Social movement literature has long focused on the tactics of movements without examining the broader question of strategies, what I conceptualize as the varying trajectories of tactics defined by the means collective actors use to seek influence. Literature on governance often assumes a predisposition of civil society toward participatory institutions or other means of institutionalized voice within the state, which does not recognize the diversity of preferences of actors engaged in collective action. The typology I develop here serves to move beyond examining tactics alone and allows for reflection on the means of influence community organizations find most suitable and effective without presuming a preference for inside voice.

The overall hypothesis for this analysis was that we should see organizations adopting inclusionary strategies in response to global calls for inclusive governance. Among these case studies, however, only in São Paulo did housing organizations use institutions reflecting the ethos of inclusive participation to propose new housing programs, refine the scope of programs, and develop a new master plan for the city. Though institutions similar in name exist in Rio de Janeiro, the Residents' Association of Vila Autódromo and other NGO leaders with whom I spoke did not trust these spaces as instruments un-coopted by the city government and therefore did not seek to influence policies or programs through these mechanisms. In Washington, D.C., the Housing for All Campaign relied heavily on the tactic of providing testimony to the City Council as a means of swaying members' votes on the city budget, but organizers did not call for institutions in which to formalize their voices in decision making. In Atlanta, leaders of the HDDC expressed interest in a permanent oversight committee including members from civil society, but they were not adamant in their desire to prioritize the formation of such an institution.

Even if inclusive governance existed in greater measure across these cities, leaders would likely still rely on indirect strategies—bilateral meetings, mobilization among constituents, testimony to the city council, protest, and occupations—as a means of influencing the decisions of public officials. At some point, public officials and community organizations need to communicate their interests, and the electoral force of democracy will always make educating the public and disruptive actions important for generating political will. But the case of São Paulo also demonstrates how the two strategies—inclusionary and indirect—may complement one another. There, housing movements have worked within the participatory councils to elicit budgetary allocations for housing and shape inclusionary zoning rules, but protest, occupations, and bilateral meetings provide the impetus for implementation of programs when the government stalls on its promises. Activists in São Paulo have developed a model in which they make proposals, engage in public debate, and play a role in decision making within participatory institutions while also using the force of members in direct actions and relationships to public officials to push for implementation of programs. Through this model, organizations are able to be proactive in bringing their ideas to the table, exercising direct influence through voting procedures within the institution, while also following through to hold officials accountable. Though far from perfect in practice, the model provides a valuable playbook for activists in other cities.

In contrast, Vila Autódromo engaged in a model that took the means of influence outside of the city to the international community, already attuned to the country's troubles surrounding preparations for the World Cup and Olympics. While successful up to a point in preventing displacement and securing benefits for those who left the community, the course of action may not provide a workable model for most circumstances of displacement in which there is not some variety of external attention focused on a city. The international concern with the city's management of these two mega-events and the financial fallout that could have resulted from negative publicity, at least in part, persuaded the city government of Mayor Paes to respond to Vila Autódromo's demands. To be optimistic, changing public sentiment around favelas resulting from the efforts of Vila Autódromo and the community's allies could have an effect in forming a constituency around housing issues that would potentially change electoral outcomes and strengthen participatory institutions in the long run.

While in Washington, D.C., and Atlanta, leaders of community organizations expressed some interest in participatory institutions, a disposition presuming the centrality of representative democracy reduced support for measures to formally institutionalize civil society. In short, the cases do not demonstrate support for the hypothesis that community organizations are seeking greater avenues for inclusive governance.

Across countries, these case studies demonstrate that there is variation in the goals and choice of tactics, but there is also great similarity in the means by which organizations seek influence. Across cases, particularly in Washington, D.C., São Paulo, and Rio de Janeiro, organizations seek the force of law to protect residents from displacement. In Brazil, however, laws meant to remedy the long history of insecure property rights and informality are still subject to personal interpretation by judges (Fischer 2008). In both countries, though, community organizations seek to influence the outcomes of judicial actions by publicizing their cases and bringing public sympathy to their causes. The extent of the affordability crisis and the trend in these cities toward development geared to the wealthy provide compelling narratives to mobilize support among residents and public officials alike. Community organizations across cities, therefore, increasingly capitalize on the severity of the challenges to develop advocacy strategies.

Motivations for Strategies

In Chapter 2 I argued that ideology, the organization's relationship with the state, political opportunities, and resources all matter in the development of organizational strategies. In particular, I argued that an ideology based on the right to housing or the right to the city and a close relationship with the state would lead organizations to engage in inclusionary strategies, while a close relationship with the state without a rights-based ideology would lead to more indirect strategies. Political opportunities shift strategies toward influence of sympathetic officials or toward overhaul of the administration, depending on electoral and policy cycles. Finally, a lack of resources may necessitate networking and cooperation to build organizational capacity and also incentivize inclusionary strategies that involve less expenditure of money for advocacy efforts.

First, through the case studies I find that a rights-based ideology alone does not lead organizations to pursue inclusionary strategies. As demonstrated in São Paulo, a close relationship with the state, improved by the election of an allied administration, served to generate trust in participatory processes and increasing reliance on the participatory councils as spaces to prioritize efforts. But in Rio, where Vila Autódromo and the community's partners did not trust the participatory process, ideology was not enough to persuade them to seek resolution through similar institutions. While they did engage with the Defensoria Pública to pursue legal remedy, activists from Vila Autódromo knew from past experiences that the law alone would not prevent the city government from displacing the community. In Washington, D.C., the Housing for All Campaign did not adopt a strong rights-based ideology, though they did have a consistently close relationship with the city government. The close relationship motivated the campaign to seek influence with government officials through the networks created and by gathering increasing evidence of the affordability crisis in the city. Atlanta's HDDC had neither a rights-based ideology nor a close relationship with the state and did not pursue inclusionary strategies, but rather engaged in indirect strategies to limited effect. Though I hypothesized that a conservative ideology and weak relationship with the state would lead to overhaul strategies, in Atlanta this has not been the case.

The case studies lead me to conclude that in order to bring about inclusive governance in the United States, organizations will need to take a more radical stance while also working toward electing allies to office. That is not to say that government officials do not also need to change their ways of thinking about housing and inclusion, but the research in this book largely looks at the challenges of urban development from the perspective of community organizations. Though ideology alone is not a sufficient condition for organizations to pursue inclusionary strategies, it may be a necessary condition. Part of the reticence of U.S.-based organizations seems to stem from ideas about the role of civil society in government decision making. Of the nonprofit leaders I interviewed in the United States, there was a general sense that unelected members of civil society could not make a legitimate claim to direct participation within political institutions. Conversely, Brazil has a long history of corporatism and incorporation of special interests, especially unions, which has normalized the participation of civil society within the state and reduces the reticence of citizens to accept civil society's insertion in the policy arena. Moreover, to legitimize civil society inclusion in formal institutions and respond to latent criticism, participatory institutions in Brazil often do incorporate electoral selection of members. Though participatory institutions in Brazil are far from uniform, and in practice far from perfect, an exchange of best practices across contexts might generate further interest and understanding of participatory institutions in the United States.

Second, I find that community organizations are quite adept at taking advantage of political opportunities and accordingly modifying strategies to secure housing for low-income residents. In São Paulo, local movements took advantage of the political opening created by the election of a mayor from the Workers' Party to negotiate a new master plan that incorporated inclusionary zoning and expropriation of abandoned buildings for social housing. The HDDC in Atlanta also recognized an opening with the election of a new City Council member and worked with other local organizations to secure the passage of an inclusionary zoning bill, while in Washington, D.C., the Housing for All Campaign saw an opportunity with a new administration to work even harder to ensure housing was at the top of the new mayor's priorities. In the latter pair of cases, however, the pendulum did not swing toward new strategies; rather, the political opportunities presented an opening for more forceful activism to persuade new public officials of the importance of their demands. In neither case were the organizations particularly involved in the election of these new officials, meaning that their initial strategies had not involved a desire for overhauling the administration, but once there were new officeholders, the moment provided new ears to hear their requests. In Rio, both political and economic turmoil surrounding the World Cup and Olympics focused global attention on the city, to which Vila Autódromo and the community's partners deftly directed their efforts. The inflection of strategies based on political opportunities across these cases ranges from inclusionary to indirect to exit based on the circumstances of the opening and pre-existing factors, such as the presence of participatory institutions, the location of a new audience, and the scope of the opportunity. The impact of political opportunities on organizational strategies, therefore, is highly context specific, but evolving opportunities may serve to reinforce previous actions rather than incentivizing shifts in strategies.

Third, networking may be both part of an organization's strategy and a factor in determining the strategies an organization may pursue. In Rio, a lack of resources led the residents' association of Vila Autódromo to seek assistance from more well-connected academics and international NGOs. Given the modest scale of Vila Autódromo's single community, members knew they needed to link to higher-capacity organizations and a broader cause in order to be heard, even within their own city. I characterize Vila Autódromo's strategy as "exit" on the basis of its intent to influence global opinion first, which in turn would shape local government decisions, but the community could not have engaged in this strategy without first establishing a network of supporters within the city. In Atlanta, the HDDC has not expressly formed networks, but the community of housing organizations in the city is relatively small and activists tend to know each other. With only a small network of like-minded advocates, the HDDC has not been readily able to mobilize supporters for large-scale actions or sway elections in a meaningful way. The lack of a strong network, therefore, limits the HDDC's influence beyond conventional meetings with public officials.

In São Paulo and Washington, D.C., the UMM, FLM, and the Housing for All Campaign are umbrella organizations, in which smaller groups affiliate with the core organization to form the network. However, the effect of networking on strategies diverges across these two cities. In both cities the organizations used networks to build capacity of members and supporters to be able to participate within government institutions. The primary difference rests on the nature of the institutions and the intended influence of their voices. In São Paulo, the UMM and the FLM trained members to participate in occupations and protests as well as to become actively involved in participatory institutions and to negotiate the legal process through the Defensoria Pública. The Housing for All Campaign trained residents and other nonprofit leaders to identify and tell their own stories to public officials through testimony and visits to City Council members' offices in an effort to persuade them to invest in low-income housing and preserve existing affordable housing. In each case the networks created by the central organizations were mobilized for distinct purposes. These cases, then, demonstrate that networks alone do not influence the choice of inclusionary or indirect strategies; rather, the networks work in combination with ideological orientation and institutional context.

Outcomes

On the basis of these cases, what can we conclude about the impact of community organizations on preventing displacement, providing affordable housing, and strengthening institutions related to housing? In none of these cases did housing advocacy produce new institutional forms. But in all of the cases, on the basis of the efforts of local organizations, governments did provide some measure of increased resources toward housing and took steps to prevent the displacement of current low-income residents. For example, in two instances—Atlanta and São Paulo—new or improved inclusionary zoning laws were enacted. The strategies of the community organizations under study often yielded success in explicit goal achievement, but the narrow confines of these goals also inhibited greater demands for inclusive governance, thereby limiting the long-term structural effects of their efforts. In addition, the cases show the limitations of civil society influence in the face of insufficient government capacity or because of grassroots organizations' internal characteristics.

Perhaps the most disappointing outcome among the cases was the forced removal of the majority of residents from Vila Autódromo. Provision of nearby public housing, market-rate indemnity payments, and the eventual urbanization of the community for the remaining twenty residents do represent small victories, but these outcomes are far from the call of "no to all removals" originally articulated by the Residents' Association. Whether Vila Autódromo serves as a precedent for future removals or broader reforms remains uncertain. The community's exit strategy served the purpose in the moment, in that residents received far greater benefits than they would have if their story remained untold. In the long term, it may be that the public awareness generated by the global campaign to explain the value of favelas as a source of affordable housing and stable communities may change the hearts of voters. But with the two mega-events completed, international attention has shifted away from Rio, removing the financial consequences of negative press that brought about the positive benefits the community did receive. Though further study among a larger number of cases will be necessary, judging from this case alone, an exit strategy does not appear to generate lasting change in local politics or inclusive urban development. The community will need to regroup and continue networking across the city and the globe for long-term transformation, perhaps prioritizing the improvement of existing participatory institutions.

In São Paulo, where urban reform movements did employ a mix of inclusionary and indirect strategies, programs to reclaim city center buildings and reform inclusionary zoning laws are considerably more advanced when compared to the cities in which indirect strategies alone predominated. But the case of São Paulo also shows us that inclusionary strategies are imperfect as mechanisms for reform given other intervening variables. The shift toward more innovative policies and programs largely relied on the allied city administration in power, and as a new more conservative administration took over in 2017, the future of these innovations was in jeopardy. In addition, the shaky financial capacity of the city undeniably creates a tension between promises made and actual implementation. Inclusionary strategies, then, may bring about innovative policies and programs, but political change, money, and the will to prioritize housing in times of crisis limit the real effect of inside voice. Civil society influence is still only one factor among many determining policies and programs.

With financial resources for the time being plentiful, the City Council of Washington, D.C., responded positively to the Housing for All Campaign's requests for increasing funding, particularly to the Housing Production Trust Fund. Leaders built the campaign over the course of five years, knowing that, as the financial position of the city improved after the 2008 financial crisis, they would need to be ready with the capacity to persuade the council to prioritize their agenda. The civic capacity of the campaign, built on the governmental and nongovernmental experiences of the organizers, also enabled the success of the strategy to persuade government officials of the urgency of the housing crisis. The campaign defined their goals narrowly in terms of expanding resources for existing programs and was successful in their efforts. If they had instead sought to reform the housing bureaucracy in the city or implement more radical programs, they likely would have faced greater resistance. For-profit developers in the city do not necessarily agree with the increase in funding for the Housing Production Trust Fund, which keeps buildings for sale from entering the open market, but the program also does not disrupt their business model in serving the high-end market. The campaign set goals conservatively in terms of scope, though ambitiously in terms of fiscal allocation, and their indirect strategies paid off.

In Chapter 2, I argued that each type of strategy would have distinct outcomes, and the case studies largely bear out this conclusion: inclusionary strategies in São Paulo did lead to the adoption of policies and programs proposed by the organizations themselves; indirect strategies in Washington, D.C., did lead to increasing investment in

188 \ Chapter 7

existing programs; and an exit strategy in Rio did address the situation at hand without immediate, broader impact. The tenacity, commitment, and experience of the leadership in each of the organizations increased their ability to succeed in achieving their goals and adeptly implementing their chosen strategies. Alliances with local NGOs, global actors, concerned citizens across demographics, public officials, and private-sector interests also improved their ability to persuade government officials to meet their demands. In Brazil, the 2016 financial recession and political turn to the right limits the capacity and will of city governments to respond to concerns of low-income housing and further tests the ability of the judicial system to interpret legal provisions in favor of residents in informal settlements. In Washington, D.C., the political and economic tides are on the side of increasing investment in social programs, but at the same time increasing municipal revenues will continue to depend on increasing profits from development. The tension between civil society and private-sector interests remains strong.

Among these cases, Atlanta is an outlier in that indirect strategies have not yet succeeded in increasing investment in existing programs, but the efforts of the HDDC have been a part of the adoption of a new inclusionary zoning law and the creation of a housing trust fund. New political leadership and the new reality that housing prices are increasingly unaffordable to most residents have pushed the City Council to enact reform, but the HDDC leaders still struggle to mobilize support among neighborhood residents and city officials. Inadequate funding for housing programs limits their ability to act as a community development corporation within the Old Fourth Ward, and to date they are still grappling with a plan to prevent further erosion of affordable housing in the neighborhood. A formal institution to collectivize knowledge and debate about gentrification and displacement might allow the HDDC to generate the solutions for which they are searching.

All of these organizations were skilled in shaping their goals and activities to match the realities in which they existed. In doing so they elicited public benefits for residents and the promise of laws that should promote inclusive urban development into the future. The challenge, however, will be in promoting inclusive governance to enable bottom-up rather than top-down development. Cities may invest in more programs that allow low-income residents to stay within the bounds of the city, but without greater political voice from below to propose new programs and policies, cities still will not truly belong to the people. The increasing influence of community organizations, particularly in the United States, does indicate that we are living in "a new era," as Stone and his colleagues asserted (2015), but this new era is still vulnerable to breakdown and incomplete in terms of the institutions that will enable formalized voice by civil society.

Conclusions

Inclusive cities will not form on their own, but to become reality will require massive, concerted effort, especially by community organizations with the most at stake. The ideal, of course, may remain just that: a vision for the type of city we would want if we could choose. But this research points to a number of straightforward conclusions to direct future strategies of community organizations. First, think big. While an ideology that favors the promotion of the right to housing or the right to the city is not sufficient to create structural change, establishing the goal of structural change in the city is a vital step toward transforming urban development. Second, elect allies. A strong relationship with the state is necessary for establishing open dialogue and respect across community organizations, the private sector, and government actors, and too often, it appears, housing organizations are not getting involved in campaigns to elect leaders they can trust as allies. Third, build alliances both locally and globally. Building networks of global knowledge and support strengthens the ability of community organizations to influence local politics, but local supporters are also critical to reshaping politics within cities. Fourth, and finally, "lean in." Even when city officials are allies and access to them seems assured, don't underestimate the importance of who is making final decisions and seek greater influence from inside the halls of power.

While the study of urban politics has to date neglected comparisons across cities that vary by political and economic history, the truth is that cities today face similar challenges despite seeming differences, and we cannot forgo comparison because of an ingrained bias toward controlling for all potentially confounding variables. The case studies in this book demonstrate the challenges of comparing diverse cities, but until we make these comparisons, we cannot know whether and how differences in cities matter for political behavior and policy outcomes. Cities in the United States and Brazil vary considerably in terms of settlement types, existing institutions, and ideas regarding the role of civil society, but as this study illustrates, these cities are all facing significant challenges in resolving the contradictions in the aims and consequences of development. Community organizations across cities will play a substantial role in resolving these contradictions toward greater democratic urban development on the basis of the means they find for influence and the political will they generate for positive solutions.

Notes

Introduction

1. For further information, see the *Washington City Paper* and the *Washington Post,* which have followed this case extensively. See, e.g., https://www.washingtonpost.com/news/local/wp/2016/02/25/residents-of-low-income-chinatown-building-are-still-fighting-to-stay-in-the-neighborhood/.

2. Estimates come from Garau, Sclar, and Carolini 2005.

3. Study presented by Dr. Shlomo Angel, professor at New York University, to the United Nations Habitat III Conference in Quito, Ecuador, October 2016. Data available at atlasofurbanexpansion.org.

4. For example, in a study of New York City, Lance Freeman and Frank Braconi (2004) found that gentrification did not lead to displacement of low-income residents, though they did find that when rental units became available, they were more likely to be leased to middle- and upper-income households, gradually leading to the decrease of low-rent housing. Kathe Newman and Elvin Wyly (2006) then broadened the time horizon of this study and found that, in fact, 6–10 percent of all moves in New York City were the result of economic displacement.

5. For example, residents of a low-income apartment building in D.C.'s Chinatown filed a lawsuit against the owner when they were told they would have to either purchase the building for an exorbitant amount or leave. See the August 7, 2014, *Washington Post,* at http://www.washingtonpost.com/local/black-and-asian-residents-unite-to-savelow-income-building-on-edge-of-chinatown/2014/08/06/552accf0-189c-11e4-85b6-c1451e622637_story.html.

6. I use plural pronouns to refer to groups to emphasize that they represent individuals rather than corporate entities.

Chapter 1

1. For further details, see Chapter 5 on São Paulo.

2. Available at http://portal.hud.gov/hudportal/HUD?src=/about/mission, accessed February 10, 2015.

3. From the website of the Caixa Economica Federal, which administers the Minha Casa Minha Vida Program, available at http://www.caixa.gov.br/voce/habitacao/minha-casa-minha-vida/urbana/Paginas/default.aspx.

4. From an article posted on RioOnWatch, available at http://www.rioonwatch.org/?p=14887. According to the article, about half of the units in Rio were to house residents forcibly removed from favelas in the time leading up to the World Cup and the Olympics. Many residents contended that these units are generally far from their original homes, are smaller in size, and are increasingly controlled by militias.

5. For a discussion and text of the Statute of the City in English, see Pólis Institute 2001.

6. The Low-Income Housing Tax Credit (LIHTC) was created by the U.S. Congress as the Tax Reform Act of 1986. According to HUD, "The LIHTC program gives state and local LIHTC-allocating agencies [generally Housing Authorities] the equivalent of nearly $8 billion in annual budget authority to issue tax credits for the acquisition, rehabilitation, or new construction of rental housing targeted to lower-income households." HUD then maintains a public database of affordable rental units. See https://www.huduser.gov/portal/datasets/lihtc.html.

7. For further details on the Minha Casa Minha Vida Program, see, in Portuguese, "Minha Casa Minha Vida: Recursos FAR," from the Caixa Econômica Federal, available at http://www.caixa.gov.br/poder-publico/programas-uniao/habitacao/minha-casa-minha-vida/Paginas/default.aspx, or, in English, "Minha Casa Minha Vida: An Overview of New Public Housing in Rio," from RioOnWatch, available at http://www.rioonwatch.org/?p=14887.

8. Between twenty-five and eighteen respondents out of seventy-five cited these factors as having "significant influence" on local policies. For further information, see https://urbangovernance.net/en/.

Chapter 2

1. For a discussion of the increasing commodification of housing and the need to prioritize housing as "home" rather than real estate, see Marcuse and Madden 2016. The authors of this work detail the history of housing and mobilization in New York City.

2. See, e.g., Almeida and Johnston 2006; Auyero 2007; Auyero, Lapegna, and Poma 2009; Giarracca 2001; Giraudy 2007; Levitsky 2003; López-Maya and Lander 2006; Shefner, Pasdirtz, and Blad 2006; Stokes 2005; Svampa and Pereyra 2009; Tarrow 1994.

Chapter 3

1. For an analysis of removals in Rio under the dictatorship, see Valladares 1978.

2. Reported by the Brazilian newspaper *Folha* from a study by the Savills real estate company. Available at http://www1.folha.uol.com.br/mercado/2014/09/1521749-

rio-e-a-cidade-que-mais-encareceu-no-mundo-aponta-pesquisa.shtml, accessed July 6, 2015.

3. Bus Rapid Transit (BRT) involves dedicated bus lanes to facilitate faster transport. The construction of BRTs requires additional land and may require expropriations.

4. See, e.g., *New York Times* 2012 and Watts 2013.

5. For a characterization of the Barra da Tijuca neighborhood, see Herzog 2013.

6. For further discussion of the community's history (in English) and a comparison to Atlanta's experience with the 1996 Olympics, see Vale and Gray 2013.

7. According to Rio de Janeiro's Secretariat for Housing (Secretaria Municipal de Habitação, Cidade do Rio de Janeiro 2010), approximately thirty thousand residents completed the regularization of tenure process between 1994 and 2010.

8. As evidence of the continuous coverage of Vila Autódromo, a search for the community on *The Guardian* website in July 2016 resulted in forty-six related articles.

9. Data from the Brazilian Tribunal Superior Eleitoral, available at http://www.tse.jus.br/.

10. The Urban Age Program at the London School for Economics awarded the community a cash prize to support urbanization according to the Popular Plan.

11. In 2012 President Rousseff and former president Lula da Silva endorsed Paes for mayor.

12. Datafolha survey following protests, July 1, 2013, available at http://www.datafolha.folha.uol.com.br.

13. This information comes from author correspondence with Giselle Tanaka, member of the Popular Committee for the World Cup and the Olympics, in 2014, and LISTSERV announcements from the NGO Centro Vivo following the June protests.

14. For example, an article from *The Guardian* quoted Altair Guimarães of Vila Autódromo: available at http://www.theguardian.com/global-development/2013/jun/18/brazil-protests-peoples-cup-evictions, accessed March 13, 2015. The *New York Times* has also published a number of articles referring to Vila Autódromo; see, e.g., *New York Times* 2012.

Chapter 4

1. But see the work of Michael Rich, who finds largely positive results. See, e.g., Rich 2015.

2. On the median rental price and increase, see data from 2008 to the present at http://www.zillow.com/atlanta-ga/home-values/.

Chapter 5

1. Irregular settlements are those in which residents have access to basic services and infrastructure but do not have proper land titles. The area may have

been illegally subdivided or constructed. Favelas generally lack access to some basic services and infrastructure, are incrementally built by squatters, and lack basic land rights. I use the terms "informal settlements" or "favelas" to refer to communities lacking land rights.

2. President Getúlio Vargas established the minimum salary (i.e., minimum wage) for Brazil in 1936. Today, the amount needed to "attend to the basic necessities of workers and their families, including housing, food, education, health, leisure, hygiene, transportation, and social welfare" as guaranteed by the constitution equals approximately four to five times the minimum salary, according to DIESSE (Departamento Intersindical de Estatística e Estudos Socioeconômicos) 2005 statistics (see http://www.dieese.org.br/).

3. I have chosen to use the term "informal communities" here to include residents who live in a variety of circumstances, including city center building occupations, unserviced squatter settlements, and neighborhoods that started as occupations but now have some form of legal right to land use. To monitor and study these new incidences of removals, a group of faculty members from the Department of Architecture and Urbanism at the University of São Paulo started the Observatório das Remoções. Using news reports, academic research, and violations reported to the United Nations Special Rapporteur for Adequate Housing, the group documented 177 communities in the metropolitan region that had either been removed or notified of potential removal by the municipal government (Observatório de Remoções 2012). Of these, approximately half were engaged in some form of dispute with the initiator of the removal, whether the state government, the municipal government, or a private property owner. The great majority of these conflicts involved communities for which the justification for removal was the construction of public works projects. Communities in which residents were being removed for urbanization projects or because their homes were deemed to be in areas of risk were somewhat less common and less likely to generate disputes among the parties. This may be because the majority of the community members were able to remain in place, while only a portion of the community members were threatened with removal to make room for improvements. Though some of these removals were tied to construction for the 2014 World Cup, the majority of them were a result of general processes of development and gentrification in the city.

4. The federal government began the Minha Casa Minha Vida (My House My Life) Program in 2009 in order to stimulate the construction sector amid the global financial crisis. The program provides financing and funds construction, targeting citizens earning up to ten minimum salaries, or approximately $3,000 per month. Units are targeted to either those earning from ten to seven, six to four, or under three minimum salaries. As of 2014, about $23 billion was made available for housing production, with 60 percent of funds going to those earning between three and ten minimum salaries, even though this group represents only 9 percent of the housing deficit (Cruz Rufino 2016, 223).

5. As described above, Brazil's minimum salary is regulated by federal law and is frequently used as a measure to categorize income. The current minimum salary is approximately $300 per month.

6. The movements refer to "dignified" housing (*moradia digna*) as their primary goal. "Dignified" housing includes basic amenities—kitchen, bathroom, bedroom, and living space—and offers residents physical security and a measure of respect within the city.

7. For instance, Bruhn (2008) found that during several administrations of the Workers' Party, the housing movements believed they had adequate access to officials through institutional channels and hence had no need to protest.

8. The movements lack trust in the judiciary to fairly resolve property conflicts involving property owners, and the evidence appears to confirm their perception of bias. For instance, Maria Laura de Souza Coutinho (2010) reviewed five hundred decisions involving the right to housing issued by the São Paulo Court of Appeals from 2000 to 2010 and found that almost all of the cases were decided in favor of property owners.

9. In the 1980s in Brazil, Mainwaring (1987) found that common identity formation was difficult to cultivate among heterogeneous social movements and that many people believed change would come through their own individual circumstances rather than political participation.

Chapter 6

1. I remember, as a child growing up in the D.C. Metropolitan Region in the 1980s, the presence of drug addicts on the streets, the nighttime desolation of the streets among the surrounding downtown federal government offices, and the rats that took over abandoned lots.

2. Available at http://dcinno.streetwise.co/2015/02/10/percent-renters-wash ington-dc-nationwide/, accessed February 13, 2015.

3. For example, residents of a low-income apartment building in D.C.'s Chinatown filed a lawsuit against the owner when they were told they would either have to purchase the building for an exorbitant amount or leave. See the August 7, 2014, *Washington Post*, available at http://www.washingtonpost.com/local/black-and-asian-residents-unite-to-savelow-income-building-on-edge-of-chinatown/20 14/08/06/552accf0-189c-11e4-85b6-c1451e622637_story.html.

4. The campaign budget requests for 2015 were the dedication of $100 million to the Housing Production Trust Fund, an increase of $8 million for the Home Purchase Assistance Program (HPAP) and an increase of the maximum allowable loan amount, an increase of $11.9 million to the Housing First Program, an increase of $5 million for the project-based and sponsor-based Local Rent Supplement Program (LRSP) to produce new housing for individuals and families with extremely low incomes, and $5 million for the tenant-based LRSP vouchers.

References

Abers, Rebecca. 1996. "From Ideas to Practice: The Partido dos Trabalhadores and Participatory Governance in Brazil." *Latin American Perspectives* 23 (4): 35–53.

Abers, Rebecca Neaera, and Margaret E. Keck. 2009. "Mobilizing the State: The Erratic Partner in Brazil's Participatory Water Policy." *Politics and Society* 37 (2): 289–314.

Acharya, Arnab, Adrian Gurza Lavalle, and Peter Houtzager. 2004. "Representation in the Participatory Budget and Deliberative Councils of São Paulo, Brazil." *Institute for Development Studies Bulletin* 35 (2): 42–48.Ackerman, John. 2004. "Co-governance for Accountability: Beyond 'Exit' and 'Voice.'" *WD World Development* 32 (3): 447–463.

Alexander, James. 2015. Interview by the author. May. Atlanta.

Alinsky, Saul. 1969. *Reveille for Radicals*. New York: Vintage Books.

Almeida, Paul D., and Hank Johnston, eds. 2006. *Latin American Social Movements: Globalization, Democratization, and Transnational Networks*. Lanham, Md.: Rowman and Littlefield.

American Community Survey (ACS). 2014. "American FactFinder—Results." *American FactFinder*. U.S. Census Bureau. Available at https://factfinder.census.gov/faces/tableservices/jsf/pages/productview.xhtml?src=bkm.

Andranovich, Greg, Matthew J. Burbank, and Charles H. Heying. 2002. "Mega-Events, Urban Development, and Public Policy." *Review of Policy Research* 19, no. 3 (Fall): 179–202.

Angotti, Tom. 2013. "Urban Latin America: Violence, Enclaves, and Struggles for Land." *Latin American Perspectives* 40 (2): 5–20.

Arias, Enrique Desmond. 2004. "Faith in Our Neighbors: Networks and Social Order in Three Brazilian Favelas." *Latin American Politics and Society* 46 (1): 1–38.

—. 2006. *Drugs and Democracy in Rio de Janeiro: Trafficking, Social Networks, and Public Security*. Chapel Hill: University of North Carolina Press.

Arretche, Marta. 2012. Interview by the author. May. São Paulo.

Atlanta BeltLine. 2017. "How the BeltLine Is Funded." *Atlanta BeltLine*. Available at http://beltline.org/about/the-atlanta-beltline-project/funding/.

Auyero, Javier. 2007. *Routine Politics and Violence in Argentina: The Gray Zone of State Power*. New York: Cambridge University Press.

Auyero, Javier, Pablo Lapegna, and Fernanda Page Poma. 2009. "Patronage Politics and Contentious Collective Action: A Recursive Relationship." *Latin American Politics and Society* 51 (3): 1–31.

Avritzer, Leonardo. 2009. *Participatory Institutions in Democratic Brazil*. Baltimore: Johns Hopkins University Press.

Axelrod, Robert. 1997. *The Complexity of Cooperation: Agent-Based Models of Competition and Collaboration*. Princeton, N.J.: Princeton University Press.

Azevedo, Lena, and Lucas Faulhaber. 2015. "SMH 2016: Remoçoes no Rio de Janeiro Olimpico." Rio de Janeiro: Mórula Editorial.

Baiocchi, Gianpaolo. 2001. "Participation, Activism, and Politics: The Porto Alegre Experiment and Deliberative Democratic Theory." *Politics and Society* 29 (1): 43–72.

—. 2005. *Militants and Citizens: The Politics of Participatory Democracy in Porto Alegre*. Palo Alto, Calif.: Stanford University Press.

Baiocchi, Gianpaolo, Patrick Heller, and Marcelo Silva. 2011. *Bootstrapping Democracy: Transforming Local Governance and Civil Society in Brazil*. Stanford, Calif.: Stanford University Press.

Banaszak, Lee Ann. 2010. *The Women's Movement inside and outside the State*. Cambridge: Cambridge University Press.

Barbosa, Benedito Roberto. 2013. Interview by the author. January. São Paulo.

—. 2015. Interview by the author. April. São Paulo.

Barros, Ciro. 2013. "Altair enfrenta a terceira remoção da vida pelas Olimpíadas." *A Pública*, June 21. Available at http://www.apublica.org/2013/06/altair-en frenta-terceira-remocao-da-vida-pelas-olimpiadas/.

BBC. 2016. "Rio Shanty Town Cleared for Olympics." February 27. Available at http://www.bbc.co.uk/newsround/35670737.

Belda-Miquel, Sergio, Jordi Peris Blanes, and Alexandre Frediani. 2016. "Institutionalization and Depoliticization of the Right to the City: Changing Scenarios for Radical Social Movements." *International Journal of Urban and Regional Research* 40:321–339.

Belisário, Adriano. 2014. "As quatro irmás (The four sisters)." *Pública*. June 30. Available at http://apublica.org/2014/06/as-quatro-irmas/.

Berta, Ruben. 2015. "Apesar de indenizações milionárias, prefeitura não consegue acabar com a Vila Autódromo: Em meio a escombros, cerca de 170 famílias ainda vivem na comunidade, que é vizinha ao Parque Olímpico da Barra da Tijuca." *O Globo*, May 14. Available at http://oglobo.globo.com/rio/apesar-deindenizacoes-milionarias-prefeitura-nao-consegue-acabar-com-vila-autodro mo-16153064.

Berube, Alan, and Natalie Holmes. 2015. "Some Cities Are Still More Unequal than Others—An Update." *Brookings.* March 17. Available at https://www.brookings .edu/research/some-cities-are-still-more-unequal-than-others-an-update/.

Bilonick, Marla. 2016. Presentation by the executive director of the Latino Economic Development Center during the CNHED Monthly Meeting regarding the CNHED report "Vision to Action: How CNHED's Housing for All Campaign Led DC from Drastic Cuts to Momentous Investments in Affordable Housing." January 21. Washington, D.C.

Bobo, Kimberley A., Jackie Kendall, and Steve Max. 2001. *Organizing for Social Change: Midwest Academy Manual for Activists.* 3rd ed. Santa Ana, Calif.: Seven Locks Press.

Borges, Osmar. 2015. Interview by the author. April. São Paulo.

Brenner, Neil, Peter Marcuse, and Margit Mayer, eds. 2012. *Cities for People, Not for Profit: Critical Urban Theory and the Right to the City.* New York: Routledge.

Briggs, Xavier de Souza. 2008. *Democracy as Problem Solving: Civic Capacity in Communities across the Globe.* Cambridge, Mass.: MIT Press.

Brookings Institution. 2012. "São Paulo Metropolitan Area Profile." *Brookings.* Available at http://www.brookings.edu/about/programs/metro/.

Bruhn, Kathleen. 2008. *Urban Protest in Mexico and Brazil.* New York: Cambridge University Press.

Buraco Quente Community Residents. 2013. Interview by the author. January 20. São Paulo.

Caldeira, Teresa P. R. 2001. *City of Walls: Crime, Segregation, and Citizenship in São Paulo.* Berkeley: University of California Press.

Cardoso, Auduto Lúcio, and Cleber Lago do Valle. 2000. "Habitação e governança urbana: Avaliação da experiência em 10 cidades brasileiras" [Housing and urban governance: Evaluation of the experience in 10 Brazilian cities]. *Cadernos Metrópole* 4:33–63.

Castells, Manuel. 2009. *The Rise of the Network Society: The Information Age: Economy, Society, and Culture.* Vol. 1. 2nd ed. Chichester, U.K.: Wiley-Blackwell.

Castro, Julian. 2016. Presentation to Habitat III: The United Nations Conference on Housing and Sustainable Development. October. Quito, Ecuador.

Charner, Flora. 2016. "Rio 2016: Neighborhood Demolished to Clear Path for the Olympics." CNN, March 10. Available at http://edition.cnn.com/2016/03/10/ sport/rio-olympics-2016-favela-demolition/index.html.

Clos, J. 2016. Presentation to Habitat III: The United Nations Conference on Housing and Sustainable Development. October. Quito, Ecuador.

CNHED. 2014. "What Is the Housing for All Campaign?" Coalition for Nonprofit Housing and Economic Development. Available at https://www.cnhed.org/ housing-for-all-campaign/.

———. 2016. "Vision to Action: How the Housing for All Campaign Led Washington, DC from Drastic Cuts to Momentous Investments in Housing Funding." Coalition for Nonprofit Housing and Economic Development and the Center for Community Change. Available at http://h4all.cnhed.org/wp-content/uploads/2016/02/H4AllCaseStudy_Online.pdf.

COHAB. 2015. Interview by the author. April. São Paulo.

Colomb, Claire, and Johannes Novy, eds. 2016. *Protest and Resistance in the Tourist City*. Abingdon, U.K.: Routledge.

Committee on Housing and Community Development of the D.C. City Council. 2015. Performance Oversight Hearing. February 26. Washington, D.C.

Coslovsky, S. V. 2015. "Beyond Bureaucracy: How Prosecutors and Public Defenders Enforce Urban Planning Laws in São Paulo, Brazil." *International Journal of Urban and Regional Research* 39 (6): 1103–1119.

Coutinho, Maria Laura de Souza. 2010. "Ativismo judicial: Uma análise a partir do direito à moradia" [Judicial activism: An analysis of the right to housing]. Master's thesis, Fundação Getúlio Vargas, São Paulo.

Crouch, Heather. 2015. Interview by the author. March. Washington, D.C.

Cruz Rufino, Maria Beatriz. 2016. "Transformação da periferia e novas formas de desigualdades nas metrópoles brasileiras: Um olhar sobre as mudanças na produção habitacional." *Cadernos Metrópoles* 18 (35): 217–236.

Cury Construction Executive. 2012. Interview by the author. May. São Paulo.

DC Fiscal Policy Institute. 2015. "Going, Going, Gone: DC's Vanishing Affordable Housing." March 12. Available at http://www.dcfpi.org/going-going-gone-dcs-vanishing-affordable-housing-2.

DC Preservation Network. 2014. "Maintaining Economic Diversity and Affordability: A Strategy for Preserving Affordable Rental Housing in the District of Columbia." Washington, D.C.: Preservation Strategy Working Group.

DeFilippis, James. 2001. "The Myth of Social Capital in Community Development." *Housing Policy Debate* 12 (4): 781–806.

DHCD (Washington, D.C., Department of Housing and Community Development). 2016. "Mission and Vision." DC.gov. Available at https://dhdc.dc.gov/page/mission-and-vision-DHCD.

Dickens, Andre. 2016. Interview by the author. Atlanta.

District, Measured. 2015. "Homeownership in the District." *District, Measured: Posts from the District of Columbia's Office of Revenue Analysis*. Available at http://districtmeasured.com/2015/05/page/2/.

District of Columbia. 2015. "2016 DC Budget." Available at http://cfo.dc.gov/sites/default/files/dc/sites/ocfo/publication/attachments/2016_DCBudget_V2_Opt.pdf. Accessed August 15, 2016.

———. 2016. "Pathways to the Middle Class: FY 2016 Proposed Budget and Financial Plan." https://cfo.dc.gov/sites/default/files/dc/sites/ocfo/publication/attachments/2016_DCBudget_V3_Opt_2.pdf.

Donaghy, Maureen. 2013. *Civil Society and Participatory Governance: Municipal Councils and Social Housing Programs in Brazil*. New York: Routledge.

Dosh, Paul Gandhi Joseph. 2010. *Demanding the Land: Urban Popular Movements in Peru and Ecuador, 1990–2005*. University Park: Pennsylvania State University Press.

Dowbor, Monika. 2012. "A arte da institucionalização: Estratégias de mobilização dos sanitaristas (1974–2006)" [The art of institutionalization: Mobilization strategies of the Sanitarista Movement in São Paulo (1974–2006)]. Ph.D. thesis, Universidade de São Paulo.

Eckstein, Susan, and Manuel Antonio Garretón Merino, eds. 2001. *Power and Popular Protest: Latin American Social Movements*. Berkeley: University of California Press.

Editorial Board. 2014. "Sky's the Limit for Atlanta Rents: Ponce City Market Leases Are Just a Sampling." *Creative Loafing Atlanta*, April 23. Available at http://clatl.com/atlanta/skys-the-limit-for-atlanta-rents/Content?oid=10985233.

Evans, Peter, ed. 2002. *Livable Cities? Urban Struggles for Livelihood and Sustainability*. Berkeley: University of California Press.

Falcon, Elizabeth. 2015. Interview by the author. February. Washington, D.C.

———. 2016. Interview by the author. January. Washington, D.C.

FASE Coordinators. 2012. Interview by the author. July. Rio de Janeiro.

Fason, James. 2015. Interview by the author. May. Atlanta.

Fidelity Investments. 2013. "Are the Olympics a Golden Opportunity for Investors?" Available at https://www.fidelity.com/binpublic/060_www_fidelity_com/documents/Are%20the%20Olympics%20a%20Golden%20Opportunity%20for%20Investors_Fidelity.pdf.

Fischer, Brodwyn M. 2008. *A Poverty of Rights: Citizenship and Inequality in Twentieth-Century Rio de Janeiro*. Stanford, Calif.: Stanford University Press.

Fix, Mariana. 2001. *Parceiros da exclusão: Duas histórias da construção de uma "nova cidade" em São Paulo: Faria Lima e Água Espraiada*. São Paulo: Boitempo Editorial.

Flor, Katarine, and Gláucia Marinho. 2013. "A favela agora virou a alma do negócio." *Brasil de Fato*, January 8. Available at http://www.brasildefato.com.br/node/11477.

Fosse, Farah. 2015. Interview by the author. April. Washington, D.C.

Foweraker, Joe. 2005. "Towards a Political Sociology of Social Mobilization in Latin America." In *Rethinking Development in Latin America*, edited by Charles H. Wood and Bryan R. Roberts, 115–135. University Park: Pennsylvania State University Press.

Fox, Jonathan. 1996. "How Does Civil Society Thicken? The Political Construction of Social Capital in Rural Mexico." *World Development* 24 (6): 1089–1103.

Freeman, Lance, and Frank Braconi. 2004. "Gentrification and Displacement: New York City in the 1990s." *Journal of the American Planning Association* 70 (1): 39–52.

Frey, Klaus. 2007. "Governança urbana e participação pública" [Urban governance and public participation]. *RAC-eletrônica* 1:136–150.

Friendly, Abigail. 2013. "The Right to the City: Theory and Practice in Brazil." *Planning Theory and Practice* 14 (2): 158–179.

Fundação João Pinheiro. 2013. "Déficit habitacional municipal no Brasil 2010." Available at http://www.fjp.mg.gov.br/index.php/docman/cei/deficit-habitacional/216-deficit-habitacional-municipal-no-brasil-2010/file.

———. 2015. "Déficit habitacional no Brasil 2011–2012." Available at http://www.fjp.mg.gov.br/index.php/docman/cei/559-deficit-habitacional-2011-2012/file.

Fung, Archon. 2009. *Empowered Participation: Reinventing Urban Democracy.* Princeton, N.J.: Princeton University Press.

Fung, Archon, and Erik Olin Wright. 2003. *Deepening Democracy: Institutional Innovations in Empowered Participatory Governance.* New York: Verso.

Gallaher, Carolyn. 2016. *The Politics of Staying Put: Condo Conversion and Tenant Right-to-Buy in Washington, DC.* Philadelphia: Temple University Press.

Gamson, William A. 1990. *The Strategy of Social Protest.* 2nd ed. Belmont, Calif.: Wadsworth.

Garau, P., E. D. Sclar, and G. Y. Carolini. 2005. *A Home in the City: United Nations Millennium Project Task Force on Improving the Lives of Slum Dwellers.* London: Earthscan. Available at www.unmillenniumproject.org/documents/Slumdwellers-complete.pdf.

Garcia-Navarro, Lulu. 2016. "As the Olympics Loom, Brazil Lurches from One Crisis to the Next." NPR, March 14. Available at http://www.npr.org/sections/parallels/2016/03/14/470116613/as-the-olympics-loom-brazil-lurches-from-one-crisis-to-the-next.

Gay, Robert. 1994. *Popular Organization and Democracy in Rio de Janeiro.* Philadelphia: Temple University Press.

Giarracca, Norma. 2001. ¿Una *nueva ruralidad en América Latina?* Buenos Aires: CLACSO.

Giraudy, Agustina. 2007. "The Distributive Politics of Emergency Employment Programs in Argentina (1993–2002)." *Latin American Research Review* 42 (2): 33–55.

Gittell, Ross, and Avis Vidal. 1998. *Community Organizing: Building Social Capital as a Development Strategy.* Thousand Oaks, Calif.: SAGE Publications.

Glaude, Steven. 2016. Presentation by the executive director of CNHED during the CNHED Monthly Meeting regarding the CNHED report "Vision to Action: How CNHED's Housing for All Campaign Led DC from Drastic Cuts to Momentous Investments in Affordable Housing." January 21. Washington, D.C.

Goldman, Michael. 2014. "Development and the City." In *Cities of the Global South Reader,* edited by Faranak Mirftab and Neema Kudva, 55–64. New York: Routledge.

Goodwin, Jeff, and James Jasper, eds. 2004. *Rethinking Social Movements: Structure, Meaning and Emotion.* Lanham, Md.: Rowman and Littlefield.

Greene, Solomon. 2003. "Staged Cities: Mega-Events, Slum Clearance, and Global Capital." *Yale Human Rights and Development Law Journal* 6 (1): 161–187.

Griffin, Jo. 2016. "Change Beckons for Vila Autódromo, the Favela that Got in the Rio Olympics' Way." *The Guardian,* April 26, Global Development section. Available at https://www.theguardian.com/global-development/2016/apr/26/rio-de-janeiro-favela-change-vila-autodromo-favela-olympics.

Guimarães, Altair. 2012. Interview by the author. July. Rio de Janeiro.

Hall, Kwanza. 2016. Interview by the author. May. Atlanta.

Hall, Nina L., and Ros Taplin. 2007. "Revolution or Inch-by-Inch? Campaign Approaches on Climate Change by Environmental Groups." *The Environmentalist* 27 (1): 95–107. doi:10.1007/s10669-007-9022-y.

Hankins, Katherine, Mechelle Puckett, Deirdre Oakley, and Erin Ruel. 2014. "Forced Mobility: The Relocation of Public-Housing Residents in Atlanta." *Environment and Planning* 46 (12): 2932–2949.

Harsch, Ernest. 2009. "Urban Protest in Burkina Faso." *African Affairs* 108 (431): 263–288. doi:10.1093/afraf/adp018.

Harvard University Joint Center for Housing Studies. 2016. "The State of the Nation's Housing 2016." Available at http://www.jchs.harvard.edu/sites/jchs .harvard.edu/files/jchs_2016_state_of_the_nations_housing_lowres.pdf.

Harvey, David. 2003. "The Right to the City." *International Journal of Urban and Regional Research* 27 (4): 939–941.

Helwege, Ann. 2015. "Social Polarization and Economic Instability: Twin Challenges for Enduring Reform." In *Enduring Reform: Progressive Activism and Private Sector Responses in Latin America's Democracies,* edited by Jeffrey W. Rubin and Vivienne Bennett, 27–52. Pittsburgh: University of Pittsburgh Press.

Herzog, Lawrence A. 2013. "Barra Da Tijuca: The Political Economy of a Global Suburb in Rio de Janeiro, Brazil." *Latin American Perspectives* 40 (2): 118–134.

Hirata, Marcia. 2012. "Márcia Hirata: Sem o direito à cidade, a cidade não vale a pena." *Viomundo,* November 26. Available at http://www.viomundo.com .br/politica/marcia-hirata-sem-o-direito-a-cidade-a-cidade-nao-vale-a-pena .html. Accessed January 13, 2017.

Hirschman, Albert O. 1970. *Exit, Voice, and Loyalty: Responses to Decline in Firms, Organizations, and States.* Cambridge, Mass.: Harvard University Press.

Historic District Development Corporation (HDDC). 2016. "HDDC.net." Available at http://www.hddc.net/home.

Hochstetler, Kathryn, and Margaret E. Keck. 2007. *Greening Brazil: Environmental Activism in State and Society.* Durham, N.C.: Duke University Press.

Holston, James. 2008. *Insurgent Citizenship: Disjunctions of Democracy and Modernity in Brazil.* Princeton, N.J.: Princeton University Press.

Horak, Martin. 2007. *Governing the Post-Communist City: Institutions and Democratic Development in Prague.* Toronto: University of Toronto Press.

HUD. 2017. "Affordable Housing—CPD—HUD." *Affordable Housing.* U.S. Department of Housing and Urban Development. Available at https://portal .hud.gov/hudportal/HUD?src=/program_offices/comm_planning/afford ablehousing/. Accessed January 10.

IBGE. 2014a. "An Analysis of the Living Conditions of the Brazilian Population 2014." Brazilian Institute of Geography and Statistics. Available at http://www .ibge.gov.br/english/estatistica/populacao/condicaodevida/indicadores minimos/sinteseindicsociais2014/default_tab_xls.shtm. Accessed December 30.

———. 2014b. "Cidades: Rio de Janeiro." Brazilian Institute of Geography and Statistics. Available at http://cidades.ibge.gov.br/xtras/perfil.php.

Immergluck, Dan. 2015. "Examining Recent Declines in Low-Cost Rental Housing in Atlanta, Using American Community Survey Data from 2006–2010 to 2009–2013: Implications for Local Affordable Housing Policy." Available at https://www.scribd.com/document/284775500/Loss-of-Low-Cost-Rentals-Atlanta-by-Dan-Immergluck-Oct-2015.

Immergluck, Dan, Ann Carpenter, and Abram Lueders. 2016. "Declines in Low-Cost Rented Housing Units in Eight Large Southeastern Cities." Community and Economic Development Discussion Paper. Community and Economic Development Department of the Federal Reserve Bank of Atlanta.

Invest Atlanta. 2015. "Housing Strategy." Available at https://www.investat lanta.com/about-invest-atlanta/public-information/strategies-plans/hous ingstrategy/.

———. 2016. "Press Release: New Affordable Housing Policy." Available at http:// www.investatlanta.com/news-press/press-releases/press-release-new-af fordable-housing-policy/.

Jasper, James M. 2004. "A Strategic Approach to Collective Action: Looking for Agency in Social Movement Choices." *Mobilization: An International Quarterly* 9 (1): 1–16.

Jones-Correa, Michael, and Diane Wong. 2015. "Whose Politics? Reflections on Clarence Stone's Regime Politics." *Urban Affairs Review* 51 (1): 161–170.

Justiça Global. 2012. "Moradores removidos por obra olímpica há dois anos continuam sem indenização no Rio de Janeiro." Available at http://global.org .br/programas/moradores-removidos-por-obra-olimpica-ha-dois-anos-con tinuam-sem-indenizacao-no-rio-de-janeiro/.

Katz, Bruce, and Richard M. Daley. 2013. "Atlanta Can Flourish in Global Economy." *Brookings.* April 22. Available at https://www.brookings.edu/opinions/ atlanta-can-flourish-in-global-economy/.

Keck, Margaret E., and Kathryn Sikkink. 1998. *Activists beyond Borders: Advocacy Networks in International Politics.* Ithaca, N.Y.: Cornell University Press.

Kennedy, Phil. 2015. Interview by the author. April. Washington, D.C.

Khomami, Nadia, and Josh Halliday. 2015. "Shoreditch Cereal Killer Cafe Targeted in Anti-gentrification Protests." *The Guardian,* September 27, UK News section. Available at https://www.theguardian.com/uk-news/2015/ sep/27/shoreditch-cereal-cafe-targeted-by-anti-gentrification-protesters.

Lefebvre, Henri. (1968) 1995. "The Right to the City." In *Writings on Cities,* edited by E. Kofman and E. Lebas, 63–181. Oxford, U.K.: Blackwell. First published as *Le Droit à la Ville* by Anthropos.

Levitsky, Steven. 2003. "From Labor Politics to Machine Politics: The Transformation of Party-Union Linkages in Argentine Peronism, 1983–1999." *Latin American Research Review* 38 (3): 3–36.

Lichbach, Mark Irving. 1987. "Deterrence or Escalation? The Puzzle of Aggregate Studies of Repression and Dissent." *Journal of Conflict Resolution* 31 (2): 266–297.

Little, Kate. 2015. Interview by the author. May. Atlanta.

Loeffler, Christian. 2016. "Demolishing a Favela to Make Way for the Olympics." *Bloomberg News,* March 9. Available at http://www.bloomberg.com/news/photo-essays/2016-03-09/demolishing-a-favela-to-make-way-for-the-olympics.

Logan, John R., and Harvey Luskin Molotch. 1987. *Urban Fortunes: The Political Economy of Place.* Berkeley: University of California Press.

London School of Economics. 2016. "Urban Governance Project." In *How Cities Are Governed.* Available at https://urbangovernance.net/en/about/.

Lopes, J. 2012. "Sobre arquitetos e sem-tetos." Ph.D. thesis, São Carlos, IAH/University of São Paulo.

López-Maya, Margarita, and Luis E. Lander. 2006. "Novedades y continuidades de la protesta popular en Venezuela." *Revista Venezolana de Economía y Ciencias Sociales* 12 (1): 11–30.

Luke, Dawn. 2016. Report to the Invest Atlanta Board Meeting. Atlanta.

Mainwaring, Scott. 1987. "Urban Popular Movements, Identity, and Democratization in Brazil." *Comparative Political Studies* 20 (2): 131–159.

Maney, Gregory M., Rachel V. Kutz-Flamenbaum, Deana A. Rohlinger, and Jeff Goodwin, eds. 2012. *Strategies for Social Change.* Minneapolis: University of Minnesota Press.

Marcuse, Peter. 2009. "From Critical Urban Theory to the Right to the City." *City* 13 (2–3): 185–197.

Marcuse, Peter, and David Madden. 2016. *In Defense of Housing: The Politics of Crisis.* New York: Verso Books.

Marques, Eduardo. 2013. "Government, Political Actors and Governance in Urban Policies in Brazil and São Paulo: Concepts for a Future Research Agenda." *Brazilian Political Science Review* 7 (3): 8–35.

Masliansky, Nechama. 2016. Senior advocacy advisor of SOME, Inc., as member of panel to discuss the CNHED report "Vision to Action: How CNHED's Housing for All Campaign Led DC from Drastic Cuts to Momentous Investments in Affordable Housing." CNHED Monthly Meeting. January 21. Washington, D.C.

Mayer, Margit. 2009. "The 'Right to the City' in the Context of Shifting Mottos of Urban Social Movements." *City* 13 (2–3): 362–374.

McAdam, Doug. 1982. *Political Process and the Development of Black Insurgency, 1930–1970.* Chicago: University of Chicago Press.

McAdam, Doug, and Hilary Boudet. 2012. *Putting Social Movements in Their Place: Explaining Opposition to Energy Projects in the United States, 2000–2005.* Cambridge: Cambridge University Press.

McAdam, Doug, John D. McCarthy, and Mayer N. Zald. 1996. *Comparative Perspectives on Social Movements: Political Opportunities, Mobilizing Structures, and Cultural Framings*. Cambridge: Cambridge University Press.

McAdam, Doug, Sidney Tarrow, and Charles Tilly. 2001. *Dynamics of Contention*. Cambridge: Cambridge University Press.

McCall, Nathan. 2008. *Them: A Novel*. New York: Washington Square Press.

McCann, Bryan. 2014. *Hard Times in the Marvelous City: From Dictatorship to Democracy in the Favelas of Rio de Janeiro*. Durham, N.C.: Duke University Press.

McCarthy, John D., and Mayer N. Zald. 1977. "Resource Mobilization and Social Movements: A Partial Theory." *American Journal of Sociology* 82 (6): 1212–1241.

McFarland, William. 2015. Interview by the author. May. Atlanta.

McGarry, Aidan, and James Jasper, eds. 2015. *The Identity Dilemma: Social Movements and Collective Identity*. Philadelphia: Temple University Press.

Mehrotra, Karishma. 2014. "Atlanta's Popular BeltLine Trail Still Has Miles to Go." *Wall Street Journal*, July 31. Available at http://www.wsj.com/articles/atlantas-popular-beltline-trail-still-has-miles-to-go-1406837184.

Melucci, Alberto. 1995. "The Process of Collective Identity." In *Social Movements and Culture*, edited by Hank Johnston and Bert Klandermans, 41–63. Minneapolis: University of Minnesota Press.

Meyer, David S. 2014. *The Politics of Protest: Social Movements in America*. New York: Oxford University Press.

Ministry of Cities. 2013. *Portaria*, no. 317, July 18. Available at http://www.lex.com.br/legis_24624228_PORTARIA_N_317_DE_18_DE_JULHO_DE_013.aspx.

Mitchell, Don. 2003. *The Right to the City: Social Justice and the Fight for Public Space*. New York: Guilford Press.

Mollenkopf, John H. 1983. *The Contested City*. Princeton, N.J.: Princeton University Press.

Molotch, Harvey. 1976. "City as a Growth Machine: Toward a Political Economy of Place." *American Journal of Sociology* 82 (2): 309–332.

———. 1979. "Capital and Neighborhood in the United States: Some Conceptual Links." *Urban Affairs Quarterly* 14 (3): 289–312.

Morris, Aldon D. 1984. *The Origins of the Civil Rights Movement: Black Communities Organizing for Change*. New York: Free Press.

Mossberger, Karen, and Gerry Stoker. 2001. "The Evolution of Urban Regime Theory: The Challenge of Conceptualization." *Urban Affairs Review* 36 (6): 810–835.

Moulden, Dominic. 2015. Interview by the author. April. Washington, D.C.

Nadeau, Brianne. 2016. Speech to members of the Housing for All Campaign on Advocacy Day to the Council. Washington, D.C.

Netto, Vinicius de Moraes, Maira Soares Pinheiro, and Roberto Bousquet Paschoalino. 2015. "Segregated Networks in the City." *International Journal of Urban and Regional Research*, 39, 1084–1102.

New Communities Initiative. 2015. "Annual Program Report 2014." Available at http://dcnewcommunities.org/.

Newman, Kathe, and Elvin K. Wyly. 2006. "The Right to Stay Put, Revisited: Gentrification and Resistance to Displacement in New York City." *Urban Studies* 43 (1): 23–57.

New York Times. 2012. "Slum Dwellers Are Defying Brazil's Grand Design for Olympics." March 4. Available at http://www.nytimes.com/2012/03/05/world/americas/brazil-faces-obstacles-in-preparations-for-rio-olympics.html.

Nicholls, Walter J., and Justin R. Beaumont. 2004. "The Urbanisation of Justice Movements? Possibilities and Constraints for the City as a Space of Contentious Struggle." *Space and Polity* 8 (2): 119–135.

Numbeo. 2015a. "Property Prices in Rio de Janeiro." June 25. Available at http://www.numbeo.com/property-investment/city_result.jsp.

———. 2015b. "São Paulo." Available at http://www.numbeo.com/property-investment/city_result.jsp.

Oakley, Deirdre. 2015. Interview by the author. May. Atlanta.

Oakley, Deirdre, Erin Ruel, and Lesley Reid. 2013. "Atlanta's Last Demolitions and Relocations: The Relationship between Neighborhood Characteristics and Resident Satisfaction." *Housing Studies* 28 (2): 205–234.

Observatório das Remoções. 2012. "Mapa das remoções." Available at http://observatorioderemocoes.blogspot.com.br/.

Oliver, Pamela, and Hank Johnston. 2005. "What a Good Idea! Ideology and Frames in Social Movement Research." In *Frames of Protest: Social Movement and the Framing Perspective,* edited by Hank Johnston and John A. Noakes. 185–204. Lanham, Md.: Rowman and Littlefield.

Oliver, Pamela, and Daniel Myers. 2002. "The Coevolution of Social Movements." *Mobilization: An International Quarterly* 8 (1): 1–24.

Orren, Karen, and Stephen Skowronek. 1994. "Beyond the Iconography of Order: Notes for a New Institutionalism." In *The Dynamics of American Politics: Approaches and Interpretations,* edited by Lawrence C. Dodd and Calvin C. Jillson, 311–330. Boulder, Colo.: Westview Press.

Parkin, Benjamin. 2014. "Housing Crisis in São Paulo: Affected Families Take Action." RioOnWatch. Available at http://www.urbem.org.br/.

Pateman, Carole. 2012. "Participatory Democracy Revisited." *Perspective on Politics* 10 (1): 7–19.

Perlman, Janice. 1976. *The Myth of Marginality: Urban Poverty and Politics in Rio de Janeiro.* Berkeley: University of California Press.

———. 2010. *Favela: Four Decades of Living on the Edge in Rio de Janeiro.* Oxford: Oxford University Press.

Pierre, Jon, and Guy Peters. 2012. "Urban Governance." In *The Oxford Handbook of Urban Politics,* edited by Peter John, Karen Mossberger, and Susan E. Clarke, 71–86. New York: Oxford University Press.

Pólis Institute. 2001. "The Statute of the City: New Tools for Assuring the Right to the City in Brazil." Available at http://www.polis.org.br/uploads/916/916.pdf. Accessed January 13, 2016.

Popular Committee for the World Cup and Olympics in Rio. 2012. "Megaeventos e violações dos direitos humanos no Rio de Janeiro: Dossiê do Comitê Popular da Copa e Olimpíadas do Rio de Janeiro." Available at http://comi tepopulario.wordpress.com/2012/04/20/baixe-agora-dossie-megaeventos-e-violacoes-dos-direitos-humanos-no-rio-de-janeiro/.

———. 2013. "Megaeventos e violações dos direitos humanos no Rio de Janeiro: Dossiê do Comitê Popular da Copa e Olimpíadas do Rio de Janeiro." Available at http://comitepopulario.wordpress.com/2013/05/15/baixe-agora-dos sie-megaeventos-e-violacoes-de-direitos-humanos-no-rio-de-janeiro-2a-edicao-revisada-e-atualizada/.

———. 2015. "Mega-Events and Human Rights Violations in Rio de Janeiro Dossier: Rio 2016 Olympics: The Exclusion Games." Available at https://issuu.com/mantelli/docs/dossiecomiterio2015_eng_issuu.

Purcell, Mark. 2002. "Excavating Lefebvre: The Right to the City and Its Urban Politics of the Inhabitant." *GeoJournal* 58 (2–3): 99–108.

———. 2008. *Recapturing Democracy: Neoliberalization and the Struggle for Alternative Urban Futures.* New York: Routledge.

———. 2014. "Possible Worlds: Henri Lefebvre and the Right to the City." *Journal of Urban Affairs* 36 (1): 141–154.

Putnam, Robert D. 1993. *Making Democracy Work: Civic Traditions in Modern Italy.* Rev. ed. Princeton, N.J.: Princeton University Press.

Reed, Jenny. 2012. "Disappearing Act: Affordable Housing in DC Is Vanishing amid Sharply Rising Housing Costs." Available at http://www.dcfpi.org/wp-content/uploads/2012/05/5-7-12-Housing-and-Income-Trends-FINAL.pdf.

Resident Leadership Team. 2015. Interview by the author. Washington, D.C.

Ribeiro, Luiz Cesar de Queiroz. 2012. "As metrópoles brasileiras no milênio—Resultados de um projeto de pesquisa" [Brazilian metropolitan areas at the millennium—Results of a research project]. Rio de Janeiro: Instituto de Pesquisa e Planejamento Urbano e Regional da Universidade Federal do Rio de Janeiro/Observatorio das Metropoles. Available at http://observatoriometropoles .net/download/metropoles_milenio.pdf.

Rich, Michael. 2015. "Panel Paper: Pathways to Self-Sufficiency: Lessons from Atlanta's MTW Demonstration." Paper presented to the Annual APPAM Conference. Available at https://appam.confex.com/appam/2015/webprogram/Pa per13657.html. Accessed January 13, 2017.

Right to the City Alliance. 2015. *Right to the City.* Available at http://rightto thecity.org/.

RioOnWatch. 2013. "Favela Não Se Cala Continues Mobilizing Awareness in Providência and Horto." Available at http://www.rioonwatch.org/?p=9116.

———. 2014. "Caminhos divergentes: Moradores da Vila Autódromo resistem, seguem o caminho, ou aguardam." Available at http://rioonwatch.org.br/?p=12090.

———. 2015a. "Mayor Announces Eminent Domain in Vila Autódromo as MIT Report Criticizes City Policy." Available at http://www.rioonwatch.org/?p=20983.

———. 2015b. "Resistance in Vila Autódromo Continues against Pressure from the Municipal Government, and Opens Historical Precedent for Market-Rate Indemnities." Available at http://rioonwatch.org.br/?p=13342.

Rivadulla, María José Álvarez. 2012. "Clientelism or Something Else? Squatter Politics in Montevideo." *Latin American Politics and Society* 54 (1): 37–63.

Roberts, Bryan R., and Alejandro Portes. 2006. "Coping with the Free Market City: Collective Action in Six Latin American Cities at the End of the Twentieth Century." *Latin American Research Review* 41 (2): 57–83.

Roberts, Kenneth M. 1997. "Beyond Romanticism: Social Movements and the Study of Political Change in Latin America." *Latin American Research Review* 32 (2): 137–151.

———. 2002. "Social Inequalities without Class Cleavages in Latin America's Neoliberal Era." *Studies in Comparative International Development* 36:3–33.

Rodrigues, Anaí. 2012. Interview by the author. January. São Paulo.

Rubin, Jeffrey W., and Vivienne Bennett, eds. 2015. *Enduring Reform: Progressive Activism and Private Sector Responses in Latin American Democracies.* Pittsburgh: University of Pittsburgh Press.

Rupp, Leila, and Verta Taylor. 1987. *Survival in the Doldrums: The American Women's Rights Movement, 1945–1960.* New York: Oxford University Press.

Saegert, Susan. 2006. "Building Civic Capacity in Urban Neighborhoods: An Empirically Grounded Anatomy." *Journal of Urban Affairs* 28 (1): 275–294.

Saegert, Susan, Phillip Thompson J., and Mark R. Warren, eds. 2002. *Social Capital and Poor Communities.* New York: Russell Sage Foundation.

Samora, Patricia Rodrigues, and Márcia Saeko Hirata. 2012. "Participatory Urban Plans for 'Special Zones of Social Interest' in São Paulo: Fostering Dense Central Areas." Available at http://www.academia.edu/2571040/Participatory_urban_plans_for_Special_Zones_of_Social_Interest_in_S%C3%A3o_Paulo_Fostering_dense_central_areas.

Samuels, Robert. 2013. "In District, Affordable-Housing Plan Hasn't Delivered." *Washington Post,* July 7. Available at https://www.washingtonpost.com/local/in-district-affordable-housing-plan-hasnt-delivered/2013/07/07/789f1070-bc03-11e2-97d4-a479289a31f9_story.html?utm_term=.0c311d603d27.

Sandbrook, Richard, Marc Edelman, Patrick Heller, and Judith Teichman. 2007. *Social Democracy in the Global Periphery: Origins, Challenges, Prospects.* Cambridge: Cambridge University Press.

Santos Júnior, Orlando Alves dos. 2002. "Democracia, desigualdades e governança local: Dilemas da reforma municipal no Brasil" [Democracy, inequality, and local governance: Dilemmas for municipal reform in Brazil]. *Cadernos Metrópole* 8:87–103.

Santos Júnior, Orlando Alves dos, Luiz Cesar de Queiroz Ribeiro, and Sergio de Azevedo. 2004. *Governança democrática e poder local: A experiência dos conselhos municipais no Brasil* [Democratic governance and local power: The experience of municipal councils in Brazil]. Rio de Janeiro: Revan, Fase.

Sassen, Saskia. 1988. *The Mobility of Labor and Capital: A Study in International Investment and Labor Flow.* Cambridge: Cambridge University Press.

———. 1991. *The Global City: New York, London, Tokyo.* Princeton, N.J.: Princeton University Press.

———. 2011. *Cities in a World Economy.* 4th ed. Thousand Oaks, Calif.: SAGE Publications.

Schelling, Thomas C. 1960. *The Strategy of Conflict.* Cambridge, Mass.: Harvard University Press.

Schwartz, Alex F. 2015. *Housing Policy in the United States.* New York: Routledge.

Schwartzman, Paul, Abigail Hauslohner, and Scott Clement. 2015. "Poll: White Residents in D.C. Think Redevelopment Helps Them. Black Residents Don't." *Washington Post,* November 20. Available at https://www.washingtonpost .com/local/poll-white-and-wealthy-residents-in-dc-think-redevelopment-helps-them-black-and-poor-residents-dont/2015/11/19/bb7acbca-8ed6-11e5-ae1f-af46b7df8483_story.html.

Scopelliti, Demetrio M. 2014. "Housing: Before, during, and after the Great Recession." Spotlight on Statistics. U.S. Bureau of Labor Statistics. Available at https://www.bls.gov/spotlight/2014/housing/pdf/housing.pdf.

Scruggs, Greg. 2013. "New São Paulo Mayor Shelves Massive Development Project." *Next City.* Available at https://nextcity.org/daily/entry/new-S.

SECOVI Executive. 2012. Interview by the author. May. São Paulo.

Secretaria Municipal de Habitação, Cidade do Rio de Janeiro. 2010. "Regularização fundiaria." Rio de Janeiro: Prefeitura do Rio de Janeiro. Available at http://www.rio.rj.gov.br/web/smh/exibeconteudo.

Secretaria Municipal de Habitação, Cidade de São Paulo. 2008. "Urbanização de favelas: A experiência de São Paulo." São Paulo: Prefeitura da Cidade de São Paulo.

Secretaria Municipal de Urbanismo e Licenciamento de São Paulo. 2014. "Plano Diretor Estratégico." Available at http://www.prefeitura.sp.gov.br/cidade/sec retarias/urbanismo/legislacao/plano_diretor/index.php?p=201105. Accessed January 13, 2017.

Shah, Phoram, Ellen Hamilton, Fernando Armendaris, and Lee Heejoo. 2015. "Inclusive Cities Approach Paper." AUS8539. World Bank.

Shefner, Jon, George Pasdirtz, and Cory Blad. 2006. "Austerity Protests and Immiserating Growth in Mexico and Argentina." In *Latin American Social Movements: Globalization, Democratization, and Transnational Networks,* edited by Paul Almeida and Hank Johnston, 19–42. Lanham, Md.: Rowman and Littlefield.

Sigolo, Leticia. 2015. Interview by the author. April. São Paulo.

Silva, Luiz da. 2012. Interview by the author. July. Rio de Janeiro.

———. 2016. Interview by the author. June. Rio de Janeiro.

Silva, Valério da. 2012. Interview by the author. July. Rio de Janeiro.

Silver, Hilary, Alan Scott, and Yuri Kazepov. 2010. "Participation in Urban Contention and Deliberation." *International Journal of Urban and Regional Research* 34 (3): 453–477.

Smith, Michael Peter, and Michael McQuarrie, eds. 2011. *Remaking Urban Citizenship: Organizations, Institutions, and the Right to the City.* Vol. 1. New York: Transaction Publishers.

Smith, Neil. 1996. *The New Urban Frontier: Gentrification and the Revanchist City.* New York: Routledge.

Souza, Nelson de Cruz. 2013. Interview by the author. São Paulo.

Souza, Sandra Maria de. 2016. Interview by the author. June. Rio de Janeiro.

Stoecker, Randy. 1997. "The CDC Model of Urban Redevelopment: A Critique and an Alternative." *Journal of Urban Affairs* 19 (1): 1–22.

———. 2003. "Understanding the Development-Organizing Dialectic." *Journal of Urban Affairs* 25 (4): 493–512.

Stoker, Gerry. 1998. "Governance as Theory: Five propositions." *International Social Science Journal* 50 (155): 17–28.

Stokes, Susan C. 1991. "Politics and Latin America's Urban Poor: Reflections from a Lima Shantytown." *Latin American Research Review* 26 (2): 75–101.

———. 2005. "Perverse Accountability: A Formal Model of Machine Politics with Evidence from Argentina." *American Political Science Review* 99 (3): 315–325.

Stone, Clarence N. 1976. *Economic Growth and Neighborhood Discontent: System Bias in the Urban Renewal Program of Atlanta.* Chapel Hill: University of North Carolina Press.

———. 1989. *Regime Politics: Governing Atlanta, 1946–1988.* Lawrence: University Press of Kansas.

———. 1993. "Urban Regimes and the Capacity to Govern: A Political Economy Approach." *Journal of Urban Affairs* 15 (1): 1–28.

———. 2001. "Civic Capacity and Urban Education." *Urban Affairs Review* 36 (5): 595–619.

———. 2015. "Reflections on Regime Politics from Governing Coalition to Urban Political Order." *Urban Affairs Review* 51 (1): 101–137.

Stone, Clarence N., Robert P. Stoker, John Betancur, Susan E. Clarke, Marilyn Dantico, Martin Horak, Karen Mossberger, Juliet Musso, Jeffrey M. Sellers, Ellen Shiau, Harold Wolman, and Donn Worgs. 2015. *Urban Neighborhoods in a New Era: Revitalization Politics in the Postindustrial City.* Chicago: University of Chicago Press.

Sturtevant, Lisa. 2014. "The New District of Columbia: What Population Growth and Demographic Change Mean for the City." *Journal of Urban Affairs* 36 (2): 276–299.

Suderman, Alan. 2012. "Bowser Defends Corporate Giving, and Lots of It." *Washington City Paper,* June 20. Available at http://www.washingtoncity paper.com/news/loose-lips/blog/13132959/bowser-defends-corporate-giv ing-and-lots-of-it.

Svampa, Maristella, and Sebastián Pereyra. 2009. *Entre la ruta y el barrio: La experiencia de las organizaciones piqueteras*. Buenos Aires: Editorial Biblos.

Tanaka, Giselle. 2014. Personal e-mail communication with the author.

Tarrow, Sidney. 1994. *Power in Movement: Social Movements, Collective Action and Politics*. New York: Cambridge University Press.

Tatagiba, Luciana. 2010. "Desfios da relação entre movimentos sociais e instituições políticas: O caso do movimento de moradia da cidade de São Paulo." *Columbia Internacional* (January–June): 60–83.

Tatian, Peter. 2015. "A Preservation Strategy Will Help DC Residents Meet Their Needs." *Urban Wire*. Urban Institute. Available at http://www.urban.org/urban-wire/preservation-strategy-will-help-dc-meet-affordable-housing-needs. Accessed January 13, 2017.

Tatian, Peter, and S. Lei. 2015. "Washington, DC: Our Changing City." Urban Institute. Available at http://datatools.urban.org/features/OurChangingCity/demographics/.

Taylor, Alan. 2016. "America's Tent Cities for the Homeless." *The Atlantic*. February 11. Available at http://www.theatlantic.com/photo/2016/02/americas-tent-cities-for-the-homeless/462450/.

The Telegraph. 2012. "Slum Eviction Plans in Haiti Spark Protests," July 25, World section. Available at http://www.telegraph.co.uk/news/worldnews/centralamericaandthecaribbean/haiti/9425214/Slum-eviction-plans-in-Haiti-spark-protests.html.

Tendler, Judith. 1998. *Good Government in the Tropics*. Baltimore: Johns Hopkins University Press.

Tilly, Charles. 1978. *From Mobilization to Revolution*. Reading, Mass.: Addison-Wesley.

———. 1995. "To Explain Political Processes." *American Journal of Sociology* 100 (6): 1594–1610. doi:10.1086/230673.

———. 2004. *Social Movements, 1768–2004*. Boulder, Colo.: Routledge.

———. 2006. *Regimes and Repertoires*. Chicago: University of Chicago Press.

———. 2008. *Contentious Performances*. New York: Cambridge University Press.

Torres, Haroldo da Gama, Eduardo Marques, Maria Paula Ferreira, and Sandra Bitar. 2003. "Pobreza e espaço: Padrões de segregação em São Paulo." *Estudos Avançados* 17 (47): 97–128. doi:10.1590/S0103-40142003000100006.

Touchton, Michael, and Brian Wampler. 2014. "Improving Social Well-Being through New Democratic Institutions." *Comparative Political Studies* 47 (10): 1442–1469.

Tribunal Superior Eleitoral. 2014. "Prestação de contas." Available at http://www.tse.jus.br/eleicoes/eleicoes-anteriores/eleicoes-2014/prestacao-de-contas-eleicoes-2014.

United Nations Habitat. 2012. "Global Campaign on Urban Governance: Progress Report of the Executive Director." HS/UF/1/13—Dialogues/I/Paper 7. New York: United Nations.

———. 2016. "Habitat III: New Urban Agenda." Draft Outcome of the United Nations Conference on Housing and Sustainable Urban Development (Habitat III). Quito, Ecuador: United Nations.

United Nations Preparatory Committee for United Nations for Habitat III. 2016. "Policy Paper 10: Housing Policies." A/CONF.226/PC.3/23. http://habitat3.org/wp-content/uploads/PU10-HABITAT-III-POLICY-PAPER.pdf.

U.S. Census Bureau. 2011. "City of Atlanta: 2010 Summary Census Report." Available at http://www.atlantaga.gov/modules/showdocument.aspx.

———. 2015. "QuickFacts: Atlanta, GA." Available at http://www.census.gov/quickfacts/table/PST045215/1304000.

Vainer, Carlos. 2012. Interview by the author. July. Rio de Janeiro.

Vale, Lawrence, and Annemarie Gray. 2013. "The Displacement Decathlon." *Places Journal* (April). doi:10.22269/130415. Available at https://placesjournal.org/article/the-displacement-decathlon/.

———. 2015. "Displaced by the Olympics: Can Favela Residents Gain Market-Rate Compensation in Rio?" *MIT Displacement Research and Action Network.* March 20. Available at http://displacement.mit.edu/displaced-by-the-olympics-can-favela-residents-gain-market-rate-compensations-in-rio-de-janeiro/.

Valladores, Licia do Prado. 1978. "Working the System: Squatter Response to Resettlement in Rio de Janeiro." *International Journal of Regional and Urban Research* 2 (104): 12–25.

Vila Autódromo. 2013. "A Vila Autódromo vive! Nota pública, Vila Autódromo conquista sua permanência." *Comunidad Vila Autódromo.* Available at dromo.blogspot.com/.

Vila Autódromo Residents. 2012. Interview by the author. July. Rio de Janeiro.

Vincent, Carol Hardy, Laura A. Hanson, and Jerome P. Bjelopera. 2014. "Federal Land Ownership: Overview and Data." 7-5700. Congressional Research Service. Available at https://fas.org/sgp/crs/misc/R42346.pdf.

Walker, Christopher J., and Mark Weinheimer. 1998. "Community Development in the 1990s." Washington, D.C: Urban Institute. Available at wealth.org/sites/clone.community-wealth.org/files/downloads/report-walker-weinheimer.pdf.

Wampler, Brian. 2010. *Participatory Budgeting in Brazil: Contestation, Cooperation, and Accountability.* University Park: Pennsylvania State University Press.

———. 2015. *Activating Democracy in Brazil.* Notre Dame, Ind.: University of Notre Dame Press.

Watts, Jonathan. 2013. "Brazil Protests Take to the Pitch as People's Cup Highlights Evictions." *The Guardian,* June 18, Global Development section. Available at https://www.theguardian.com/global-development/2013/jun/18/brazil-protests-peoples-cup-evictions.

Weise, Barry. 2016. Interview by the author. May. Washington, D.C.

WIEGO. 2016. "About the Inclusive Cities Project." *Inclusive Cities.* Accessed January 10. Available at http://www.inclusivecities.org/about_us/.

Wiener, Aaron. 2015. Interview by the author. February. Washington, D.C.

Williamson, Theresa. 2016. Interview by the author. June. Rio de Janeiro.

———. 2015a. "Madonna and the Risks of Land Titling." RioOnWatch. January 29. Available at http://www.rioonwatch.org/.

———. 2015b. "A New Threat to Favelas: Gentrification." *Architectural Review*, May 30. Available at https://www.architectural-review.com/rethink/a-new-threat-to-favelas-gentrification/8682967.article.

Woetzel, Jonathan, Ram Sangeeth, Jan Mischke, Nicklas Garemo, and Shirish Sankhe. 2014. "A Blueprint for Addressing the Global Affordable Housing Challenge." McKinsey Global Institute. Available at https://www.canback.com/files/2014_MK_Affordable_housing_Full%20Report.pdf.

Wolford, Wendy. 2015. "Rethinking the Revolution: Latin American Social Movements and the State in the Twenty-First Century." In *Enduring Reform: Progressive Activism and Private Sector Responses in Latin America's Democracies*, edited by Jeffrey W. Rubin and Vivienne Bennett, 53–80. Pittsburgh: University of Pittsburgh Press.

Wrede, Catharina. 2014. "Ex moradores da Vila Autódromo festejam a vida no parque." *O Globo*. Available at http://oglobo.globo.com/rio/ex-moradores-da-vila-autodromo-festejam-vida-no-parque-carioca-12311245.

Youngblood, Mtamanika. 2015. Interview by the author. Atlanta.

———. 2016. Interview by the author. May. Atlanta.

Zap. 2015. "Indicé Fipe Zap." Available at http://www.zap.com.br/imoveis/fipe-zap-b/.

Zillow. 2015. "Home Values: Atlanta, GA." Available at http://www.zillow.com/atlanta-ga/home-values/.

Zumper. 2015. "February 2015 Rent Report." Available at https://www.zumper.com/blog/wp-content/uploads/2015/03/Zumper-February-2015-National-Rent-Report.pdf.

Index

MAUREEN M. DONAGHY is an Assistant Professor of Political Science at Rutgers University and the author of *Civil Society and Participatory Governance: Municipal Councils and Social Housing Programs in Brazil*.

Also in the series *Urban Life, Landscape, and Policy*: